Library of
Davidson College

*Politics and Public Policy
in America:* AN INTRODUCTION

THE LIPPINCOTT SERIES IN AMERICAN GOVERNMENT
Under the editorship of William C. Havard,
Virginia Polytechnic Institute and State University

DAVID A. CAPUTO, Purdue University

Politics and Public Policy in America: AN INTRODUCTION

J. B. LIPPINCOTT COMPANY
Philadelphia New York Toronto

Copyright © 1974 by J. B. Lippincott Company.
All rights reserved.

With the exception of brief excerpts for review, no part of this book may be reproduced in any form or by any means without written permission from the publisher.

ISBN 0-397-47306-0
Library of Congress Catalog Card Number: 73-20245
Printed in the United States of America

Library of Congress Cataloging in Publication Data
Caputo, David A.
   Politics and public policy in America.
   (The Lippincott series in American government)
   Includes bibliographical references.
   1. United States—Politics and government—Handbooks, manuals, etc. I. Title.
JK274.C272   320.4'73   73-20245
ISBN 0-397-47306-0

for my Mother and Father

TABLE OF CONTENTS

PREFACE xv

SECTION I. Introduction

1 Some Basic Questions 3
  Focal Points 5
  Power and Legitimacy 5   Nature of Government 7
  Types of Change 10   Layers of Government 13
  Leadership Responsibility 15   Citizen Responsibility 16
  Summary 17

2 Change: A Historical Perspective of American Politics 21
  Voting Rights and Representation 21
  Minority Rights 26
  Civil Rights 29
  Summary 37

SECTION II. American National Political Institutions

Introduction 41

3 The United States Congress and Public Policy 49
  Five Common Characteristics 49
  The Legislative Process 58
  Criticisms of Congress 60

4 **The Court System and the Judicial Process** 69
  The Supreme Court 69
  Other Federal Courts 78
  State Courts 79
  Implications 80

5 **The Contemporary Presidency** 85
  Presidential Selection 88
  Presidential Power 93
  Presidential Problems 99

6 **The Federal Bureaucracy and Political Interaction** 105
  The Bureaucracy 105
  Political Interaction Among the Four Branches 111
  The Future of American Institutions 114

SECTION III. Subnational Politics

7 *American Federalism* 119
  Two Contrasting Views 119
  Integration, Responsibility, and Distribution 124

8 *State and Urban Politics in America: An Overview* 141
  Introduction 141
  Metropolitan America 145
  State Politics 150

Epilogue: Persistent and Unresolved Problems 156

SECTION IV. Group and Party Politics in America

Introduction 163

9 *Group Politics* 165
    The "Powerful" 170

10 *Political Parties and the 1972 Elections* 181
    Political Parties 181
    The 1972 Elections 189

The Primaries 190   Conventions 193   Campaign Strategies 195

    The Outcome 197

    SECTION V.   *Public Policy*

11 *Public Policy: Importance and Implications* 205
    Introduction 205
    Civil Disturbances 210
    Southeast Asia 217
    Implications 224

12 *The Future of American Politics* 233
    Introduction 233
    Current Setting 238
    Indicators of Change 242
    Three Possible Future Scenarios 247
    Individual Future Participation 253

    APPENDIX.   *The Constitution of the United States* 257

TABLES, MAPS, FIGURES

1-1 Types of Government   8
1-2 Types of Change   11
2-1 Voting Participation in the United States   24
2-2 Black Population of Selected American Cities: 1971   30
2-3 Developmental Periods in American Politics   34
II-1 Comparative Information on Major American Institutions   42
3-1 Standing Committees of the Congress of the United States   51
3-2 Data on Standing Committee Chairmen, 93rd Congress, 1st Session, 1973   54
3-3 1972 Congressional Districts in Indiana   66
4-1 Supreme Court Justices: December 1972   76
5-1 Recent Presidential Popular and Electoral College Votes   90
5-2 1972 Presidential Popular and Electoral College Results by State   91
5-3 Cost of Living Index: August 1970 to August 1972   95
6-1 The Federal Bureaucracy: A Historical Perspective   106
6-2 Civil Service Ratings and Salaries: 1971   108

7-1   Two Contrasting Views of American Federalism   120
7-2   Functional Distribution of Expenditures by Governmental Levels   131
7-3   Selected State Expenditures by Function: 1966–1967   132
7-4   Selected Local Expenditures by Function: 1966–1967   133
8-1   Estimate of 18- to 20-Year-Olds' Vote Potential   142
8-2   Governmental Units in the United States   144
8-3   Rural-to-Urban Population Movement: 1890–1970   145
8-4   Proportions of State Populations in Metropolitan Counties   146
8-5   Metropolitan Population Growth in the United States   148
8-6   Population Distribution by Race in SMSAs: 1970   149
9-1   Migration to the United States: A Historical View   166
9-2   Income Comparisons of White and Nonwhite Americans   170
9-3   Family Income Distribution in the United States   172
9-4   Corporate Assets in the United States: 1968   173
10-1 Party Preferences of the American Electorate   186
10-2 Selected 1972 Democratic Presidential Primary Outcomes   192
10-3 Comparisons of Recent Presidential Elections   198
11-1 A "Systems" Model for Political Analysis   206
11-2 Civil Disturbances and Their Effects   211

11-3	American Combat Troops in Vietnam: 1960–1972	219
11-4	American Casualties in Vietnam	223
11-5	Participation Justification: A Schematic View	227
12-1	Futuristics: A Summary	236
12-2	Continuum of Individual Responsibility	247
12-3	Possible Future Scenarios	248

PREFACE

This volume is a result of considerable discussion with and teaching of undergraduate students in my introduction to American government courses. The book is not encyclopedic; for this reason it is easy to supplement with the many excellent related paperbacks available today, and it can be used in a wide variety of introductory American government courses. The book's main purpose is to introduce the student to the complexities of American politics without overwhelming him with less important information and data. The suggested readings, listed at the end of each chapter, should be explored by those interested in a particular subject or area. Every effort has been made to provide the reader with the necessary information and analyses to begin to think about and to analyze American politics.

While I have definite views on the nature and style of American politics, I have attempted to make this a volume which encourages students to develop their own positions and to place current developments within the historical contexts presented here. This, then, is a departure from many contemporary treatments of American politics which attempt to indoctrinate or support a particular ideological position. The attempt here is to stimulate critical thought and careful consideration of American politics.

In any writing endeavor debts are many, and thanks are due to those who assisted me. My undergraduate students at Purdue University proved a constant stimulus and sounding board for my ideas and thoughts. Lisa Weiland read and suggested changes in the manuscript. Dean William C. Havard, Virginia Polytechnic Institute, provided excellent editorial assistance, as did Robert Pace and John Hoey of Lippincott. Ms. Karen Stevens and Ms. Dotty Eberle provided outstanding typing assistance combined with extreme patience; they have my appreciation for their efforts. Any writer has to make personal sacrifices to accomplish his tasks, and my parents, Mr. and Mrs. Armand Caputo, wife, Alice, son, Christopher, and daughter, Elizabeth, were especially understanding of my prolonged absences and preoccupations. I accept full responsibility for what follows and hope the reader finds it as rewarding as I did writing it.

SECTION 1
Introduction

1. Some Basic Questions

For most of you, this is probably the first book you have read introducing you to the complexities and characteristics of the American political system. In most cases, you have either recently reached voting age or have just begun to vote. Think for a few minutes of the questions you have and the answers you are seeking from this course and from your readings about the American policy process and the decisions which affect you and other American citizens. The following list probably includes at least some and, in many cases, most of these concerns.

(1) How and by whom are decisions made regarding foreign and domestic policy? Who has influence, and what roles do publicly elected officials have in the determination of governmental policy?

(2) How does an individual citizen get involved in "politics," and what are his chances for success? What resources are available to him, and how might he use them?

(3) What roles do political parties in the United States play, and why do we have only two major parties? What are the chances for the development of new political parties?

(4) How does the American political system respond to demands for change by various groups in the system? What are the consequences of this response?

(5) What effect does the electoral process have on candidates and subsequent policy development dealing with environmental quality and other pressing social issues? Are

government leaders responsive to public opinion and sentiment?
(6) Does an individual have basic rights which cannot be withdrawn or restricted by the government? What has been the American experience in the area of societal versus individual rights?
(7) What effect has the American historical experience had in shaping present American institutions and political behavior? Does past development reduce the policy alternatives available in the future?
(8) What can social scientists tell us about American politics? Do they provide techniques which may help us better understand the nature of American society and the dynamics of change?

Obviously these questions are not exhaustive, but they highlight the matters discussed here. In this short volume, I hope to provide you with sufficient information and background to answer, at least tentatively, your more important questions and to encourage you to continue your study of the American political process. You are encouraged to think critically and pursue your favorite topics in greater detail by following the suggestions for additional reading at the end of each chapter.

While the following chapters provide diverse and, at times, perhaps confusing bits of information, there are a number of ways to increase your understanding of the following pages. Perhaps the best is to think about and understand thoroughly each of the following "focal points" before continuing with your reading. They may seem difficult, but if you carefully consider them now the information which follows will have greater meaning to you. The six focal points used here to analyze the American political system can be used to study a variety of other political organizations. You should return to them whenever you feel a review of the theoretical explanation of politics would increase your understanding and knowledge of everyday events.

FOCAL POINTS

Power and Legitimacy

We need basic definitions of the terms *power* and *legitimacy* if we are to understand their uses and complexities.* For our purposes, power can be defined in very simple terms. POWER IS THE ABILITY OF A PERSON, GROUP OF PEOPLE, OR INSTITUTION TO GET ANOTHER PERSON, GROUP OF PEOPLE, OR INSTITUTION TO DO SOMETHING WHICH THAT SECOND PERSON, GROUP OF PEOPLE, OR INSTITUTION WOULD NOT HAVE DONE IF THE FIRST PERSON, GROUP OF PEOPLE, OR INSTITUTION HAD NOT ACTED. If an individual were to face east and command the sun to rise, would we agree that it was his power over the sun which caused it to rise? Probably not, since we know the sun would have risen despite the person's command.

Another example illustrates this point. Jones has power over Smith whenever Smith does something *because* Jones wants him to, which Smith would not have done without Jones's insistence. Substitute other persons, groups of people, and institutions for Jones and Smith, and other power relationships are envisioned. For instance, the president may have power over Congress by getting it to adopt a specific proposal he wants, one Congress would not have adopted unless he had pushed for it.

Despite the simplicity of this notion of power, it has a large number of variations. For instance, power relationships can be

---

* An asterisk indicates that you should refer to the end of the chapter for suggested readings you may wish to pursue.

found, by definition, in institutions and organizations that are not normally thought of as political. For instance, is there any doubt in your mind who has the power in your family or among your friends? It soon becomes apparent that power relationships may be so complicated and universal that their study becomes highly complex. When this happens, it may be wise to study the components that make up the relationship. A specific example should prove useful.

City councilmen A and B both want the mayor to appoint their "man" to a newly created city job. The mayor does not want to lose the support of either councilman, but each has told the mayor that unless the decision is in his favor he will withdraw his support. What are the mayor's alternatives? One, he could appoint another nominee to the position or simply decide to let it go unfilled. This would not likely bring favorable reaction from either of the two councilmen. Two, he could appoint one of the nominees and hope that the disappointed councilman would not long be unhappy nor attempt to "repay" the mayor for his decision.

So, in this case, what may appear to be a very simple power relationship is actually quite complicated. There are at least five participants (the mayor, the two councilmen, and the two nominees) and probably a great deal of personal interaction. Keep in mind that great amounts of interaction and energy are spent during the decision-making process and that promises or threats of reward and punishment (usually called sanctions) may occur during the negotiation process. What appears to be a very simple act of appointment may actually be the result of a long and complicated bargaining process involving a great deal of time and personal contact.

Because of this complexity, any analysis of power relationships should be made cautiously. By simply assuming Jones has power over Smith because Smith did what Jones wanted him to do does not reflect a power relationship. The observer must also be able to show that Smith would not have acted as he did without Jones's influence. In order to understand power relationships, the analysis must go beyond what *appears* to be accurate. There must be careful analysis and consideration of the entire situation.

Related to the difficult question of power is the question of legitimacy. For our purposes, LEGITIMACY CAN BE DEFINED AS THE ACCEPTANCE OF POLITICAL POWER BY THOSE AFFECTED BY IT. In the United States, for example, most people accept the government's power to levy taxes and perform other such duties granted to various persons occupying governmental offices. Two questions concerning legitimacy should be considered. First, who has the legitimate power in a society? Second, do significant segments of that society refute or refuse to recognize that legitimacy? By attempting to answer these questions, the student of American politics will gain a better and more thorough understanding of the American historical experience and the contemporary unrest within the political system. Quite often the unrest is caused by a basic questioning of those in power and the legitimacy they have in governing.

After analyzing and understanding both power relationships and legitimacy, you should have a much deeper appreciation of American politics. Such analysis permits you to view society as a dynamic set of relationships and to understand the forces at work.

Nature of Government

Two of the recurring themes in any discussion of the American political system are: who controls political institutions, and who actually governs?* Throughout American history, frequent debates and arguments have arisen over the nature of American government.[1] Rather than going into great depth and detail about the arguments, Table 1-1 summarizes the essential characteristics of three "ideal" types of government. Some observers have argued the United States is a mixture of the three; others have argued the emphasis is on one particular type.[2]

Table 1-1
Types of Government

ELITIST	PLURALIST	DEMOCRATIC
Small group of people dominates.	Views expressed by and through groups representing wide interests.	Individual choice and participation open to all who want it.
Selection of elite may be based on variety of things: education, wealth, merit, influence, status.	Group power determined by resources (including potential members) available to the group.	Extensive individual participation in all phases of political expression.
Decisions made by elite; elite defines public interest.	Extensive bargaining and compromise essential. Emphasis on group benefits. These may coincide with general public needs.	Common perception of good dominates decisions. Disagreements resolved.
Decisions accepted by or imposed on rest of populace.	Group concepts dominate; group influences implementation of decisions.	Individualistically oriented; adherence often a matter of individual conscience.

Table 1-1 indicates the extensive differences in the various descriptions offered on the nature of the American political system. Each deserves careful consideration. To begin, many assume the United States was organized as a democracy. This is only partially correct. The United States was organized as and has evolved into a *representative* democracy in which citizens elect representatives to conduct and decide policy matters. This is contrasted with a participatory democracy in which citizens meet collectively to discuss and decide issues. In a country as diverse and large as the United States, participatory democracy in its "ideal" form is difficult to envision.

In addition to questions about the democratic nature of American government, there has been considerable debate in recent years about the pluralist-elitist view of American government. While democratic government is based on a common perception of community good and individual responsibility, pluralism and elitism stress different characteristics.

Those who maintain the United States is in reality an elitist system offer the following points to support their contentions.[3] They maintain that public decision-making is usually dominated by a small number with private interests, who have values different from the majority of the citizens. Hence, government decisions, since they are made by members of this group, benefit this small minority. In addition, it is argued that the elite is composed of those with enough wealth and influence to be in the "upper classes" of American society. Finally, it is believed that the elite not only have the ability to decide and influence policy matters, but they are also capable of establishing which issues will be publicly discussed and decided. In short, this view maintains that the vast majority of citizens have a very limited and inactive role in an elitist political system. In such a system, wealth and status determine who will have political power, and those in power will decide policy matters in such a way as to benefit themselves, not the majority of citizens.

This position can be contrasted with that offered by the pluralists, who maintain that groups dominate policy-making and that the individual citizen has extensive participatory power, because he either belongs or may belong to a large number of groups.[4] Under the pluralist concept, emphasis is on group bargaining and compromise. The bargaining and compromise permit everyone to achieve some level of satisfaction and thus prevent extensive alienation by the majority of citizens. The pluralists maintain that this analysis permits greater understanding of politics in America and does not waste time by looking for an elite which does not exist.

Elitists argue there is little citizen involvement; pluralists argue it occurs through group activity; and those advocating participatory democracy maintain it takes place in the form of individual participation. But does the nature of government make any difference in terms of what it does or citizen satisfaction with its policies? Does an elitist government have policies different from a pluralist or participatory democratic government? Do the citizens have significantly different reactions to the three types? If the same policies and satisfactions (or dissatisfaction) develop from all three, does it make much difference which is in effect? The answers to these questions will help you decide what type of change you may wish to implement and how you would implement it.

Types of Change

One certainty in this world is that things are always changing.* Popular books are constantly being published which consider the ramifications and types of change. Yet many observers fail to realize, since governmental institutions are composed of people and since problems affect these institutions, that governments and governmental structures are often likely to bring about change or to change themselves. Table 1-2 depicts three types of change which can occur.

Table 1-2
Types of Change

CHARACTERISTICS	Incremental	TYPES OF CHANGE Major	Revolutionary
People in governmental positions	Little change	Extensive change	Nearly complete or complete change
Governmental policy	Minor adjustments	Extensive adjustments and adoption of new policies	Total abandonment of old policies and adoption of new
Governmental institutions	Minor adjustments	Restructuring and reorganizing of many aspects	Abolition of old institutions and adoption of new
Means used	Traditional methods	Traditional, plus justification for extensive change based on "crisis" situation	New and different means used, based on extreme "crisis" situation

As Table 1-2 indicates, change can be categorized, in most cases, into three general types: incremental, major, and revolutionary. In addition, by examining the characteristics found in each type, one can quickly see the differences among the types.

Incremental change has been dominant in the American political system. Many observers have argued that this type of change is predominant in social and political organizations. Why should institutions and policies change in a major or revolutionary fashion if they are doing what is expected of them? In the "real" world, incremental change is most likely to occur, because enough citizens or groups have impressed upon government officials the need to make policy adjustments. An excellent example of an incremental decision is the periodic increase in Social Security benefits usually voted by Congress. The increase in benefits represents an adjustment, not a major change.

Incremental change can be contrasted with major change, which involves extensive personnel adjustments and/or the adoption of major new programs. Major change is often brought about because of the existence of a crisis situation. For instance, the wide-ranging institutional and program changes which characterized the New Deal of Franklin D. Roosevelt in the 1930s placed emphasis on creation of new programs (many of them later determined unconstitutional by the Supreme Court) and new policies which would benefit a large number of individuals. In this case, the crisis created by the Great Depression was instrumental in bringing about the change. Major change usually occurs when the crisis becomes serious enough to threaten the continued existence of a political system unless change does take place.

Contrasted with these first two types of change is revolutionary change. Probably least likely to occur in any society or political system, it involves basic and massive realignments. People, policies, and institutions are changed in drastic ways. In addition, the situation bringing on revolutionary change is usually extremely violent and causes a great deal of hardship to both the society and its members. The birth of the American republic is usually cited as a truly revolutionary change. Can you think of others?

Since these three types of change are "ideal" types, analysis of change in the political world will probably reveal fewer clear-cut distinctions. Also, remember that the terms themselves are neutral; simply to describe change as incremental, major, or revolutionary is *not* to imply that such change is either good or bad. That type of judgment is up to the person viewing the system and most likely will reflect the individual's underlying values and his view of the society about him. Thus, one individual may decide incremental change is best, while others may opt for major or revolutionary change.

Up to this point, the three focal points discussed have dealt with the abstract subjects of power and legitimacy, the nature of government, and types of change. The following focal points deal more directly with individual and systemic (that is, pertaining to the political system itself) qualities, and should encourage you to think about their ramifications and implications.

Layers of Government

To many observers, politics in the United States focuses only on presidential or national politics. This is a critical oversight. Consider for a moment which levels of government students have most contact with on a regular basis. True, students pay federal income tax, register with the Selective Service, and use postal services. Despite this, they are probably more closely in contact with state and local governments. If they attend a publicly supported college or university, the bulk of that support comes from state and local sources. Their children may be educated in public schools financed, for the most part, by state and local governments. Personal habits in drinking, driving, and behavior are largely under state and local jurisdiction. Cars and property are subject to taxation by state and local officials.

For our purposes, consider the American system as having three layers: national, state, and local. The national layer includes all the agencies and personnel of the federal government; the state layer includes the institutions and personnel of the 50 state governments, and the local layer includes municipalities, counties, regional authorities, and special districts such as school boards. The point is not to negate the importance of the national layer, but to stress the very large and direct roles the other two layers of government play in our lives.

Thus, if we wish to influence or modify the rules and regulations affecting us, we may want to be active at the local or state levels. One of the most compelling arguments for the decentralized nature of the American political system is that it encourages diversity and the implementation of policies conducive to the health and well-being of particular sections or localities of the country. In addition, decentralization may result in greater citizen participation by increasing the opportunities for participation.

Keep in mind that each of the other focal points may be used to investigate each of these layers of government. For instance, it is possible to have different types of change at the various levels. In addition, power may be distributed in different fashions at the various levels. This analysis permits a better understanding of American politics.

As examples, consider the urban violence which affected many American cities in the mid and late 1960s. Each city had a unique set of circumstances at work, and the responses (change) of various governmental institutions to the violence differed greatly from city to city. In similar fashion, what occurs at one level of government affects the other levels. An excellent example of this was the 1972 decision to "share" a percentage of federal tax revenues with state and local governments. Thus, Congress established another financial link among the various levels of government and somewhat altered the distribution of power.

Remember that the American political system has many layers of government and that a statement accurately describing aspects of one layer may be inaccurate regarding any other. If you ignore the importance and diversity of the other layers, any analysis and understanding of American politics will be at best superficial and probably inaccurate.

Leadership Responsibility

While it is doubtful that many students of this course hold an elected public office, most have probably voted for a candidate for a particular office. What should we expect of political leaders? It can be assumed that we do not want them to take off with the funds in the treasury or be in any way dishonest in their dealings, but there are a variety of other relationships we might expect to have with them.*

The relationship might be a consulting or direct one. Do we want our elected representative, regardless of the issue involved, to canvass those he represents before he makes a decision or takes a particular course of action? Some critics of political leaders have stressed that an elected representative should be bound by the recommendations and feelings of his constituents. It is usually argued that such a practice will insure public policy reflective of the general will by stressing the direct relationship between the representative and those he represents.

A second possible relationship is the people's implicit trust in the elected representative to act in what he feels are his constituents' best interests in every case. He determines the position most likely to benefit those he represents and then follows that course of action. His constituents pass judgment by examining his record and expressing their satisfaction or dissatisfaction at election time. If satisfied, he would continue in office. If the constituents were significantly dissatisfied, they would vote him out of office. His longevity in office or subsequent success depends on his ability to interpret correctly his constituents' best interests.

A third relationship permits the elected representative to exercise his own judgment on most matters, but encourages him to consult with his own constituents on matters of great importance to them. The representative in this case, not the constituents, decides when he needs advice and counsel.

These relationships are obviously ideal types, so they do permit certain questions to be raised. For instance, do we want our leaders at the local level to follow one of these relationships, and those at the state and national levels to adopt another? Does the relationship the leader has with his constituents make an important difference in policy matters? We cannot expect to fault public officials for their decisions if we do not have a clear understanding of what we expect from them. This leads to the final focal point.

Citizen Responsibility

In any political system, what are the responsibilities of the individual citizen? Before answering that he must obey the laws and participate in legally prescribed ways, consider the words of the Declaration of Independence on the conditions under which the citizen is obligated to take violent action.

> *We hold these truths to be self-evident, that all men are created equal, that they are endowed by their Creator with certain unalienable Rights, that among these are Life, Liberty and the Pursuit of Happiness. That to secure these rights, Governments are instituted among men, deriving their just powers from the consent of the governed. That whenever any form of Government becomes destructive of these ends, it is the*

Right of the People to alter or abolish it, and to institute new Governments.[5]

Without advocating violence as a legitimate method of change, we must keep in mind that unless we have a clear understanding of what we feel individual citizen responsibility is, we cannot evaluate various responses citizens might follow. For instance, is it the individual's responsibility to accept the will of the majority when that individual is convinced that the majority is wrong? If so, under what conditions must he submit to the will of the majority?

This raises a basic question about intensity of feelings. Most of us are likely to go along with the majority when the matter involved is not of great importance to us, but what happens when such a matter is of utmost importance? Are we obligated to go along, or do we have a more basic obligation to resist? If so, how do we accomplish it? Finally, is there a "higher law" that man must answer to?

Unless we can investigate and analyze why individual citizens act as they do, our understanding of American politics will be limited to a very static and narrow amount of information and shallow beliefs. But before we can consider the feelings of others, it is important to have a clear understanding of our own. What *are* our responsibilities and obligations to the American system? Can we fulfill them?

SUMMARY

The six focal points noted above help to organize the study of American politics. In addition, they are helpful in an analysis of American politics. If you consider them carefully and try to think clearly about their implications, they will serve as useful organizing devices as you study the following material. They are not easy to master, but they are essential to a sound understanding of the American political process.

18 Introduction

If we carefully consider the various aspects of the preceding focal points, as they apply to the American experience, one theme quickly becomes predominant—change. Change has been the most characteristic aspect of the American political experience. The next chapter summarizes what types of change have occurred in the United States and how.

SUGGESTED READINGS

Power and Legitimacy: The dual concepts of power and legitimacy have created considerable controversy. For excellent, but complicated theoretical considerations of these terms, see: Carl J. Friedrich, *Constitutional Government and Politics* (New York: Harper, 1937); John Locke, *Second Treatise on Civil Government*, ed. Thomas P. Peardon (New York: Bobbs-Merrill, 1952); Harold Lasswell and Abraham Kaplan, *Power and Society* (New Haven: Yale University Press, 1950); and Jean Jacques Rousseau, *The Social Contract*, tr. Willmoore Kendall (Chicago: H. Regnery, 1960).

Who Governs and Controls: For a spirited understanding of the concerns over who governs and who controls, browse the following in this order: Floyd Hunter, *Community Power Structure* (Chapel Hill: University of North Carolina Press, 1969); Robert A. Dahl, *Who Governs* (New Haven: Yale University Press, 1961); and Peter Bachrach and Morton S. Baratz, *Power and Poverty* (New York: Oxford University Press, 1970). A volume which is both interesting and provocative is C. Wright Mills, *The Power Elite* (New York: Oxford University Press, 1956).

Change: On the question of political and social change, see: Aldous Huxley, *Brave New World* (New York: Harper and Brothers, 1932) and George Orwell, *1984* (New York: Harcourt-Brace, 1949); for the dangers of technological change, see: Michael Crichton, *The Andromeda Strain* (New York: Alfred A. Knopf, 1969); and for a probing look into the implications of change for human development, see: Alvin Toffler, *Future Shock* (New York: Random House, 1970).

Leadership Relationships: For a discussion of leadership types, see: John C. Wahlke et al., *The Legislative System* (New York: Wiley, 1962). For a provocative discussion of the role of leaders in a democracy, read the short but spirited volume: E. E. Schattschnider, *Semisovereign People* (New York: Holt, Rinehart and Winston, 1960). For a view of leadership which emphasizes citizen participation and interaction, see: Alan Altshuler, *Community Control* (New York: Pegasus, 1970).

NOTES

1. For the early debates, see: Alexander Hamilton, et al., *The Federalist* (Garden City, New York: Anchor Books, 1966); John C. Calhoun, *A Disquisition on Government*, ed. Richard K. Crolle (New York: P. Smith, 1943). For a differing economic interpretation of American society, see: Charles A. Beard, *An Economic Interpretation of the Constitution of the United States* (New York: Macmillan, 1923).

2. See: Walter Lippman, *Public Opinion* (New York: Harcourt-Brace, 1922); David B. Truman, *The Governmental Process* (New York: Alfred A. Knopf, 1951); and Thomas R. Dye and L. Harmon Zeigler, *The Irony of Democracy* (Belmont, California: Duxbury Press, 1972).

3. Dye and Zeigler, pp. 4–24, 343–360.

4. For a comprehensive discussion of group activity, see: David B. Truman, *The Governmental Process* (New York: Alfred A. Knopf, 1951).

5. Henry Steele Commager, *Documents of American History* (New York: Appleton-Century Crofts, 1958), p. 100.

2. Change: A Historical Perspective of American Politics

Anyone familiar with historical depictions of the American experience will recall that historians usually divide our past into eras, such as Jacksonian democracy, the rise of big business, the New Deal, and the New Federalism.* Rather than provide a comprehensive overview of what has occurred in the United States since its founding, this section focuses on three distinctive yet interrelated areas that have undergone extensive change. Keep in mind that the changes described here are continuing and that other areas have also undergone change.

VOTING RIGHTS AND REPRESENTATION

Even the pre-independence days of the United States were characterized by considerable concern over who was entitled to vote and how representation was to be accomplished. For instance, the Boston Tea Party was an overt act against "taxation without representation" during the colonial era. After independence was declared in 1776, general discussion followed about who would vote and what was to be the method of representation. Both deserve our consideration.

The United States has continually broadened suffrage (the right to vote); it has been extended to more and more Americans as the nation has grown and matured. When the Constitution was originally written, free white males were the only persons entitled to vote. All women and slaves and many others were excluded from voting. The reasons were many, but one of the more important ones was the general distrust of the masses by the Founding Fathers. They maintained that men of property had a much larger stake in political decisions and therefore had an obligation and a responsibility to elect the best qualified persons to public office.[1] Although the federal Constitution leaves most rules regarding voting privileges to the states, its lack of positive statements for the groups previously mentioned is often interpreted as indicative of the Founding Fathers' lack of confidence in these groups.

Despite such an attempt by the writers of the Constitution to limit voting rights, American history has seen the gradual extension of these rights to other groups of citizens. For instance, the Fifteenth Amendment provided the Negro with the right to vote in federal elections and was the result of the strong anti-South feeling of the post-Civil War era. The Nineteenth Amendment in 1921 provided women with the right to vote and resulted partially from the well-organized, determined efforts of the "suffragettes." Finally, the Twenty-sixth Amendment provided for 18-year-olds to vote in all federal elections and came about after extensive debate and concern over the irony of permitting American youth to fight in the armed services on reaching the age of 18 but denying them voting rights till they reached 21. These changes have significantly broadened the number and characteristics of those eligible to vote, and all came about after extensive debate and controversy.

Despite the interest and governmental activity in the area of voting rights, many Americans still find it difficult to vote. One of the best reasons for this is the use of intimidation, force, or even fraud to keep qualified voters from the polls. Examples of these actions are usually drawn from the Southern black experience but are not limited to it.

What has been the result of increased suffrage in the United States? To answer this adequately, one must recognize that voting, even in national elections, is still largely under the regulation of state and local election officials. A person who wishes to vote in an election must first establish residency (although this may be changed for most elections), prove such residency if necessary, register to vote, and then actually vote. While this procedure can normally be accomplished with a minimum of effort and time, it can also serve as a very powerful deterrent to those interested in voting. Quite often, Americans with the right to vote might not be able to satisfy residency and other requirements or may be unwilling to take the time required to do so. Thus, this tends to decrease voter turnout. Table 2-1 indicates the numbers of Americans eligible to vote in a variety of recent elections, the numbers that voted, and the turnouts computed as percentages of the numbers of possible voters.

As the data indicate, American voting turnout is *not* especially high. In fact, when compared with voters in other democratic systems, American voters are less likely to exercise their franchise.[2] The result of the increased suffrage has not been massive participation.

The extension of voting rights has been one area undergoing considerable change. Another, closely related area has also been involved in extensive change; the question of the forms representation should take in America has been slow to evolve and has thus resulted in a great deal of controversy. For example, most people assume that United States senators have always been elected by direct popular vote. This is false. Prior to the Seventeenth Amendment (1913), United States senators were elected by state legislatures. Americans could influence the senatorial choice only if they had voting privileges in the election of representatives to their state legislatures. Needless to say, this indirect method of senatorial selection often effectively restricted public control.

The record of the Constitutional Convention indicates that the Founding Fathers wanted to insulate the second house of Congress, the Senate, from direct popular influence.[3] It was felt that the Senate and its members should be less disposed than the House of

Table 2-1
Voting Participation in the United States in Federal Elections

YEAR	1964[a]	1966[b]	1968[a]	1970[c]	1972[d]
Total population of voting age (millions)	113.8	112.9	120.0	120.7	139.6
Number of persons voting (millions)	70.6	62.5	73.2	65.9	76.1
% of voting-age population voting	62.1	55.4	61.0	54.6	54.5

SOURCES:

a. U.S. Department of Commerce, Bureau of the Census, *Population Characteristics*, P-20, no. 177, p. 4.
b. U.S. Department of Commerce, Bureau of the Census, *Population Characteristics*, P-20, no. 160, p. 3.
c. U.S. Department of Commerce, Bureau of the Census, *Population Characteristics*, P-20, no. 228, p. 12.
d. *Congressional Quarterly Weekly Report* (November 11, 1972) pp. 2,947–2,949.

Representatives to respond to periodic shifts of public opinion. Thus, the senators were given a six-year term in office, and the representatives, who were thought to be more responsive (or vulnerable) to abrupt changes in public opinion, were granted a two-year term.

Another aspect of representation involves the decision to base representation in the House of Representatives on state population and representation in the Senate on state equality. Among the important issues decided at the Constitutional Convention was the question of the large versus the small states. Naturally, voters from small states like Rhode Island and Delaware wanted their states to have equal representation with large states in the national legislature; however, those from large states like Pennsylvania and New York favored representation based on population size. In one of the most important compromises ever made in American history, each state was given two votes in the Senate, but its number of representatives in the House of Representatives was based on its population. Thus, Alaska, which had 300,000 residents in 1970, had the same number of United States senators that year as did California, with 19,953,000 residents. Observers of the American system usually point out this non-democratic characteristic of the American Congress.

Despite such criticism, the method of representation used in the United States and the continuing extension of voting rights has created a potential for extensive participation by Americans. This has been the result of dramatic changes that have occurred throughout our history, continuing as recently as 1970 with the ratification of the 18-year-old-vote amendment.

Related to the right to vote is the right to have one's vote count the same as every other vote. Reapportionment has gained considerable attention since the mid 1960s and will remain important in American politics.* The Constitution calls for reassigning the number of representatives a state has in the House of

Representatives every ten years, after the census is completed. This often results in partisan political attempts to redesign the congressional districts to overrepresent one political party and to underrepresent another political party. This practice will be discussed in the chapter dealing with Congress (3). It is also common practice for state legislatures and other legislative bodies to do the same thing when they are determining districts. Since the mid 1960s, the federal courts have been responsive to suits challenging the drawing of district lines or methods of representation not based on population.[4]

MINORITY RIGHTS

To many Americans, the phrase "civil rights" implies the recent attempts by various minority groups in the United States to acquire voting and other rights. This is unfortunate, because the term, while it may imply this, also includes other individual freedoms. This and the next segment of this chapter will consider both minority rights and other civil rights as coequal aspects of the concern over civil rights and as the second and third areas experiencing change in the United States.

It is very difficult for even the most well-meaning American to accept the fact that the United States was very slow to abolish and forbid slavery. Slavery, usually involving black men and women, was a long-standing practice in the colonies and states prior to the Constitutional Convention. At the convention itself, there was extensive debate and ultimately compromise concerning this question. The Constitution did not specifically forbid slavery; it simply prohibited slave importation after 1808. In addition, the Founding Fathers decided that slaves were to be counted as three-fifths of a person when determining the population as a basis for establishing congressional districts and apportioning direct taxes among the states. This acknowledged in legal terms that a slave was less than a total person, and it reflected the dominant opinion at the time. Slaves were considered to be personal property, not human beings. The reasons for such beliefs were many and varied, but the implications of these decisions for American history were, and still are, profound.

The question of slavery and the rise of a Southern economy based on it became an issue in national politics even prior to the ratification of the Constitution. During the 1800s there was extensive debate and frequent compromise on the issue. This resulted in temporary solutions imposed by the Congress and the Supreme Court. However, the question was never permanently resolved, and it ultimately plunged the nation into a devastating civil war. The Civil War produced such regional hatred and divisiveness that many argued the country would never again be truly united.

While the decision-makers created policy, the slaves were usually forced to endure conditions of physical punishment and abuse. In addition, the slave was seen as chattel and was often separated from his family. In short, the slave's survival, in both physical and emotional terms, often depended upon the reservoir of strength he carried within himself. It was not until the Civil Rights Amendments (thirteenth, fourteenth, and fifteenth) that the slave was made an American citizen, declared entitled to due process under the law, and formally provided with the right to vote. American history since the Civil War can be interpreted as an attempt to reconcile the former slave's new status with that of the rest of society.

The period from the late 1860s to the early 1930s was marked by several contradictory trends. In the first place, many black Americans were restrained, through subtle discriminatory acts such as the "grandfather clause" and violent acts extending even to lynching, from exercising their rights as citizens. In addition, economic conditions were such that most blacks remained closely tied to the Southern rural economy. Second, during the early 1900s, the large industrial cities of the North, needing inexpensive labor for industry and services, became a migratory place for many blacks. In these cities, the blacks quite often formed homogeneous residential areas, which were the forerunners of today's dilapidated and deteriorating central cities. Even then the quality of city services provided in those areas was deficient in many respects and resulted in lower standards of living for the areas' residents. Third, during this period there was increased emphasis on black nationalism. Several organizations and groups, such as the National Association for the Advancement of Colored People (NAACP) and Marcus Garvey's followers, stressed the importance of the black cultural experience, and their leaders often spoke of a return to the great black civilizations of Africa. Despite this emphasis, the quality of life among most American blacks was inferior to that enjoyed by most whites.

During the 1930s, the federal government became more involved in the affairs of the black American, and the result, extending even into the 1970s, has been increased attention and policy directed toward the relief of his plight. In 1948, President Truman ended formal segregation in all aspects of American military life by executive order. The Civil Rights Acts of 1957, 1960, and 1964 stressed the need to protect the black man's basic rights and to provide him with more equal opportunities. The 1965 Voting Rights Act, renewed for an additional five years in 1970, brought the national government directly into the process of enforcing voting rights in some state and local elections.

The 1970s promise to be of critical importance to the entire problem of black civil rights for several reasons. First, it is clear that federal policy may not continue to expand enforcement of civil rights of black Americans because of the extensive public reaction to such policy. The role played by compulsory school bussing in the 1972 presidential election is indicative of the saliency and importance of such an issue. Employment practices stressing affirmative action to recruit blacks have been criticized. In short, the larger society may not be willing to make the commitments necessary to enhance conditions for any minority group in the United States. Second, the black community is now widely divided on what it expects and hopes in the area of domestic policies. Integration, which was widely accepted in prior years, does not have the support among black leaders it once did. Black leaders now frequently argue that black separation is more beneficial than integration with white society.*

Regardless of these two trends, a third is likely to be as influential. As Table 2-2 indicates, many American cities have significant black populations. As black Americans begin to control the political structures of these cities, far-reaching change may be forthcoming. Certainly the issue of black civil rights will be one of the more important concerns of the 1970s.

It must be remembered that rights in America, for many other minority groups as well as for blacks, has been a major and controversial aspect of our political development and national heritage. There is little reason to expect this to change in the future. This is also the case with individual freedoms, more generally referred to as civil rights.

CIVIL RIGHTS

Many Americans point with pride to the democratic values of a free press, free speech, and broad individual freedoms. What is important is that the United States has a long historical tradition of stressing these rights. Of course, at various points in our history these rights were less protected and guaranteed than during other periods. A brief summary could not begin to capture the dynamic quality and importance of individual rights in United States history; the reader is encouraged to pursue this study by selecting and

Table 2-2
Black Population of Selected American Cities: 1971

CITY	BLACK % OF TOTAL CITY POPULATION
Washington, D.C.	71
Newark, New Jersey	54
Atlanta, Georgia	51
Baltimore, Maryland	46
New Orleans, Louisiana	45
Detroit, Michigan	44
Birmingham, Alabama	42
Richmond, Virginia	42
Cleveland, Ohio	38
Oakland, California	34
Philadelphia, Pennsylvania	34
Houston, Texas	26
Kansas City, Missouri	22
New York, New York	21
Indianapolis, Indiana	18
Boston, Massachusetts	16

SOURCE:

U.S. Department of Commerce, Bureau of the Census, *The Social and Economic Status of the Black Population in the United States, 1971* (Washington, D.C.: Government Printing Office, 1972), p. 124.

Change: A Historical Perspective of American Politics

reading any of the several books suggested at the close of this chapter. Instead of summarizing here the various court cases and decisions involving individual freedoms, three general areas will be discussed.

The first is the area of free speech. Many Americans feel they have the right to utter whatever they please at any time, because this is a free country. Others would argue that the country is repressive and that truly free expression of ideas would be harshly and severely dealt with by legal authorities. As is the case with most individual freedoms, you must decide which is applicable. For instance, does a speech calling for overt action and violence, which is then followed by acts of violence, constitute a violation of free speech? Or, does the heckling of the president or unproved accusations of wrongdoing against public officials come under government control?

The United States has experienced several periods of intense concern over these questions. Quite often they occur at times of involvement in wars and periods of great international or national tension. While most people would point to the major wars as times when concern over freedom of speech was at its greatest, as recently as 1972, spokesmen for the Nixon administration felt that the critics of President Nixon's peace proposal concerning the Vietnam war were "aiding and comforting the enemy." This accusation brought immediate and widespread reaction from both the public and the press, and the Nixon administration was accused of attempting to stifle dissent.

Such questions are not easy to resolve; in fact, Chapter 4's review of the Supreme Court's position on the matter will indicate that the Court has chosen to interpret the breadth of the free speech guarantee in different ways at various points in our history. As in many other aspects of America, debate and change have characterized the situation.

Another widely discussed and increasingly important area of individual rights is the obtaining of evidence by search and seizure.

The Fourth Amendment established the need for law enforcement officials to obtain a search warrant in most criminal proceedings. The idea was to protect the individual from unreasonable search and seizure. It should not surprise anyone in this era of sophisticated technology and complicated legal questions that this matter has commanded considerable attention. Two examples illustrate this point.

In recent years, concern has been expressed over the growth and activities of various organized crime syndicates. Because the participants usually work from personal memory and individual contact, law enforcement agencies often find it difficult to obtain useful and important evidence to support their charges. Thus, one of the techniques most frequently used in crime detection has been electronic eavesdropping. The question is whether such a practice violates the constitutional rights of the suspects; the courts have yet to establish a clear policy on this point. If law enforcement officials are allowed to maintain electronic surveillance over suspected organized crime figures, should they also have the same right regarding other suspected wrongdoers?

A second example, an area in which the courts have established clearer precedents, involves a person who is stopped by a police officer for a traffic violation and is subsequently found to have an illegal drug in his possession. Can the prosecution of this person on an illegal drug possession charge be permitted, even though he was originally stopped because of a traffic violation? The courts have ruled that it can, because discovery of the illegal drug came during a search relevant to the traffic violation.[5]

While the courts are still weighing the evidence and considering the constitutional implications of their decisions in the area of search and seizure, they have clearly delineated their position in a third area: what rights the accused have regarding legal counsel.

In the *Gideon* case in 1964, the Supreme Court ruled that persons charged with crimes who are unable to afford legal counsel have the right to counsel and that counsel must be provided by the state prosecuting them. This decision reaffirmed long-standing decisions of federal courts. In several other decisions, most notably the *Escabedo* and *Miranda* cases, the Court has ruled that the criminal suspect has the right to have his attorney present during interrogation and prior to actually being charged with a crime. In addition, the suspect has to be told of his right to counsel and his right to remain silent.

A related aspect of the question of search and seizure is the extension of the protection provided by the Bill of Rights to other levels of government. When the Bill of Rights was adopted, it specifically gave certain rights to the individual and denied the federal government the power to infringe on them. Over the years, the Supreme Court has ruled that the protection provided by the Bill of Rights also prevents state and local governments from infringing on citizens' rights.

Careful reading and consideration of the three areas discussed above make it obvious that questions involving individual rights are bound to cause a great deal of passionate and spirited debate. Many people disagree on at least one or more of these points. Given the complexities of American society and the diverse feelings of Americans, one can appreciate the difficulties the Supreme Court has in deciding such complex and interrelated questions.

The discussion of individual freedoms is important, because it sheds some light on one of two major areas yet to be included in this chapter. That is the question of political change and how it occurs in the United States. Consider the following question for a moment: what type of change occurs in the United States? What appears to be an uncomplicated question can easily become quite involved. Reconsider, for a moment, the distinctions depicted in Table 1-2 among the three types of change. These initial distinctions may prove quite interesting and useful in understanding the American political past.

Despite the objections that can be raised, it seems clear that American political life is vastly different today than it was in the early 1800s or 1900s. The American political system has undergone drastic changes since its inception nearly 200 years ago, but the important point is that these changes have occurred over an extended period of time and cannot be considered revolutionary in nature. In fact, change in American political behavior and institutions has been largely incremental, with occasional major developments.

Table 2-3 lists several periods in American history which historians argue were important to the growth and development of American politics.

Table 2-3
Developmental Periods in American Politics

HISTORICAL PERIOD	IMPORTANT DEVELOPMENTS
1789–1820	National government strengthened. National power in banking and commerce established.
1840–1865	Economic and social aspects of slavery result in Civil War.
1877–1910	Industrial expansion and growth.
1930–1945	New Deal capitalism and World War II.
1946–1972	Economic growth and material gains.

Each of these periods, with the possible exception of the Civil War era, is characterized by incremental or major political change. Personnel shifts did occur in leadership, but they did not result in drastic changes in public policy decisions. Whatever the reasons,

Change: A Historical Perspective of American Politics   35

and they will be discussed later, one can conclude that American political change, since our successful attempt to gain independence, has not been revolutionary. This has an effect on America's role in assisting other nations to develop which demands explanation.

Citizens of the newly developing, Third World nations frequently look to other nations as examples of how they might develop politically. America's past, despite its revolutionary beginning, often fails to provide a meaningful example because of its subsequent less revolutionary development. The result is that many nations may reject the American form of representative democracy and economic system of capitalism for a developmental model which they feel provides them with a more efficient, quicker path to economic and political strength. This does not necessarily mean they reject the American system, but they find it inapplicable in their own set of conditions.

Since revolutionary change is an inadequate explanation for the growth and development of the American system, two additional explanations will be briefly explored. The first involves the so-called "frontier" explanation of American politics. Popularized by a historian, Frederick Jackson Turner, this explanation maintains that the availability of relatively inexpensive land resulted in a unique set of circumstances influencing American historical development.[6] By providing an incentive for migration and by serving as a safety valve for those disenchanted with their present situations, the frontier concept permitted settlement of new land and a constant renewing of the American character. Thus people could gain new opportunities by seeking the new lands which were frequently made available by the federal government. This interpretation of the American past is change-oriented and permits a dynamic analysis of why the United States developed as it did.

A second explanation of the American experience stresses the role of technology as the basic requisite and driving force in American development. It emphasizes the early American inventors

(Whitney, Clemens, Morse, Colt) and the roles their inventions played in conquering the vast territorial expanse which was so crucial to the economic development of America. This view of the American past usually maintains it was the scientific and technological successes which provided the country with its basis for industrial and commercial development of unprecedented magnitude. Using this explanation, we can readily account for many of the changes occurring throughout American society. Books such as *Brave New World*, *1984*, *Future Shock*, and *The Andromeda Strain* offer glimpses into the future of a heavily technological and scientific society.[7]

The crucial point is not whether one single explanation for American development can be all-inclusive, but that any explanation of the American political past must include more than a single variable. If the complexities of the American historical past are ignored, as the preceding two examples illustrate, the analysis will be much too simplistic.

Many observers of America's past have chosen either to ignore or deemphasize a very important and basic ingredient of the American experience. Violence, both individual and group, has also long characterized the American political experience. Presidents Lincoln, Garfield, McKinley, and Kennedy were assassinated. In 1968 and 1972, presidential candidates were targets for assassins' bullets. There have been numerous incidents of internal strife; Shay's rebellion in the early 1780s and the violence associated with the labor movement in the 1930s and 1940s are excellent examples. In addition, the American Civil War exemplified the role of violence in the American system. And, what American cannot recall the tragedy of urban unrest which marked the 1960s with extensive damage and death?

Little is gained by refusing to accept the fact that political change in the United States has been and is often accompanied by violence. To ignore violence and the role it plays is to deny the existence of a basic American characteristic. This volume does not intend to condemn or condone violence, for that is an individual stand we must each take; it does intend to place violence in perspective as part of the American experience. To do any less would be to ignore an important American characteristic and bias any explanation of American politics.

SUMMARY

Chapter 2 has provided a brief overview of the important questions and possible considerations the rest of the volume will develop. You may want to refer back to this chapter as you proceed. One central conclusion is now possible; the American political experience is constantly changing and is characterized by diversity and complexity. The remainder of the book attempts to raise as many questions and offer as many answers as possible concerning this national experience.

SUGGESTED READINGS

Historical Eras: For examples of historians who divide the American past into eras, see: Richard Hofstadter, *The American Political Tradition* (New York: Alfred A. Knopf, 1948); Richard Hofstadter, *The Age of Reform* (New York: Alfred A. Knopf, 1955); Arthur M. Schlesinger, *Political and Social History of the United States* (New York: Macmillan, 1925). Two excellent "era" histories are: Arthur M. Schlesinger, *The Age of Jackson* (Boston: Little, Brown, 1945), which describes Andrew Jackson's tenure as president and the resulting social changes; and John D. Hicks, *Republican Ascendancy: 1921–1933* (New York: Harper and Brothers, 1960), which presents a comprehensive view of the 1920s in American life.

Reapportionment: Two interesting and readable considerations of reapportionment are: Malcolm E. Jewell, ed., *The Politics of Reapportionment* (New York: Atherton Press, 1962) and Andrew Hacker,

Congressional Districting (Washington, D.C.: Brookings Institution, 1964). For a series of essays dealing with future apportionment politics, see Nelson W. Polsby, ed., *Reapportionment in the 1970s* (Berkeley: University of California Press, 1971).

Black Political Strategy: For a variety of viewpoints, perspectives, and strategies, see Eldridge Cleaver, *Soul on Ice* (New York: McGraw-Hill, 1968); Martin Luther King, *Why We Can't Wait* (New York: Harper and Row, 1964); Stokely Carmichael and Charles V. Hamilton, *Black Power* (New York: Random House, 1968); and Malcolm X, *By Any Means Necessary* (New York: Pathfinder Press, 1970). For a collection of these positions and viewpoints, see Robert Penn Warren, *Who Speaks for the Negro* (New York: Random House, 1965).

NOTES

1. Alexander Hamilton, John Jay, James Madison, "Federalist #10," *The Federalist* (New York: The Modern Library, n.d.), pp. 53–62.
2. In England, participation usually averages 80 percent, as described by Richard Rose, *Politics in England* (Boston: Little, Brown, 1964), pp. 85–90. In Germany, voting is often in excess of 85 percent; see Arnold J. Heidenheimer, *The Governments of Germany* (New York: T. Y. Crowell, 1966), pp. 107–110.
3. *The Federalist* #63 and #64, pp. 400–407, 407–416.
4. See the *Westbury* v. *Sanders* (1964) decision for an example of the Supreme Court's reasoning.
5. This entire area of search and seizure has been the subject of many controversial court decisions and is in a constant state of flux.
6. Frederick Jackson Turner, "The Significance of the Frontier in American History," *Frontier and Section* (Englewood Cliffs, N.J.: Prentice-Hall, 1961), pp. 37–62.
7. See the suggested readings on change at the end of Chapter 1.

SECTION II
American National Political Institutions

INTRODUCTION

Most American government texts provide the beginning student with detailed and complicated explanations of the institutional arrangements of American government.* This requires an emphasis on structural matters, procedural rules, and historical precedents. By contrast, this chapter will introduce the important institutional information in a less comprehensive way, but in a way that should encourage the reader to explore it more thoroughly through other sources. Following this brief introduction, each of the major national government institutions will be summarized and discussed. A fourth branch, the federal bureaucracy, has been included with the Congress, the Supreme Court, and the presidency. While the federal bureaucracy has not traditionally been considered a "branch" of government, it has developed to the point where it makes major and important contributions, not only to the administration of public policy but also to the formulation of that policy. Because of this, a thorough explanation of the American bureaucracy is in order.

The institutional characteristics discussed in this chapter are products of extensive historical development and are subject to future change. The "proper" roles of the various institutions have been explored extensively throughout American history and are still being interpreted as social conditions alter, new issues arise, and different persons occupy the seats of power. Before each of the institutions is presented in some depth, you should review Table II-1, which presents comparative information on the four branches.

Note, for example, the age requirements for the House of Representatives and the Senate. It is possible to explain or anticipate the likely composition of those legislative bodies based solely on the formal age requirements? Except for the bureaucratic offices, which have diverse civil service criteria, the requirements

Table II-1
Comparative Information on Major American Institutions

INSTITUTION	NO. OF MEMBERS	HOW SELECTED	REQUIREMENTS FOR HOLDING OFFICE	LENGTH OF TERM
Congress House of Representatives	435	By popular election in congressional districts	25 years old; citizen for 7 years	2 years; no limit on succession
Senate	100	2 by popular election in each state	30 years old; citizen for 9 years	6 years; no limit on succession
President	1	Indirect: popular vote and electoral college	35 years old; natural citizen	4 years; limit of two terms
Supreme Court	9	Appointment by president; confirmed by Senate	No formal requirements	Life
Regulatory Commissions	7 Commissions	Appointment by president	No formal requirements	Varies

for the various offices are set forth by the Constitution (see Appendix) and are therefore subject to change by the amendment process detailed in the Constitution. The amending process is, then, one means through which change takes place. For example, the Seventeenth Amendment provides for the direct election of United States Senators rather than election by the various state legislatures, as prescribed in the Constitution.

The Constitution provides two specific ways for amendments to be proposed and two ways for proposed amendments to be ratified. The fact that the Constitution has been amended only 26 times in almost 200 years indicates either that the American people have been well satisfied with its basic provisions or that the amending process is such a difficult and arduous procedure that it makes amending nearly impossible.

Amendments to the Constitution may be *proposed* by a two-thirds vote of the members of the House and Senate (acting separately) or by the delegates sent to a convention called by Congress upon petition by two-thirds of the state legislatures. The latter method of proposing amendments has never been used. An amendment is *adopted* whenever three-fourths of the states ratify the proposal through their state legislatures or by means of conventions called by the state legislatures. Notice that there is always the need for more than a simple majority (which is 50 percent plus 1) in order to propose or adopt an amendment. In addition, by requiring that both the House and the Senate and the various state legislatures act on an amendment, the amount of time involved is quite long. Many state legislatures meet only every other year. Any person who hopes for a speedy adoption of an amendment misunderstands the amending process in the United States. A good case in point is the recent struggle over the amendment on equal rights for women.*

Passed by Congress in 1972, the equal rights amendment states, "Equality of rights under the law shall not be denied or

abridged by the United States or by any state on account of sex."
The amendment is to go into effect two years after it is ratified by
three-fourths of the state legislatures, who have till 1979 to ratify
it. By April 1973, 30 states had ratified the amendment, but 12 had
rejected it. Thus, no one additional state can reject it if the
amendment is to achieve the 38 states needed for ratification.

The struggle for ratification or rejection varied from state to
state, but in most cases it stirred public feeling. The Nebraska
legislature ratified the amendment, then later rejected it. This
reversal prompted a legal controversy over the constitutionality of
such an action. Connecticut's legislature first rejected the amendment
and then ratified it—a constitutionally acceptable practice. It
remains difficult to predict whether the amendment will become
the twenty-seventh to the Constitution, but the evolutionary process
of the amendment through congressional debate and action and
subsequently to each of the 50 state legislatures for its decision is
indicative of the exceedingly slow and time-consuming process
necessary to amend the Constitution. In addition, those favoring
the amendment, while able to muster considerable support at the
national level, have found it more difficult to gain support in many
of the state legislatures. The decentralizing aspect of the amendment
process makes change difficult, unless there is general support
for that change throughout the states.

A careful reading of the amendments (Appendix) indicates
few formal changes in the provisions setting forth requirements for
public office or the conduct of affairs in those offices. There has
been, however, extensive informal change in the various national
institutions and in the behavior of the individuals who are part of
those institutions. Custom and personal preference have played
large roles in these changes. Our attention will focus on what is,
not what has been. But first, we might ask, why is it important to
understand the institutional arrangements of the American national
government and their complicated interrelations? Although not

exhaustive, several mutually supporting answers may be offered to this question.

First, the institutions depicted in Table II-1 are responsible for the important national decisions affecting the personal security and freedom of the residents of this country. For example, whether we like to admit it or not, the tremendous destructive power and capability of the American military establishment affects us all. It is of critical importance who controls and decides when and how that military power will be used. An excellent example of this importance is the national selective service system. Congress and the president directly control who gets inducted and the type of service expected. In recent years the Supreme Court has become involved in deciding the constitutionality of the selective service laws; thus the institutions at the national level make decisions which affect us in dramatic ways. In essence, they are life-and-death decisions.

Second, the institutions should not be seen as independent actors, each operating in its own sphere, without any pressures or interplay from the other institutions. Rather, after each institution is understood as it is in itself, then the interplay and interaction among the various institutions should be carefully explored. Furthermore, these institutions and the arrangements among them are subject to public scrutiny and public opinion. Observers often seek specific decisions or legislation and attempt to rally public support for or against them. This process is best understood when the institutional arrangements themselves are clearly understood.

Third, a thorough understanding of the institutions and the relationships among them is essential if one wishes to take a position regarding the balance of power in the American system. The drafters of the Constitution created a system that "checked" and "balanced" various institutions. Thus, the presidency was created as a unique blend of executive authority and restricted power. In similar fashion, Congress and the Supreme Court were established. The Founding Fathers devised a system of "separation of powers";

that is, it was envisioned that each branch would have authority in its area. The president would enforce the laws established by Congress, and the Supreme Court would consider disputes.

In today's complex world, and even in the early days of the nation, such separation of function and responsiblity would be impossible. Unless you understand the various institutions, you cannot really assess the various powers of one vis-à-vis the other. For instance, some observers of the American system claim that our current problems in foreign affairs are due to a decline in the relative power of the Congress and an increase in the president's power. Regardless of the reasons for holding that position, it is an interesting argument. But to understand and evaluate such a judgment, one must have a basic knowledge of the institutions: what they do and how they do what they do.

Finally, one other point needs mentioning. As was discussed in the preceding chapter, the American system is often regarded as an example to the rest of the world. Unless one understands the specifics of the institutional arrangements through which this system works and what is responsible for their operation, this type of comparison becomes meaningless. This section is designed to present the unique features of American political institutions and to examine how the arrangements among them affect the development of public policy in the United States.

SUGGESTED READINGS

American Government Texts: James M. Burns and Jack W. Peltason, *Government by the People* (Englewood Cliffs, N.J.: Prentice-Hall, 1972); Marian D. Irish and James W. Prothro, *The Politics of American Democracy* (Englewood Cliffs, N.J.: Prentice-Hall, 1971); and Austin Ranney, *The Governing of Men* (New York: Holt, Rinehart and Winston, 1966). For an interesting and worthwhile discussion of the theoretical and philosophical implications of American institutions, see: Robert A. Dahl, *Pluralist Democracy in the United States: Conflict and Consent* (Chicago: Rand-McNally, 1967).

Women's Rights: For a variety of viewpoints and specific plans of action, the following feminist literature is suggested: Betty Friedan, *The Feminine Mystique* (New York: Norton, 1963); Kate Millett, *Sexual Politics* (New York: Avon, 1971); and Germaine Greer, *The Female Eunuch* (New York: Bantam, 1972). Also, *Ms.* magazine warrants careful reading, as it presents contemporary feminist perspectives.

3. The United States Congress and Public Policy

The Congress of the United States is a *bicameral* legislative body; that means that it has two separate chambers or houses, each having its own powers and responsibilities.* In order for a bill to be enacted into law, it must be passed by both houses. The Senate of the United States is composed of two popularly elected senators from each state. The House of Representatives is made up of members elected from 435 congressional districts within the 50 states. One member is elected from each congressional district, and the number of congressmen assigned each state is determined on the basis of population, following each decennial census. The state draws the lines for the districts, but recent court decisions require the districts within each state to be as nearly equal in population as possible. In addition to the 435 voting members of the House, a representative from the District of Columbia has speaking rights but can not vote on legislation before the House.

FIVE COMMON CHARACTERISTICS

Although the two houses are based on different principles of representation and vary in size, they do share certain common characteristics. First, since both the House and the Senate must pass a bill if it is to become law, the members of both houses are in the midst of the legislative process. Second, because of certain constitutional provisions, each house often finds itself directly involved with the other branches of government. Two examples serve to illustrate this point. When a vacancy occurs in the Supreme Court, the president has the authority to appoint a person to the Court; however the appointment is subject to senatorial confirmation, so the president must be aware of the type of person the Senate is likely to confirm. This usually involves some very complicated political interaction between the Senate and the president. This occurred in the late 1960s, when President Nixon attempted to fill several Supreme Court vacancies. The president nominated Clement F. Haynesworth, Jr. and G. Harold Carswell. Both nominees were rejected by the Senate after a series of bitter conflicts; this was the first time the Senate had ever failed to ratify two consecutive presidential nominees for the Supreme Court.

In similar fashion, the House of Representatives has frequent interaction with the president. The Constitution stipulates that all legislation dealing with revenue must originate in the House of Representatives. This does not mean that the Senate does not have to approve it, only that the House must originate the action. Thus, if a president wants congressional approval to spend money for domestic, defense, or foreign purposes, he must have someone introduce legislation in the House of Representatives requesting such expenditures.

Another shared characteristic is that both houses tend to be organized in a way which promotes expertise among individual members in only a few areas, and usually in just one area. Given the complexity and vast amounts of information pertaining to any subject, it is understandable that a senator or representative will concentrate on one particular program or several aspects of it. To accomplish this, both houses have established *standing committees*. These are permanent committees which initially consider all legislative proposals on a given subject. Table 3-1 lists the various standing committees in both houses; note how they correspond with specific areas of interest.

Individual senators and representatives are assigned to various standing committees. Normally one keeps his committee assign-

Table 3-1
Standing Committes of the Congress of the United States

HOUSE OF REPRESENTATIVES	SENATE
Agriculture	Aeronautical and Space Sciences
Appropriations	Agriculture and Forestry
Armed Services	Appropriations
Banking and Currency	Armed Services
District of Columbia	Banking, Housing and Urban Affairs
Education and Labor	
Foreign Affairs	Commerce
Government Operations	District of Columbia
House Administration	Finance
Interior and Insular Affairs	Foreign Relations
Internal Security	Government Operations
Interstate and Foreign Commerce	Interior and Insular Affairs
Judiciary	Judiciary
Merchant Marine and Fisheries	Labor and Public Welfare
Post Office and Civil Service	Post Office and Civil Service
Public Works	Public Works
Rules	Rules and Administration
Science and Astronautics	Veterans' Affairs
Standards of Official Conduct	
Veterans' Affairs	
Ways and Means	

ments throughout his tenure in Congress; however it is possible to change committee assignments and, within limits set by legislation and party regulations, a member may serve on additional ones as openings develop. By being on a committee, a congressman is expected to develop expertise in that particular area of legislation. For instance, a representative or senator serving on the agriculture committee of his chamber is expected to understand the implications of various governmental policies dealing with price supports and agricultural programs. It should be obvious that representatives often want to be on committees which reflect their constituents' interests and needs. This provides them with the opportunity to directly influence legislation in areas of political importance to them.

Another related and important point concerning the role of the committees in both houses cannot be overemphasized. Breaking the fairly large membership of the two houses into committees permits the Congress to conduct hearings and consider policy in groups of manageable size, and this in turn fosters free and open discussion. In addition, it means that a great deal of the congressional work is done in committee and not by the total membership. Thus, the agriculture or education committee will consider a particular proposal and make a recommendation to the larger body. Quite often the full House or Senate will base its decision on whether to oppose or support this legislation on the committee's report or the division within the committee. This is due to the time pressures on the congressman; since he cannot devote the time necessary to be an expert, he will often assume the committee has carefully considered the problem and acted accordingly. The legislation adopted by Congress is usually not the result of extensive development and discussion by the full body; in most cases it is the result of long and often tedious work by a committee or committees.

A fourth characteristic common to both houses is the role

partisan political organization plays in decision-making. *Partisan* means using party labels as a basis for organization and to identify various voting blocs. For instance, each congressional committee reflects the underlying party divisions in Congress. Suppose, for example, there are 60 Democratic and 40 Republican senators. In that case, the Democrats would have approximately six-tenths of the positions on the various Senate standing committees and the Republicans the rest. In the House, membership on the standing committees also reflects the underlying partisan division. For all practical purposes, each political party determines which of its members will serve on which committee. Thus the political party becomes an important organizational device in the American Congress.

This also means that partisan politics play a major role in congressional decision-making; if the Democrats control one chamber, it can be expected that on most issues the Democrats should be able to muster enough votes to get their policy adopted or a Republican proposal defeated. However, on questions involving considerable controversy or items of national interest, party allegiance alone is often not sufficient to produce a desired outcome. We will return to this point later when we consider political parties. What is important now is to realize that Congress is intensely partisan and political.

The fifth and last common characteristic to be discussed here is that to gain power in either house of Congress, political and physical longevity is required because of the role played by seniority. *Seniority* is simply the length of time an individual continuously serves in the same position. A representative who has served the same district for 22 continuous years has more seniority than a representative who has served one for 20. The reason seniority is important is that both houses of Congress use it as an organizing device and as a way to structure power relationships. One becomes a committee chairman if he belongs to the party which has a majority

Table 3-2
Data on Standing Committee Chairmen, 93rd Congress, 1st Session, 1973

HOUSE OF REPRESENTATIVES

COMMITTEE	CHAIRMAN	STATE	AGE	YEARS OF SERVICE
Agriculture	William R. Pogue	Texas	74	36
Appropriations	George H. Mahon	Texas	73	38
Armed Services	F. Edward Hebert	Louisiana	72	32
Banking and Currency	Wright Patman	Texas	80	44
District of Columbia	Charles C. Diggs, Jr.	Michigan	51	18
Education and Labor	Carl D. Perkins	Kentucky	61	24
Foreign Affairs	Thomas E. Morgan	Pennsylvania	67	28
Government Operations	Chet Horlifield	California	70	30
House Administration	Wayne L. Hays	Ohio	62	24

Interior and Insular Affairs	James A. Haley	Florida	74	20
Internal Security	Richard H. Ichord	Missouri	47	12
Interstate and Foreign Commerce	Harley O. Staggers	West Virginia	65	24
Judiciary	Peter W. Rodino, Jr.	New Jersey	64	24
Merchant Marine and Fisheries	Leonor K. Sullivan	Missouri	70	20
Post Office and Civil Service	Thaddeus J. Dulski	New York	58	14
Public Works	John A. Blatnik	Minnesota	62	27
Rules	Ray J. Madden	Indiana	81	30
Science and Astronautics	Olin E. Teague	Texas	63	26
Standards of Official Conduct	Melvin Price	Illinois	68	30

Continued

Table 3-2—*Continued*

HOUSE OF REPRESENTATIVES

COMMITTEE	CHAIRMAN	STATE	AGE	YEARS OF SERVICE
Veterans' Affairs	William Jennings Bryan Dorn	South Carolina	57	22
Ways and Means	Wilbur D. Mills	Arkansas	64	34

SENATE

COMMITTEE	CHAIRMAN	STATE	AGE	YEARS OF SERVICE
Aeronautical and Space Sciences	Frank E. Moss	Utah	62	14
Agriculture and Forestry	Herman E. Talmadge	Georgia	60	17
Appropriations	John L. McClellan	Arkansas	77	30
Armed Services	John C. Stennis	Mississippi	72	26

Banking, Housing and Urban Affairs	John J. Sparkman	Alabama	74	27
Commerce	Warren G. Magnuson	Washington	68	29
District of Columbia	Thomas F. Eagleton	Missouri	44	5
Finance	Russell B. Long	Louisiana	55	25
Foreign Relations	J. William Fulbright	Arkansas	68	28
Government Operations	Sam J. Ervin, Jr.	North Carolina	77	19
Interior and Insular Affairs	Henry M. Jackson	Washington	61	20
Judiciary	James O. Eastland	Mississippi	69	30
Labor and Public Welfare	Harrison A. Williams, Jr.	New Jersey	54	14
Post Office and Civil Service	Gale W. McGee	Wyoming	58	14
Public Works	Jennings Randolph	West Virginia	71	15
Rules and Administration	Howard W. Cannon	Nevada	61	14
Veterans' Affairs	Vance Hartke	Indiana	54	14

in that house and if he has served longer on that particular committee than any other member of his party. This is a relatively simple rule, and this simplicity is usually cited as the reason for maintaining the system of seniority.

The implications are obvious. Seniority results in congressional leadership largely dominated by men in their old age. Table 3-2 presents the ages of the various committee chairmen for the Ninety-third Congress.

Proponents of the seniority system maintain that it permits those with the most expertise and experience to lead, and, by providing a simple and automatic selection process, it eliminates other alternatives which could damage morale and affect policy decisions. Opponents argue that the seniority system guarantees that committees will be headed by those who are least representative of shifts in public opinion and who may actually be too physically incapacitated to conduct their duties.

These five common characteristics illustrate the complexity involved in any discussion of Congress but are important to any understanding of the legislative process.

THE LEGISLATIVE PROCESS

The term *legislative process* refers to the various procedures a proposal is subject to and the variety of forces which can affect it if it is to be enacted into a law. What follows is a brief summary rather than a comprehensive and detailed explanation of the process. The suggested supplementary readings provide excellent detailed accounts of the legislative process.*

In order for a bill to become a law, it must first be introduced by a member of either house of Congress. Proposals for legislation are limited to members of Congress, though it is common practice for the president and the heads of the various executive departments to prepare desired legislation and then have it introduced by an appropriate member of Congress. Mere introduction of a bill, regardless of who prepared it or introduced it, does not guarantee passage.

After the bill has been introduced, it is usually assigned to the appropriate standing committee for consideration. Most bills which are introduced and referred to a committee are "pigeonholed" (ignored) by the committee, and no further action is taken on them. However, if the committee decides to consider a bill, hearings on the bill are usually scheduled, and proponents and opponents can testify before the committee. Once this is completed, the committee will usually hold closed meetings to draft a report and prepare the legislation in final committee form.

The bill is then scheduled for consideration by the entire membership of that house, at which point it is debated and resolved on the floor by the entire house membership. If defeated, it may be sent back to committee for changes, or it may simply be dropped altogether. If amended or passed, it must go to the other house, for that body must pass it before it can become a law. There the procedures are repeated, and the same outcomes are possible. If the second house adopts the same bill, it can then go to the president for his signature or veto. If the second house passes the bill in a different version from the one adopted by the original house, it then goes to a conference committee, which attempts to reach a compromise that must be approved by both houses before it can go to the president for his signature.

Few Americans know or understand the intricacies of the legislative process. Each of the steps mentioned above is governed by a complicated and often unwritten set of rules and procedures which one learns by participating in the actual process. The legislative process in Congress is often criticized; what follows is a discussion of the most commonly voiced criticisms.* Based on your knowledge of the process, do you think these are valid and legitimate criticisms?

CRITICISMS OF CONGRESS

First, critics often contend that Congress and most of its policy decisions cater to special and well-organized interests. For example, by placing so much emphasis on the committee's work and recommendation, Congress makes it easier for special interests to concentrate their efforts. Thus "big business" or "big labor" can focus its efforts on the individual committee members and in many cases, so the argument goes, have a greater impact than if it had to appeal to a larger group.

In addition to the committee arrangement, critics often cite two other factors which help to increase the effectiveness of large economic and political interests. The first of these is the fact that to become a law, a bill must go through so many steps that only those interests with sufficient personnel and economic resources are capable of following its progress. Thus they have an advantage, because they can supposedly "shepherd" their legislation through the entire process, while a poorly financed and loosely organized group will not be able to monitor the progress of its legislation as carefully. The second, closely related, factor is that, because of the many steps a piece of legislation goes through, large amounts of time are consumed. In some cases this can amount to several years, but usually involves several months. Again, those with extensive resources are seen as being able to afford this time lag. The "have-nots" supposedly cannot afford to devote the necessary time and attention to insure final enactment of their proposed legislation.

While the argument over the dominance of large interests has a great appeal to many Americans, the evidence in its support is usually inconsistent. For instance, an important study of lobbyists (those hired to try to influence the votes and actions of senators and representatives) indicated that lobbyists mainly talked only to those congressmen they knew supported them. They did not try to influence those opposed to them. Other observers argue that a lobbyist does not have to change votes: he only has to influence enough people in key positions to affect legislation. Probably the most convincing argument concerning the dominance of large economic interests is that governmental policy, including congressional legislation, favors large economic interests, but another point critics often ignore requires explanation.

One should not think for a moment that large industrial corporations are the only organizations attempting to influence congressional decision-makers. Since the 1930s, organized labor has developed an extensive and usually effective lobbying organization which attempts to influence any legislation pertaining to labor. Civil rights groups have done the same, and educational groups attempt to influence congressional policy in the field of education. For instance, Congress included large amounts of money for higher education in the major education legislation of 1972. Educators appeared before congressional hearings and worked hard to be sure those provisions were in the final legislation. So, large industrial corporations do not have a monopoly on lobbying. Perhaps it is referred to by a different name when other groups do it, but the activity is still an attempt to bring collective influence to bear on legislation.

The second general criticism leveled at Congress is that it is just plain cumbersome and outmoded. Many argue that in a world filled with rapid change the techniques and procedures used by Congress should be replaced by more modern methods. Critics contend that the formal procedures of committee reports and the use of parliamentary techniques to delay legislation simply must be eliminated. They also cite the waste of time caused by the duplicate action in both houses on the same piece of legislation. Finally, these critics contend that congressional action is so detailed and complex that it becomes impossible for anyone to know exactly what is going on at a particular point in time. Two examples will illustrate this problem.

Before any money can be spent for any purpose, Congress must first pass an authorization bill and then an appropriations bill. The distinction is important. An authorization bill gives the agency involved the authority to spend funds for a particular program; the appropriations bill actually makes the money available for spending. Thus a governmental program, such as foreign aid, has first to receive authorization, then the appropriation of funds by both houses of Congress. Each step involves all the procedures described earlier. The point critics make is that the decision-making process could be simplified by combining these two procedures into one.

A related example concerns the "rules" each house uses to conduct and manage its business. The Constitution clearly states that the members of each house shall establish the rules which will be followed in that house. In the case of the Senate, this has meant the development of the filibuster, as a result of its rule that a member is entitled to unlimited debate on a measure. The Senate is proud of the fact that, except in the rarest of cases, any of its members is entitled to free speech at all times. The only way debate can be cut off in the Senate, if a senator wants to continue, is by a vote for cloture. *Cloture* means debate on that particular bill cannot continue and a vote must be taken. To obtain cloture, a two-thirds majority is necessary, and this is often difficult to obtain because many senators are reluctant to vote against another colleague's right to unlimited speech. The result, especially in the 1960s on civil rights legislation, was lengthy delays and inaction. Critics contend that the cloture rule is a poor substitute for efficient and orderly conduct of business. They argue the difficulty in obtaining cloture really means that a minority, even a minority of one, may be able to keep the Senate from its business.

Before we are too quick to agree that the complexity and organizational aspects of Congress need reform, consider the following. First, is there anything to be said for the use of procedures which insure that legislation will not be the result of momentary and temporary swings in public opinion or attitudes? One could argue that reason is more likely to prevail if congressional debate is not subject solely to arguments of efficiency and neatness. Regarding the Senate rule permitting unlimited debate, one could maintain that in a democracy there should be some institution in which a publicly elected leader has the opportunity to defend a position or point of view without worrying about a time restraint. In addition, it could be argued that although the majority may have the votes necessary to decide an issue, this does not automatically guarantee that the majority is correct—hence the need to protect the majority by safeguarding the rights of the minority to be heard. The minority can point out to the majority where it may be wrong. Thus, an argument can be made for both sides.

While the first two criticisms deal with operational and procedural aspects of Congress, the other two are philosophical in their orientation and thrust.

The first criticism is that, for a variety of reasons, Congress fails to deal effectively with the important problems facing the country. Many observers maintain that Congress usually manages to sidestep the major issues. An example often cited is congressional unwillingness to face fiscal problems in the United States. Another deals with the periodic concern over the causes and prevention of domestic violence; while Congress has enacted several gun control bills, many argue that it has failed to face the problem realistically. The reason usually cited for congressional failure to realistically resolve basic problems is an inherent need for Congress to compromise on most major issues. As was pointed out in the discussion of minority rights in Chapter 2, compromise often leads to short-term resolution of a major problem, but it also necessitates future reconsideration of the problem. Thus, a compromise reached on an issue today may lead to a new crisis in the future.

Closely related to this basic criticism of compromise is another objection. It involves extreme politicization, constant and consistent struggle for power on the most minor issues, and the fact that decisions are often reached as partisan political choices rather than as matters in the public interest.

In June of 1972, for example, Congress passed and sent to the president a bill increasing social security benefits. It was designed as part of routine legislation raising the national debt ceiling. President Nixon was faced with an impossible decision: he had to either sign the bill or veto a social security benefit in an election year and at the same time bring government spending to a halt until Congress enacted other legislation raising the debt ceiling. Imagine also the difficult position many Republican legislators had to share—the prospect of voting against increased social security benefits in an election year. Needless to say, this was not a popular position to be in. The president signed the bill, but duly noted his displeasure at the tactics used by the Democratic-controlled Congress.

This example depicts the dilemma often confronting individual congressmen, the decision between political expediency and what is conceived to be right. Granted, these may not always be separable, but still the legislator must face them. How does one define the public interest, and what should one do if his constituents wish him to act in a way inconsistent with the public interest?

Akin to this extreme politicization of the legislative process is the relationship between the two houses of Congress. Periodically, the House and Senate will act as if they were sovereign and independent nations instead of copartners in the legislative process. I remember the dispute in 1963 among the conference committee members assigned to work out a solution on the foreign aid bill. Where they were to meet and the use of proxy votes became more important than resolving the legislative difficulties. This sort of disagreement is not uncommon, and one must be careful not to assume that a United States representative has more or less power than a senator. The members of both houses are usually quick to defend the rules and stature of their respective institutions. In essence, both houses feel they are important and dislike being relegated to a secondary position. Whenever this mood prevails, the situation is likely to become increasingly politicized.

When considering these criticisms and perspectives, several additional points should be kept in mind. First, who has the ability to decide what is in the public interest? Can anyone say with certainty what is in the national interest and how decisions affecting it should be made? Chances are very good that there will be a significant relationship between one's definition of the national interest and one's personal interest. For instance, if an individual is unemployed, he almost certainly will feel that there should be greater concern with reducing unemployment. Students are usually concerned with the cost and quality of higher education, but is their concern the same as the public concern? Obviously something as abstract as public interest is difficult, if not impossible, to define. So elected representatives and senators should be expected to reflect their own views on public interest and whatever views their constituents are able to impress upon them. This is where the most serious criticism about Congress often arises, and it needs further clarification.

Congress is supposed to represent the people, and although its members stand for election at specified times, many maintain that Congress and its members are not representative of the general populace. The first argument on this point is usually based on evidence that the members of Congress are largely in upper income brackets, male, and white. Therefore, the argument continues, it is naive to expect them to understand, let alone represent, the many other groups in American society. In essence, this argument maintains that an unresponsive minority comprises Congress and that decisions are based on what is right for that minority instead of what is needed by the majority.

66 *American National Political Institutions*

Map 3-3
1972 Congressional Districts in Indiana

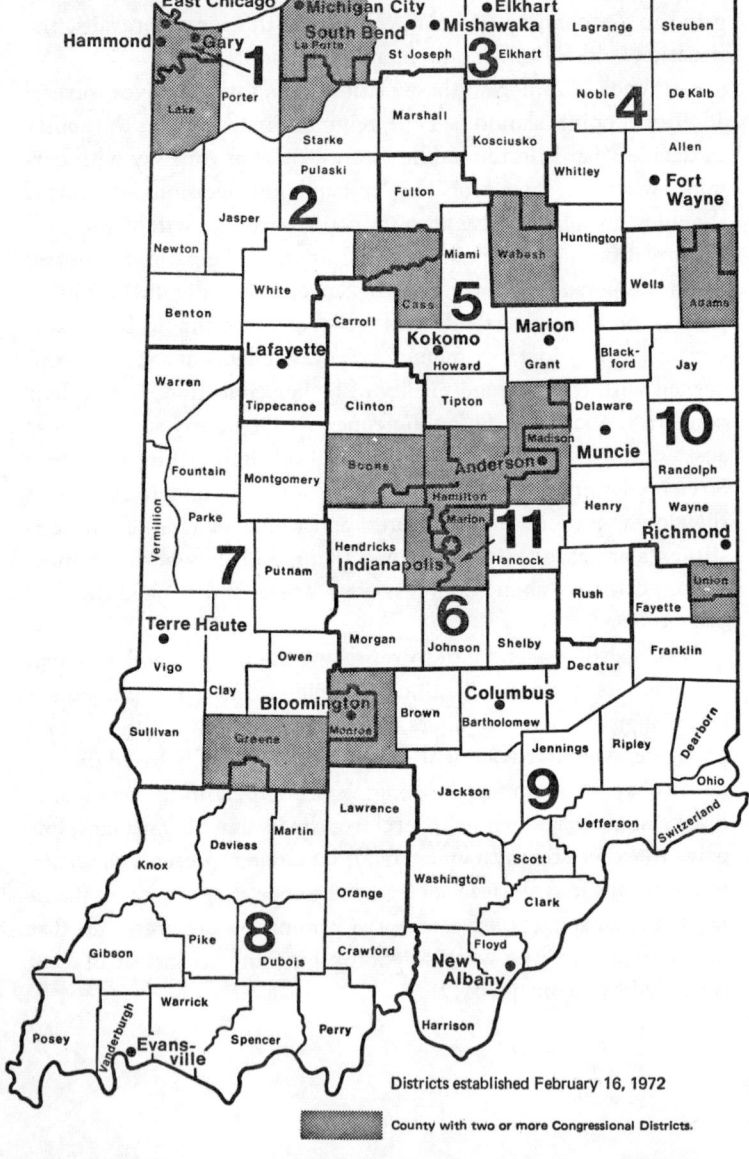

Districts established February 16, 1972

County with two or more Congressional Districts.

Related to this argument is a second one which maintains that the method of selecting senators and representatives is unfair and penalizes many interests. The discrepancy in the number of voters represented by a California senator and an Alaskan senator has already been noted. Related to this is the selection procedure for representatives. The Constitution states the House must be based on population but leaves the individual states to decide the shape of the various house districts. The Supreme Court has ruled that the "one man—one vote" concept is applicable; thus the congressional districts in a particular state must be of comparable population size. State legislatures, which are themselves quite political, determine the congressional district boundaries; the result is often strange-looking congressional districts. Map 3-3 presents the congressional districts in Indiana in 1972.

Note especially the meanderings of the 7th district, which has a city of 75,000 (basically Democrat) and rural and small town areas (basically Republican). Also note how Marion County (center of the map), in which Indianapolis is located, is divided so to influence the 5th, 6th, and 11th congressional districts. Obviously, political considerations of a partisan nature entered into drawing the boundaries of those districts. Thus, even the selection process determining congressional districts is intensely political and partisan. Why should the subsequent legislative process be any less political? Many have argued for the need to depoliticize Congress, but few suggestions have been made which would achieve this practically.

Obviously the debate over Congress will continue and be modified over time. Certainly the relative positions of the houses have changed; in recent years the Senate has been seen as a more liberal body than the House of Representatives. In addition, the power of Congress in relation to the other national institutions is ever changing. This point will be discussed in the concluding chapter of this section.

SUGGESTED READINGS

Congress: For a variety of views on Congress, see: William S. White's account of the Senate, *The Citadel* (New York: Houghton Mifflin, 1968); Lewis A. Froman, Jr., *Congressmen and Their Constituencies* (Chicago: Rand-McNally, 1963); Donald R. Matthews, *U.S. Senators and Their World* (Chapel Hill: University of North Carolina Press, 1960); and Richard Bolling, *House Out of Order* (New York: Dutton, 1965).

Legislative Process: To begin, review one of the many excellent case studies which are available: Stephen K. Bailey, *Congress Makes a Law* (New York: Columbia University Press, 1950); Raymond A. Bauer, Ithiel de Sola Pool, and Lewis Anthony Dexter, *American Business and Public Policy* (New York: Atherton, 1963); and John C. Donovan, *The Politics of Poverty* (New York: Pegasus, 1967). For a more comprehensive and theoretical view of the legislative process, see: Bertram M. Gross, *The Legislative Struggle* (New York: McGraw-Hill, 1953); David B. Truman, ed., *The Congress and America's Future* (Englewood Cliffs, N.J.: Prentice-Hall, 1965); Lewis A. Froman, Jr., *The Congressional Process: Strategies, Rules and Procedures* (Boston: Little, Brown, 1967); and George B. Galloway, *The Legislative Process in Congress* (New York: Crowell, 1953).

Congressional Criticisms: In addition to the Bolling and Truman suggestions above, see: Robert L. Peabody and Nelson W. Polsby, eds., *New Perspectives on the House of Representatives* (Chicago: Rand-McNally, 1963).

4. The Court System and the Judicial Process

The judicial system in the United States is complex and easily misunderstood.* While considerable attention is often directed at the Supreme Court, most Americans who have had personal experience with the judicial system had it with local or state courts. This is especially true of individuals involved in civil or criminal cases. An understanding of the judicial system begins by realizing that there are trial and appellate courts at both the federal and state levels. The trial and appellate courts active in the states vary in name and organization from state to state and are difficult to summarize. The federal courts consist of district courts, courts of appeal, specialized courts, and the Supreme Court. Each of these plus the state courts are discussed in the following sections.

THE SUPREME COURT

For many citizens, understanding how and why the Supreme Court operates is a difficult task. While most people have seen the president on television and many have visited the House of Representatives or Senate, few have had any contact with the Supreme Court. In addition to this lack of direct contact, there is a common misconception about the role of the Supreme Court. Many people erroneously think that the Court hears the majority of disputed cases in the United States; this is simply not true. The Supreme Court averages several hundred cases per year, which is a small fraction of the total number of cases heard by the other courts in the United States. The Supreme Court does hear many cases which set precedents; this means the decisions reached by the Court are often used by other courts in preparing or in justifying their decisions. In order to understand the Supreme Court as an institution, additional background information is required, as well as a discussion of present attitudes and practices of the Court.

To begin, the Constitution states: "The judicial Power of the United States, shall be vested in one Supreme Court, and in such inferior Courts as the Congress may from time to time ordain and establish." It should be borne in mind that the establishment of a federal Supreme Court and the possibility of other federal courts was a major victory for those favoring centralization of power at the Constitutional Convention.[1] If these provisions had not been adopted, a major institution which promoted strong national government during the republic's early days would have been missing. The Constitution does not say how many people will serve on the Court, only that the president has the power to appoint justices to the Court and that the Senate shall confirm such appointments. By an act of Congress, the present Supreme Court has nine justices. Congressional action could change this number; in fact, at various points in our history there have been both more and less than nine justices.

One of the more interesting conflicts between a president and the Supreme Court occurred in the early 1930s, when the Court consistently ruled a number of New Deal statutes initiated by Franklin D. Roosevelt unconstitutional. Roosevelt attempted to change the Court's composition by asking Congress to pass legislation which would establish a retirement age for Supreme Court justices and permit the president to appoint an additional justice for each justice who failed to retire when he reached that age. This created considerable public interest; ultimately President Roosevelt was soundly defeated by congressional refusal to pass the legislation. This type of political interaction among the branches should not be overlooked.

Another characteristic of the Supreme Court, which often proves troublesome to some observers, is that it can alter and, in many cases, change its prior position. A review of the Court's history will show that it has experienced a variety of changes; some of these coincide with general developments in the political and social characteristics of the United States. For instance, in the early 1800s, the Supreme Court, under the leadership of Chief Justice John Marshall, decided a number of important cases establishing the national government as more powerful than state government.[2] In essence, the Court added its prestige and power to the nationalist movement and was partially responsible for the development of a strong national government. In similar fashion, the Court in the late 1800s and early 1900s, consistently ruled that the corporation and other large economic interests had certain "personal" legal rights which provided them with economic advantages.[3] The Court's decisions during that time helped to promote industrial development in the United States.

While the two previous examples simply account for two historical periods, the Court's position on rights for those accused of crimes is also interesting. In a series of cases, the Supreme Court decided that a person standing trial in a federal court is entitled to such rights as the right to counsel. In many of these cases, however, the Court ruled that these safeguards did *not* apply to persons standing trial in state courts. The argument was usually made that the constitutional provisions of the Fourth (unreasonable search and seizure), Fifth (compulsory self-incrimination), Sixth (right to counsel), and Eighth (prohibitions against cruel and unusual punishment) Amendments were applicable only in federal courts.[4] Since 1961, the Supreme Court has ruled in a variety of cases that the "due process" clause of the Fourteenth Amendment guarantees the freedoms in the Bill of Rights to citizens involved in state criminal proceedings. The due process clause is contained in Section 1 of the Fourteenth Amendment and reads as follows:

> *All persons born or naturalized in the United States, and subject to the jurisdiction thereof, are citizens of the United States and of the State wherein they reside. No state shall make or enforce any law which shall abridge the privileges or immunities of citizens of the United States; nor shall any State deprive any person of life, liberty, or property, without due process of law; nor deny to any person within its jurisdiction the equal protection of the laws.*

Finally, it appears the Court may be broadening this position to include all criminal cases in state, county, or municipal courts. Obviously, this has caused considerable public controversy, since it has increased the need for the public to provide legal counsel for those unable to afford it.

A variety of explanations can be offered as to why the Court's position changes over time; two will be explored in some detail. The first is that the Court is composed of individuals; in this case, only men have served on the Court. Since these men are only human, and not possessed with godlike virtues as many think, justices change their minds and opinions just as all people do. There are a variety of reasons why a justice may change his mind. He may simply realize he was mistaken in his earlier position, or his colleagues might convince him that his position was not justified. Or the justice may gain additional information in a later case which will cause him to reach a different conclusion on the former case. Regardless of the reason, it is unrealistic to conclude that legal interpretations and decisions will remain the same because of a particular justice's prior record in such cases. In addition, of course, the composition of the Court changes over time, so subtle shifts in the majority opinion of the Court take place as individual justices are replaced.

The second, and probably more important, explanation is the fact that the United States is changing rapidly. The conditions and causes of problems and situations are apt to change over a period of several years. Because of this, the Court may decide when a problem has reached a point of gravity that it must act, and it then does so. Both of these factors, plus the fact that the composition of the Court may change, are important reasons for the Court's tendency to change its position.

While the foregoing was a brief summary of general trends, the following provides an account of how one case was heard by the Court and a look at the intricacies involved in having the decision reach the Court. Keep in mind that the Supreme Court hears both procedural and substantive cases. Procedural cases normally involve criminal suits in which a person maintains that certain basic constitutional protections, such as the right against self-incrimination, have been violated. In procedural cases, the Court does not rule on the guilt or innocence of the accused but evaluates the procedures followed and reaches a decision on their constitutionality. Too many Americans misunderstand this point. The Court does not decide that a person is guilty or innocent; it decides whether or not the procedures followed were constitutional or not. In a case involving a substantive point of law, the Court considers whether or not a constitutional provision is or is not applicable. Substantive cases usually involve noncriminal suits. The following example illustrates a substantive case.

Curt Flood was an outstanding outfielder for the St. Louis Cardinals baseball team. The Cardinals attempted to trade him to the Washington Senators, but Flood maintained that the ability of the club to trade him as they desired and without his consent reduced him to the status of property or chattel. He then filed suit against the Cardinals, maintaining that his rights had been deprived and that the Cardinals and organized baseball had no right to the "reserve clause." The reserve clause stipulates that a ballplayer is not free to negotiate terms with any baseball club other than the team which has rights to him by virtue of his contract. Thus, a ballplayer is unable to move from team to team or to let the teams "bid" for his services. Organized baseball maintains that the reserve clause is the single provision which preserves the unique aspect of baseball—balanced competition. Flood's case rested on his contention that the reserve clause restrained him unfairly in his economic negotiations and was in fact preventing him from equal protection under the laws. After a series of long and complicated lower court cases, the Flood case reached the Supreme Court. The Court decided, by a five-to-three decision, that the reserve clause did not violate Flood's constitutional rights and that baseball was in a unique economic situation.[5] The decision is important for several reasons.

First, the Flood case illustrates the long and tedious process a citizen must go through to reach the Court. It is time-consuming, and he has no assurance he will be vindicated. In the case of Flood, the long time involved and the debilitative effect of the legal struggle left its mark; he dropped out of baseball and pursued a painting career in Spain. The average case takes three to five years to reach the Court, and it does this only after a costly and tedious original trial and appeals process. The amounts of money involved are enormous; so large, in fact, that it is outside the realm of possibility for most Americans to engage in litigation unless an organization decides to help defray the expenses by providing money or legal assistance.

Second, and more important, time and economic costs are characteristic of the American judicial system and are often cited as the main reason why legal maneuvering and court action benefit the wealthy. Since the latter have both time and resources, they can afford to resort to litigation. The individual citizen in many cases has neither, and many observers maintain that his chances for justice are subsequently less. So, if someone says he'll "take it to the Supreme Court," it can be assumed that the chances of this happening are infinitesimal. One of the important challenges facing the

The Court System and the Judicial Process

American jurisprudence system, and this includes the criminal as well as civil procedures, is the development of ways to increase equity and more rapid settlement of legal disputes.

Two other matters relating to the Supreme Court deserve our attention. The first involves the political aspects of the Court and their implications. The selection process for service on the Court is highly political; after all, when the president nominates and the Senate confirms, the probability of political controversy is always present. Consider, for example, the intense political debates and controversies that erupted in the 1960s, when Presidents Johnson and Nixon had vacancies to fill on the Supreme Court. The turmoil generated by the proposed promotion of associate justice Fortas to chief justice and the attempted appointments of Haynesworth and Carswell left many wounds. No, there is little doubt that the process of appointment to the Supreme Court is extremely political in nature and will probably remain in the center of the Court's decision-making process.

To further support this point, the 1968 and 1972 presidential elections were dominated by long discussions on the role of the Supreme Court in American life. In 1968, the Court was often criticized for supposedly supporting the rights of criminals over those of the rest of society. This became a major campaign issue. In 1972, the argument was over the Supreme Court's role in the school bussing issue. Both cases illustrate how easily the Court can become involved in extensive political controversies while supposedly being above "politics."

Table 4-1 lists the present Supreme Court justices and the presidents who appointed them. Notice the extent to which Republicans and Democrats appoint members of their own parties to the Court. Are these men representative of the general populace of the United States or, also important, of the lawyers in the United States? They are not, and one could argue that their ideas and opinions are shaped by their experiences and backgrounds, there-

Table 4-1
Supreme Court Justices: December 1972

JUSTICE	POLITICAL PARTY	YEAR APPOINTED	PRESIDENT	PRESIDENT'S PARTY
William O. Douglas	D	1939	Roosevelt	D
William J. Brennan, Jr.	D	1956	Eisenhower	R
Potter Stewart	R	1958	Eisenhower	R
Byron R. White	D	1962	Kennedy	D
Thurgood Marshall	D	1967	Johnson	D
Warren E. Burger (Chief justice)	R	1969	Nixon	R
Henry A. Blackmun	R	1970	Nixon	R
Lewis F. Powell, Jr.	R	1970	Nixon	R
William H. Rehnquist	R	1970	Nixon	R

fore, the decisions they reach may not be representative of the opinions held by most Americans. Now, the question that is most interesting and deserving of careful consideration is whether the Supreme Court justices *should* be representative of the general population.

If one concludes that a Supreme Court justice should have prior legal or judicial experience, that immediately eliminates many Americans because of the formal education requirements needed to gain that type of experience. If one decides that a justice should reach his decisions free from partisan political pressures, how can this be guaranteed? It could be maintained that the present practice of presidential appointment and Senate confirmation should be eliminated, and either the president or the Senate should have the power to appoint, with no review or confirmation necessary. Would this eliminate political considerations?

The opposite position is that there is no way to guarantee that political considerations will not enter into either the selection process or the ultimate decision process. Therefore, instead of trying to eliminate them, there should be an effort to make the processes more open to the general populace. One way to do this would be to select the Supreme Court by election, say every 10 or 20 years. Thus, the Court would still be less subject to shifts in popular opinion than other officials, but it would be subject to periodic reassessment of its decisions. If the populace decided an individual justice was "out of touch" with political reality, he could be voted off the Court.

The last point concerning the Supreme Court is one that is both interesting and perplexing. The writers of the Constitution supposedly established a representative democracy, yet the Supreme Court is the final arbiter of what is constitutional or unconstitutional, and it is neither selected by election nor subject to dismissal, except through impeachment proceedings which are nearly impossible to complete successfully. It is ironic that the

Founding Fathers established an essentially nondemocratic institution to play a pivotal role in helping to maintain a representative democracy. When considerations of this position are developed and pondered, a number of perplexing and theoretical questions can be raised.

OTHER FEDERAL COURTS

As has been pointed out, the Constitution gave Congress the power to create other federal courts.* Congress has established district, appeals, and special federal courts. If an individual were involved in federal litigation, it is likely that such involvement would occur in either the district or special courts. This raises a question of jurisdiction: which court has the right to hear a particular case? Cases involving federal statutes are tried in federal courts and usually begin in district courts. The Supreme Court, as stipulated in the Constitution, has original jurisdiction in all cases ". . . affecting Ambassadors, other public Ministers and Consuls, and those in which a State shall be Party . . ." This simply means that the Supreme Court hears this type of case first; it does not have to evolve through the lower courts. In other civil (pertaining to legal action between individuals or institutions involving personal or property rights) or criminal cases, the trial court is either the appropriate state court or the federal district court.

Each state has at least one federal district court; up to 24 judges are assigned to each. District courts try varied cases, and the proportion of civil versus criminal cases varies. In 1969, approximately 70 percent of the cases heard by federal district courts were civil suits. Each of the district courts, and even the individual courts of a district, are marked by wide variations in efficiency and procedures. In fact, each court is in many ways a unique institution.

If a litigant feels the decision reached in the district court is unfair, or if he feels procedural rights have been violated, the case may be taken to the court of appeals (sometimes referred to as the circuit court). There are 11 courts of appeals in the United States and its territories; three to nine judges sit on each. These courts of appeals have only appellate jurisdiction; that is, the case must originate in a district court or a state court before it can be heard by them. The courts of appeals also hear a variety of administrative cases involving governmental regulatory commissions and agencies. Only if constitutional rights are involved can a case be appealed from the courts of appeals; thus, they are usually the last resort to most litigants.

Finally, Congress has established a variety of specialized courts, such as Customs and Claims, which hear only cases involving the special types of legal questions implied in their titles. The structure and procedure used by these special courts vary from court to court.

STATE COURTS

Each of the 50 states (and in some cases, the territories) has its own court system.* In many states, trial courts exist at several levels. For instance, local traffic courts are common in larger cities; these courts handle ordinary traffic litigation. Family, orphan, and probate courts also exist to decide matters for the affected persons or institutions. Felony and civil suits involving large sums of money are often tried in county-level courts. In these cases, the litigants are usually from the same area or the alleged criminal act occurred in that county. Again, special mention must be made that each court, regardless of its jurisdiction or location, is a unique entity in itself, and generalizations are difficult.

Finally, each state has one or more appellate courts. In 22 states, there are both appellate and state supreme courts. These courts hear appeals of decisions reached by the lower state courts and decide whether the appeal is justified or not. In many cases, the appeal process through the state appeal courts can take several years.

IMPLICATIONS

The implications behind the diversity of the various state and federal courts deserve attention. First, the selection process for judges varies considerably. As in the case of Supreme Court nominees, presidents have a tendency to nominate members of their political party when openings occur on other federal courts. State judges are selected in a variety of ways, but when appointment occurs, political factors usually play a part. In some state and local courts judges are elected. This often serves to politicize the question of justice if a particular candidate has attracted the public's attention for any reason.

Second, the American court system provides a variety of avenues for litigation. Thus, in some cases, those interested in judicial action may institute proceedings in different courts. For instance, civil rights litigation can be initiated in either federal or state courts, in most cases. The diversity often provides the litigant with an alternative which may increase the possibility of his receiving a favorable decision.

Third, this diversity of courts also means that legal interpretations of rules and procedures may vary. It is logical to assume that a Southern state court may decide a case differently than a Northern or Eastern or Western state court might. Thus, justice in America often varies, depending upon the court hearing the case. This permits local and regional variations to intervene in the administration of justice, which may be disconcerting for one interested in legal consistency.

Finally, the American court system is such that delays and expense characterize it throughout. The result is that litigation is slow, and often people and institutions must simply await the court's decision before things can be changed. This delay in changing things may work to the benefit of those interested in the status quo. A related point is that the decisions reached by one court may be overruled or modified by a higher court; thus the litigants may get an initial decision, but may have to wait for the final decision before implementing policy based on the decision. The result can be continued delay.

This chapter does not mean to present the judicial system as unresponsive, partisan, or status-quo oriented, but to counterbalance the popular image of the judicial system with its judges always using collective wisdom to decide matters. The fact of the matter is that court decisions come about only because of a serious dispute between the parties involved; the decision in effect usually favors one or the other of the litigants. In these instances, the decisions may influence public policy and even have an impact on partisan politics. The question is not whether the courts do this or not, but whether the procedures used by the courts guarantee fairness and equity for all participants. This is a major question which the United States court system and the American public must face.*

SUGGESTED READINGS

United States Judicial System: For a variety of theoretical and descriptive perspectives of the American judicial system, see: Woodrow Wilson, *Constitutional Government in the United States* (New York: Columbia University Press, 1907); Jerome Frank, *Courts on Trial: Myths and Reality in American Justice* (Princeton: Princeton University Press, 1949); Glendon A. Schubert, *Quantitative Analysis of Judicial Behavior* (New York: Free Press, 1959); Robert McCloskey, *The American Supreme Court* (Chicago: University of Chicago Press, 1960); Walter Murphy and C. Hermann Pritchett, eds., *Courts, Judges, and Politics* (New York: Random House, 1961); David

Danelski, *A Supreme Court Justice Is Appointed* (New York: Random House, 1964); Joel Grossman, *Lawyers and Judges* (New York: John Wiley, 1965); and Charles A. Black, Jr., *Perspective in Constitutional Law* (Englewood Cliffs, N.J.: Prentice-Hall, 1970).

Other Federal Courts: For both general comments about lower federal courts and descriptions of several of these courts, see: Delmar Karlen, *Appellate Courts in the United States and England* (New York: New York University Press, 1963); Richard J. Richardson and Kenneth N. Vines, "Review, Dissent and the Appellate Process: A Political Interpretation," *Law, Politics, and the Federal Courts*, ed. Herbert Jacob (Boston: Little, Brown, 1967); Kenneth N. Vines, "The Role of Circuit Courts of Appeals in the Federal Judicial Process: A Case Study," *Midwest Journal of Political Science* (1963).

State Courts: For a useful summary of state court organization, see: *State Court Systems* (Chicago: Council of State Governments, 1970). For descriptions of actual operations and decisions of state courts, see: Kenneth N. Vines, "Southern State Supreme Courts and Race Relations," *Western Political Quarterly* 18 (1965) and Beverly Blair Cook, *The Judicial Process in California* (Belmont, California: Dickinson, 1967). An interesting survey of metropolitan courts in Chicago is Albert Lepawsky, *The Judicial System of Metropolitan Chicago* (Chicago: University of Chicago Press, 1932).

The Court System and Equity: For a theoretical discussion of this point, see: Jerome Frank, *Courts on Trial* (Princeton: Princeton University Press, 1950) and Leonard Downie, *Justice Denied* (New York: Praeger, 1971). For a summary consideration of the courts and basic freedoms, see: George W. Spicer, *The Supreme Court and Fundamental Freedoms* (New York: Appleton-Century Crofts, 1967). For an interesting case study of one person's "day in court," see: Anthony Lewis, *Gideon's Trumpet* (New York: Random House, 1964). For lively discussions of the potential political uses of the judicial system, see: Jessica Mitford, *The Trial of Dr. Spock* (New York: Alfred A. Knopf, 1969) and J. Anthony Lukas, *The Barnyard Epithet and Other Obscenities* (New York: Harper and Row, 1970).

NOTES

1. For an intriguing account of one Federalist's view of the federal judiciary, see: Alexander Hamilton, *The Federalist*, #78.
2. An example of such cases was the *McCulloch* v. *Maryland* decision (1819) which granted Congress "implied power" to carry out any powers delegated to the national government. In *Gibbons* v. *Ogden* (1823), national power to regulate commerce was established even when state lines were involved.
3. The *Adkens* v. *Children's Hospital Case* (1823) was an excellent example of this. In this instance, the Supreme Court ruled that both the private corporation and the person suing it were considered as "persons" and therefore had the same right to the same legal remedies.
4. For examples of this, see the decisions on the following cases: *Nardone* v. *United States* (1937); *Wolf* v. *Colorado* (1949); *Twining* v. *New Jersey* (1908); and *Betts* v. *Brady* (1942).
5. *Flood* v. *Kuhn* (1972).

5. The Contemporary Presidency

In recent years there has been considerable discussion about and interest in the presidency, an institution which has become increasingly important and therefore deserves careful attention.* One of the more complicated aspects of the presidency is that it is not simply one job, but a combination of several arduous tasks. For our purposes, the four roles or duties that most presidents attempt to perform will be analysed in this chapter.

First, the president is seen as the head of state and, therefore, as having many ceremonial duties. He represents the United States on formal occasions; he also hosts visiting dignitaries and VIPs. By serving as head of state, the president helps to set the tone for his administration and the country. For example, the amount of attention and care a foreign dignitary receives from the president has an impact on subsequent international interaction which should not be underestimated. Constrasting the styles and methods used by Presidents Kennedy, Johnson, and Nixon in performing this role provides excellent examples of how personal tastes and styles result in different presidential behavior.

A second presidential role is that of partisan political leader. The president usually serves as the titular head of his political party and normally emphasizes his party allegiances. President Nixon has done this by stressing how his (Republican) domestic programs would return power to the people (after two Democratic presidents), rather than lead to increased centralization. The president acts as a fund raiser for his party by hosting or speaking at banquets and dinners which raise money for the party or emphasize the party's point of view. Even more important, the president assumes a partisan political role through his attempts to gain congressional approval of various items and programs. Most presidents since Franklin D. Roosevelt have had extensive staff contact with various members of Congress. The attempt is always to influence behavior and gain approval for specific legislation. One of the trade secrets of successful action by the president is his ability to persuade congressmen that their action would benefit the nation, not just the president's partisan interests. Other examples illustrating the political nature of the presidency include the president as political spokesman for and supporter of other candidates in his party. Indeed, political leadership is an important aspect of the presidency and one deserving careful attention.

A third role, one that many people feel is easy to understand, is the president as chief executive. In this role, the president is responsible for a wide range of policy and administrative decisions. These include the president's traditional leadership roles, such as commander-in-chief and treaty negotiator. Later on in this chapter, a review of American involvement in Southeast Asia will illustrate the importance of this role. As chief executive, the president often must take the responsibility and initiative in areas involving controversy and dispute. In many cases, the president must make a definitive decision on an issue and then accept the implications of that decision.

If members of a major segment of the population feel they have been unfairly treated, they usually attempt to gain presidential support for relief of their problems. This often forces the president to get involved in matters which he may prefer to avoid, but the nature of his office and his role as chief executive usually require that he be involved. Often the president has little choice about which controversies he will participate in and which he will ignore.

The fourth and final role concerns the president as "inspirational" leader for the American people and spokesman for the national interest. We have all heard a president justify his actions by maintaining that they are in the national interest and are part of the American dream. The president often justifies this judgment by asserting he is the spokesman and leader for all Americans and for the world. The president usually stresses this role when he wants to rally domestic support for a controversial policy, for example, an agreement with a foreign nation. Woodrow Wilson argued this point when he attempted to gain Senate ratification of the Treaty of Versailles, ending World War I. President Nixon also stressed this point when he concluded arms limitation talks with the Soviet Union in 1972. He stated in a message on June 13, 1972:

> *Besides enhancing our national security, these agreements open the opportunity for a new and more constructive U.S.-Soviet relationship, characterized by negotiated settlement of differences, rather than by the hostility and confrontation of decades past.*
>
> *These accords offer tangible evidence that mankind need not live forever in the dark shadow of nuclear war. They provide renewed hope that men and nations working together can succeed in building a lasting peace.*
>
> *Because these agreements effectively serve one of this Nation's most cherished purposes—a more secure and peaceful world in which America's security is fully protected—I strongly recommend that the Senate support them, and that its deliberation be conducted without delay.*

A president, if he is to be successful in rallying support by stressing this role, should be sure it is consistent with his past practices and that he does not overuse it. Otherwise, he may lose credibility and, with it, public support.

The descriptions of these four roles are oversimplified and incomplete, but they do convey an impression of the tremendous complexity involved in the office. In order to understand the reasons for the various roles, a discussion of the process for selecting the president follows. Perhaps the best way to begin it is to explain how other political systems provide for selection of the chief executive, as this is helpful in understanding the uniqueness of the American system.

PRESIDENTIAL SELECTION

All political systems have some method of determining who the political leaders will be. The procedures may vary, but leadership is still common. In democracies, elections are usually held to determine who will lead. In other nations, the various tasks and roles performed by the American president are often divided among and executed by other leaders. For instance, in parliamentary systems, the chief legislative and political leader is elected by the members of parliament, solely from within the parliament. The general public has only an indirect voice in the process—by voting for the party of their choice. The people do not vote for the specific candidates for prime minister. In addition, in most parliamentary systems another person performs the ceremonial duties associated with the head of state. In Britain, Queen Elizabeth and the royal family perform these functions; in Germany, a President of the Republic performs them. Such roles are largely ceremonial and devoid of political content, but the ceremonial head of state serves to free other officials to concentrate on more limited duties.

In the American system, the president is elected by the electoral college. Thus, if you voted in November of 1972 for Richard Nixon, George McGovern, or another presidential candidate, you actually voted for a slate of state electors pledged to that person. In early December, the electors met and cast their ballots; in most cases, their votes corresponded to the votes of their states. Each state has the same number of electors as it has senators and representatives. Thus, the more populous states (such as California, New York, Pennsylvania, Michigan, Ohio, and Illinois) have a larger say and more importance in presidential politics. In addition, the candidate who obtains the most votes in a particular state, whether it be a plurality or a majority, is entitled to all of that state's electoral college votes. This is a "winner-takes-all" system.* Table 5-1 summarizes the recent popular votes for presidents and the electoral college votes for the same elections.

Note how the electoral college tends to magnify margins of victory. The rule that the winner in each state receives all of that state's electoral college votes causes this to happen. Table 5-2 summarizes the electoral college and popular votes by states in 1972 for the major candidates.

Again note how the electoral college vote magnifies the outcome. The possibility exists under the electoral college system for a presidential candidate to lose the national popular vote but still get the necessary majority of electoral college votes. This could happen if the winning candidate were to lose a heavily populated state by a large margin and then win by narrow margins in most of the other states. Other possible ways for this to happen exist, but the important point is the tendency of the electoral college to magnify the margin of victory.

Because of the electoral college system, presidential candidates must be able to appeal to many diverse groups of people and are therefore forced to adopt policies which are widely acceptable. For example, George McGovern made modifications in his positions after the early primaries showed him to be a serious contender for the Democratic nomination. He began to move more toward the center on drug, abortion, and other controversial issues. This is not a criticism of McGovern, nor of presidential candidates in general, but a realistic depiction of what happens when candidates

Table 5-1
Recent Presidential Popular and Electoral College Votes

YEAR	CANDIDATE	PARTY	POPULAR VOTE		ELECTORAL COLLEGE VOTE	
			millions	%	total	%
1948[a]	Truman	(D)	24.104	49.5	303	57
	Dewey	(R)	21.971	45.1	189	36
	Thurmond	(States' Rights)	1.169	2.4	39	7
1952	Eisenhower	(R)	33.937	55.1	442	83
	Stevenson	(D)	27.314	44.3	89	17
1956	Eisenhower	(R)	35.589	57.3	457	86
	Stevenson	(D)	26.035	41.9	73	14
1960	Kennedy	(D)	34.221	49.7	303	56
	Nixon	(R)	34.108	49.5	219	41
1964[b]	Johnson	(D)	43.129	61.1	486	90
	Goldwater	(R)	27.178	38.7	52	10
1968[c]	Nixon	(R)	31.785	43.4	301	56
	Humphrey	(D)	31.275	42.7	191	36
	Wallace	(AIP)	9.906	13.5	46	8
1972[d]	Nixon	(R)	46.631	61.2	521	97
	McGovern	(D)	28.422	37.3	17	3

SOURCES:

a. Svend Petersen, *A Statistical History of the American Presidential Elections* (New York: Frederick Unger Publishing Co., 1963), pp. 103, 105, 106, 108, 109, 111, 113, 115.
b. Richard M. Scammon, *America Votes 6* (Washington: Congressional Quarterly, 1966), p. 1.
c. Richard M. Scammon, *America Votes 8* (Washington: Congressional Quarterly, 1970), p. 1.
d. News Election Service final returns.

Table 5-2
1972 Presidential Popular and Electoral College Results by State

STATE	POPULAR VOTE		ELECTORAL VOTE	
	Nixon	McGovern	Nixon	McGovern
Alabama	661,525	205,343	9	
Alaska	41,809	24,362	3	
Arizona	369,068	181,651	6	
Arkansas	427,014	190,598	6	
California	4,544,134	3,431,824	45	
Colorado	568,426	305,522	7	
Connecticut	763,880	507,331	8	
Delaware	139,796	91,907	3	
District of Columbia	29,697	109,974		3
Florida	1,751,210	690,565	17	
Georgia	766,899	330,607	12	
Hawaii	167,414	100,617	4	
Idaho	197,589	80,558	4	
Illinois	2,613,162	1,794,765	26	
Indiana	1,397,748	703,202	13	
Iowa	702,398	492,642	8	
Kansas	605,632	265,158	7	
Kentucky	670,937	369,082	9	
Louisiana	679,944	305,836	10	
Maine	251,327	160,845	4	
Maryland	795,358	486,195	10	
Massachusetts	1,104,310	1,323,843		14
Michigan	1,860,186	1,467,562	21	
Minnesota	881,326	789,473	10	
Mississippi	498,680	125,756	7	
Missouri	1,132,111	682,030	12	

Table 5-2—Continued

STATE	POPULAR VOTE		ELECTORAL VOTE	
	Nixon	McGovern	Nixon	McGovern
Montana	177,926	116,490	4	
Nebraska	384,157	162,600	5	
Nevada	114,593	65,258	3	
New Hampshire	212,232	115,474	4	
New Jersey	1,769,458	1,058,451	17	
New Mexico	233,036	138,756	4	
New York	4,149,761	2,884,949	41	
North Carolina	1,051,583	437,299	13	
North Dakota	166,131	94,927	3	
Ohio	3,361,238	1,524,118	25	
Oklahoma	745,910	243,388	8	
Oregon	483,229	390,867	6	
Pennsylvania	2,703,975	1,788,034	27	
Rhode Island	209,166	185,239	4	
South Carolina	468,036	184,958	8	
South Dakota	163,746	137,432	4	
Tennessee	812,484	355,817	10	
Texas	2,147,970	1,091,800	26	
Utah	318,407	124,430	4	
Vermont	115,453	67,508	3	
Virginia	982,792	439,546	12	
Washington	679,156	475,553	9	
West Virginia	471,858	271,856	6	
Wisconsin	986,751	805,726	11	
Wyoming	100,561	44,341	3	
TOTALS	46,631,189	28,422,015	521	17

are faced with the political realities of getting elected. The entire selection process involves presidential politics, which forces all contenders to adopt a variety of roles that will be transmitted to the presidential office upon the election of one of them. The nominating process will be discussed in an upcoming chapter; it, too, has an important role to play in subsequent behavior by the elected president.

While many would agree that the presidential office is complicated and that the selection process used in the United States encourages political considerations, there is more disagreement on the next aspect of the presidency to be discussed, namely, the types and extent of power the president has. To evaluate this aspect, a consideration of the president's role in domestic and international policy is required. Before that, however, a brief discussion of the relativity of power is essential.

PRESIDENTIAL POWER

In Chapter 1, the difficulty of measuring power was discussed, along with a consideration of how power often appears confusing when studied. This also applies to presidential power. On the one hand, it could be argued that the president's central position and resources make him, in fact, the most powerful person in the country. One might, on the other hand, want to argue that the president is so bound by day-to-day demands and past policies that he really has little power. Richard Neustadt, one of the most prominent students of the American presidency, maintains that the president's real power lies in his ability to persuade, not force, persons to follow his wishes.[1] Obviously, it is probably easier to be persuasive as president, but the point remains that as an individual, the president is limited or constrained from exerting total power by a wide variety of institutional and personal factors. Perhaps a brief review of one aspect of a domestic policy and one of an international policy will offer some insights into this problem.

In August of 1971, President Nixon ordered a 90-day wage-price freeze and maintained that this action was necessary in order for the country to deal with the accelerating cost of living and other inflationary tendencies in the economy. With one executive order, the entire economic situation in the United States was drastically altered. No longer could the marketplace indiscriminately determine costs and productivity; not even contracts negotiated prior to the date of the wage-price freeze could go into effect if they had not already done so.

The response to this action was most interesting. Many Americans supported the president's decision, because they felt wage-price restraints were necessary. Others, especially those who had been due for or had negotiated increased salaries or wages, protested the decision. Needless to say, partisan political factors entered into the controversy, and quite often the arguments were based on these grounds rather than on the merits of the decision. The point here, though, is the result of the president's decision. Table 5-3 illustrates the increases in the cost of living for the 24-month period from August 1970 to August 1972.

Note that the cost of living continued to increase, but at a lesser rate during the months after the president's announcement. The administration maintained that these increases would have been more drastic without the wage-price restraints. One could also argue that the restraints did not really hinder anyone, and that they were an important psychological deterrent to people involved in economic transactions. Whichever way we consider the point, the manner in which the president implemented the wage-price controls is indicative of the constraints on his power.

To begin with, a bureaucratic structure had to be organized to bear the primary responsibility for implementing the freeze guidelines. The initial public response was one of confusion; it was

Table 5-3
Cost of Living Index: August 1970 to August 1972

MONTH	INDEX
1970[a]	
August	136.0
October	137.4
December	138.5
1971[b]	
February	138.9
April	139.8
June	141.3
August	142.0
October	142.4
December	143.1
1972[b]	
February	143.9
April	144.6
June	145.4
August	146.2

SOURCES:

a. U.S. Department of Labor, Bureau of Labor Statistics, *Monthly Labor Review* (February 1971): 106.

b. U.S. Department of Labor, Bureau of Labor Statistics, *Monthly Labor Review* (December 1972): 98.

unclear from the guidelines exactly which provisions were applicable to which people. It was several months before the Wage and Price Commission succeeded in eliminating most of the confusion. President Nixon may have sensed the need for time to organize the commission's work when he maintained that the decision was necessary to protect the economic foundations of American society.

In essence, he argued that the decision was in the national interest and that both the letter and the spirit of the decision should be followed, despite the temporary bureaucratic confusion.

What happened, though, is another matter which illustrates the elusiveness of presidential power. As already mentioned, the president was subject to partisan political criticism. In addition, he personally could not make the many critical decisions necessary to administer the policy; therefore he had to set up and delegate authority to other people and institutions. Once this was done, he was subject to criticism or praise based on what the Wage and Price Commission and the other participating agencies decided, even though he might not be directly involved in those decisions. In addition, once the aura of national need and unity began to wear off, the president found his proposal under fire. Teachers throughout the country protested; in some states, state officials attempted to ignore the provisions of the freeze. In other cases, national unions began to flex their muscles and contended that if their wage settlements were not granted, there would be no work. In addition, commercial and industrial concerns were able to convince the Wage and Price Commission that prices of certain items had to be increased, due to higher costs, or the businesses involved would be faced with economic disaster.

All of these results permit some basic conclusions. Despite the formal and informal power a president has in domestic policy, he is still bound by important limitations, such as public opinion, administrative uncertainty, and political factors, which all tend to keep him from exercising his power in an arbitrary manner. This forces the president to plan carefully what he is to do and usually forces him to keep these political considerations in mind. Thus, in most domestic matters, the president is restricted, despite the formal and informal powers he might have. The next few paragraphs discuss the president's role in international affairs and offer interesting comparisons with his domestic uses of power.

From the 1940s on, the United States has been forced to make a series of difficult and troublesome decisions relating to Southeast Asia.* Operating on the general premise that the nationalist movements in Southeast Asia were controlled by outside political forces and convinced that American interests would best be served by governments friendly to the United States, this nation embarked on a policy toward Southeast Asia which has dominated and affected American political life in a staggering way. President John F. Kennedy first ordered the use of American military advisors in South Vietnam; this was followed by an extensive and massive military buildup during the administration of President Lyndon B. Johnson, with the avowed purpose of making South Vietnam militarily safe. President Nixon sharply reduced American troop strength in South Vietnam from 1969 to 1972 but increased the number of military personnel in the rest of Southeast Asia. In each case, regardless of whether you feel the presidential decisions were tragic errors or important to the survival of the free world, you must be aware of the constraints upon the presidents who made those decisions.

Consider for a moment the domestic constraints. Each president has attempted to justify his decisions in terms of protecting American interests and protecting the rights of others to make basic decisions affecting their lives. This appeal to national consciousness has been used to rally support, and, in many cases, the American public has granted that support. Despite the support they generally received, the presidents have felt the need to encourage such support and be sure that they had it.

In addition to public support, the presidents have attempted to gain congressional support. The televised coverage of Senator William Fulbright's Foreign Relations Committee's questioning of both Democratic and Republican administration spokesmen, military advisors, and cabinet officers on aspects of American policy were seen by many Americans in the 1960s and early 1970s. Usually these were sharp confrontations which had important political overtones. Also worth remembering is the fact that before the massive American military increase in the mid 1960s, President Johnson asked for and received "The Gulf of Tonkin Resolution" from Congress as a justification for his actions.[2] The need to gain both public and congressional support is an important constraint; it makes it difficult for the president to pursue a policy without at least some check on his actions. Domestic constraints, however, are often less restricting than constraints external to the United States. This requires explanation.

In the Vietnam situation, each president had to try to ascertain what responses his various policy decisions would evoke from a wide variety of international observers. For example, how would the Viet Cong (the supposedly native South Vietnamese engaged in civil war with the Saigon government) respond to American attempts to negotiate with North Vietnam? The question could also be reversed. Then came the problem of allies. How would our allies, especially European and Asian allies, respond to our policy? In most cases, special envoys were sent to explain any major changes which might be forthcoming. An attempt was usually made to insure cooperation of the allies and at least tacit approval. Needless to say, this became difficult at times, and quite often American presidents have found themselves sharply criticized by the nation's allies.

Even more perplexing and difficult to measure was the response the allies of the Viet Cong and North Vietnam would make to our policy. For instance, what would the Soviet Union's response be to American bombing which killed or injured Soviet citizens or soldiers working in North Vietnam? What would happen with communist China if any variety of possible military alternatives were pursued? Obviously the presidents could only anticipate reactions; the point is that possible reactions were important factors, and quite often constraints, in the decision-making process. While the president has great opportunity to influence American opinion and leadership, he is not likely to influence public opinion and the leaders of other countries to the full extent.

Both examples of domestic and foreign constraints offer some substantiation of the point that the president must carefully consider the constraints upon him in deciding how he might go about influencing policy. A reasonable position to take is that the president has considerable power, but that his use of it and how he develops other related resources are just as important as the formal power he has. This points out a need for blending formal and informal power, which has led to four developments, or problems, summarized below.

PRESIDENTIAL PROBLEMS

The first is obvious, but often overlooked. As the demands and complexities of American society have increased, so has the need for the president to establish both effective communication links and an advisory staff to help him perform the many complicated and difficult tasks required of him.* There was a time when the president needed little more than a personal secretary; today he requires a large number of advisory and research staff personnel if he is to be abreast of developments concerning him. How a president allocates his time is one of the most important decisions he must face.

One of the most common complaints voiced by contemporary presidents is that the job leaves little opportunity for personal contemplation or thought. In order to create more time for the president, much time is spent on assigning distinct responsibilities to staff members.[3] Once the necessary job of delegating authority is complete, the president has lost a large degree of control he might have had in those areas. Thus, it is a necessary step, but still a limiting one. Another problem is involved in staffing; if the president attempts to insure that his staff will agree with his position on most issues, he will run the risk of eliminating necessary criticism and divergence of thought from within. He must weigh the costs of internal disputes with the costs which could result from the misapplication of policy. Various presidents have differed in their approaches to this problem.

A second development which has created serious problems in the contemporary presidency is the need to make rapid decisions. No longer can a president or the country afford the luxury of contemplating policy decisions; in many cases, the "crisis syndrome" forces the president to reach decisions in quick fashion, often without knowing all of the details. For instance, should the president be faced with a decision concerning nuclear war, can he be expected to quickly and soundly decide our policy when the United States may already be under attack and facing destruction? Obviously he has to depend on rapid communications and the ability to decide priorities and policies quickly. Such a situation may force the president to follow a plan which is not as carefully thought out as it might be. Once the specific crisis has resolved itself, the president may then find himself saddled with a policy decision which hampers his other decisions. Thus, the need for rapid decision-making under crisis conditions poses severe problems for the president. It is an aspect of the contemporary presidency which should not be overlooked.

A third development, and this has already been alluded to, is the president's frequent need to use persuasion to gain approval and acceptance of his plans. In this sense, the presidency is seen as a political office in which the president must use his persuasive abilities in order to gain increased political power. Too many Americans assume that when a president wants something, he automatically gets it—not true. The president is subject to constraints and restrictions, just as other political participants are; however, he does have considerable political resources.

These resources can be used in two different but often equally effective ways. On the positive side, the president can use his prestige and power to bolster a congressman whose support he seeks by trying to positively influence the voters in that person's district or by using his influence to "deliver" material rewards, such as public works improvements. In the same vein, the president can attempt to influence other countries by offering them economic or political incentives for their cooperation and assistance.

The reverse is also true. The president can attempt to discipline or punish those opposed to him by arguing that they represent only a few, who are putting their special interests above the national interests. He can also withhold benefits from both domestic and international opponents. But again the emphasis is on the president's need to induce and persuade. For instance, the president may be able to gain support for a program by offering something a person needs or wants rather than by threatening to take something away. In international circles, tariff decisions are often used as inducements or even punishments. Domestically, public works projects and personal appearances are useful resources at the president's disposal.

The last development to be considered is the growing concern that the American presidency is too much for any single individual to handle and that the job takes too high a toll from any individual, regardless of how capable he is.[4] In essence, the point is that the presidential office, as an institution, is too complex to be managed by one man, even if he has the staff he feels is necessary. The implication is that the American political process suffers damage, not because of any particular president, but because of an unconscious tendency to avoid hard issues or to deal with them in an unsatisfactory fashion. We will return to the problems of the presidency in the closing chapter.

SUGGESTED READINGS

The Presidency: The usual starting point for anyone interested in the modern presidency is: Richard Neustadt, *Presidential Power* (New York: Wiley, 1960); this book provides an interesting and invaluable analysis of the limits of presidential power. Other books dealing with the contemporary presidency are: Louis W. Koenig, *The Chief Executive* (New York: Harcourt, Brace and World, 1968); Clinton L. Rossiter, *The American Presidency* (New York: Harcourt, Brace, 1960). Several presidential histories are worth pursuing: Lyndon B. Johnson's account of his years in office, *The Vantage Point* (New York: Holt, Rinehart and Winston, 1971); Emmett J. Hughes's account of the Eisenhower years, *The Ordeal of Power* (New York: Atheneum, 1963); and Eric F. Goldman, *The Tragedy of Lyndon B. Johnson* (New York: Knopf, 1969), in which Goldman provides his own personal view and evaluation of Lyndon Johnson.

Electoral Systems: If you are interested in the effects electoral law may have on politics and political institutions, read: Maurice Duverger, *Political Parties* (New York: Wiley, 1963).

Southeast Asia: For several excellent accounts of American policy in Southeast Asia, see: Hans J. Morgenthau, *Vietnam and the United States* (Washington: Public Affairs Press, 1965); Bernard B. Fall and Marcus G. Raskin, eds., *The Vietnam Reader* (New York: Random House, 1965); Richard H. Rovere, *Waist Deep in the Big Muddy* (Boston: Little, Brown, 1968); Chester L. Cooper, *The Last Crusade* (New York: Dodd, Mead, 1970); *The Pentagon Papers* (New York: Quadrangle Books, 1971); and David Halbestram's, *The Best and the Brightest* (New York: Random House, 1972).

Presidential Staffs: For a wide variety of views and descriptions of how individual presidents have used their staffs and cabinets, see: Richard F. Fenno, *The President's Cabinet* (Boston: Harvard University Press, 1959); Theodore C. Sorenson, *Kennedy* (New York: Harper, 1965); and Arthur M. Schlesinger, *A Thousand Days* (Boston: Houghton Mifflin, 1965).

NOTES

1. Richard E. Neustadt, *Presidential Power* (New York: Wiley, 1960), pp. 42–63.
2. Lyndon Baines Johnson, *The Vantage Point* (New York: Popular Library, 1971), pp. 112–118.
3. For an excellent example of how President Kennedy assigned his staff and cabinet different functions during a crisis, see: Robert F. Kennedy, *Thirteen Days* (New York: W. W. Norton, 1969).
4. See James D. Barber, *The Presidential Character* (Englewood Cliffs, N. J.: Prentice-Hall, 1972) for an interesting investigation into the psychological aspects of presidential power.

6. The Federal Bureaucracy and Political Interaction

THE BUREAUCRACY

The Constitution established only three branches of government, but the demands of a modern industrialized society have combined with a variety of political forces to establish a "fourth branch" of government—the bureaucracy. Table 6-1 illustrates the size of the federal bureaucracy at various times since 1821. The table records the numbers of all civilian personnel employed by the federal government; the figures exclude military personnel. Note the tremendous increases in the years associated with rapid population growth (1861–1921) or foreign or domestic crises (1941, 1956). In addition to the numbers displayed in Table 6-1, several other factual points concerning the bureaucracy are useful to consider. They include:

(1) 90 percent of the federal employees live outside of the Washington, D.C. area.
(2) Over 95 percent of the employees live in the United States.
(3) The three largest departmental employers are the Department of Defense, the Post Office, and the Veterans' Administration.
(4) Salaries, with few exceptions, are generally below those offered by private industry for similar work.

While this short background does not provide a comprehensive overview of the bureaucracy, it does point up several of the

Table 6-1

The Federal Bureaucracy: A Historical Perspective

YEAR	TOTAL NO. OF EMPLOYEES
1821[a]	6,914
1841	18,038
1861	36,672
1881	100,020
1901	239,476
1921	561,142
1941	1,437,682
1956	2,398,736
1972[b]	2,843,000

SOURCES:

a. 1821–1956 figures from U.S. Department of Commerce, Bureau of the Census, *Historical Statistics of the United States* (Washington, D.C.: Government Printing Office, 1961), p. 710.

b. 1972 figure (through April) from U.S. Bureau of the Census, *Statistical Abstract of the United States: 1972* (Washington, D.C.: Government Printing Office, 1972), p. 399.

more important questions students of American government might raise about the federal bureaucracy and its functions and effectiveness today.*

For instance, what does a bureaucrat do? Certainly anyone can think of cases in which his progress in various areas was held up by "red tape." Also, most persons have probably complained about the bureaucracy at some point. In essence, a bureaucrat's responsibility is to administer programs or policies that have already been established by legislative or executive action.[1] Most bureaucratic jobs entail highly routinized work, in which the individual employee has little if any control over broad policy matters. Thus, he administers. An example is an individual who works as a clerk in a local Social Security office. The responsibilities of such a job do not include the setting of policy on which applicants get social security but rather involve the administering of policy as established by either the Social Security Administration or the Congress. A brief discussion of four questions which periodically pop up during any consideration of the bureaucracy will help to clarify the distinction between policy-making and administration.

Most Americans are aware of the term *civil service*, but few understand what it means. In the case of the federal bureaucracy, it involves a set of rules and regulations which structure the behavior, working conditions, and benefits of federal employees. The underlying idea is that persons doing the same or similar tasks should be provided the same working conditions and benefits.

In addition, a classified, merit civil service has been established to reduce the political uses to which the federal bureaucracy was often subject. The "spoils system," a situation which existed when a newly elected administration appointed its own people to as many government jobs as possible, and patronage, whereby people are given jobs because of their political connections, were the main targets of the civil service legislation in the United States. President Andrew Jackson, although the practice existed prior to his term in office, is usually credited with firmly establishing the "spoils system" on the national level.[2] This practice continued until President Garfield was assassinated in 1881 by an individual who was denied a federal position because of his political connections. Since then, legislative efforts have been made to insure that the bureaucracy will be free from politics.* In 1939 and 1940, the federal Hatch Acts prohibited a long list of political activities from being performed by bureaucrats. It was another attempt to emphasize the bureaucracy's role of administering policy, not making it. In addition, civil service legislation insures that there is not widespread turnover in most government jobs when the administration changes.

Two questions usually arise about the civil service. One involves whether the salaries and benefits for the top administrators are competitive with those paid by private industry. Table 6-2 indicates how the various civil service ranks and salaries corresponded in the year 1971.

Table 6-2
Civil Service Ratings and Salaries: 1971

LEVEL	SALARY RANGE
GS1–4	$ 4,326 to $ 8,065
GS5–8	$ 6,938 to $12,337
GS9–11	$10,470 to $16,404
GS12–18	$15,040 to $36,000

SOURCE:

U.S. Bureau of the Census, *Statistical Abstract of the United States: 1972* (Washington, D.C.: Government Printing Office, 1972), p. 399.

While the salaries for the so-called "super-grades" appear to be large, they are not really competitive with salaries paid by large private corporations to their top executives. Some have argued that this implies that federal civil service may not be as competitive as it should be and that lower salaries may mean that only lesser qualified people will work in the federal bureaucracy.

A second question relating to civil service, and one that is interesting, is whether or not the federal bureaucracy is too civil-service oriented. A case is sometimes made for the need to permit more political appointments, not just to reinstate the power of patronage, but, more important, to insure that the policy objectives of an administration will be pursued by a bureaucracy which shares the same values and concepts. This argument maintains that in order for any policy to be effectively carried out, the bureaucrats must themselves support it. That is, a bureaucracy which is asked to do something new or different from past actions, will not function effectively. In this case, the argument contends, successful policy implementation and administration would require the appointment of new personnel in the bureaucracy.

Another argument contends that civil service makes it too difficult to dismiss or discipline any employee, regardless of how justifiable either move might be. An employee who has complaints lodged against him is able to avoid disciplinary action because of the protection offered by civil service legislation. Your reaction to this point depends a great deal on your feelings toward the role of the civil servant. The conflict between the civil servant working for the public and yet being protected from outside evaluation is evident.

A second reservation often raised concerns the size and scope of the federal bureaucracy. As has been mentioned, the bureaucracy exists to administer policy; therefore, the administration of that policy should be the same everywhere, unless the policy specifically permits variations. This makes policy national rather than adaptable to local needs and factors. For instance, the Environmental Protection Act of 1970 established guidelines in environmental quality and prescribed methods of enforcing those guidelines. The bureaucracy's task is to implement these provisions, but shouldn't it be done so as to take into consideration local conditions and factors? What about two mills fouling different rivers with industrial discharges, the one old, the other new. Can the same set of standards be applied to both? Some would argue "no"; that to try and make all policy national in scope fails to recognize the diversity of the nation. The bureaucrat is usually pictured as totally uncompromising and steadfast on this point. Should the federal official take into account local situations when attempting to administer policy?

This question raises a third point, which considers the differences between policy-making and the administration of policy—where does the one start and the other end? To begin with, policy-making is usually thought to rest with Congress or with presidential action establishing a specific program. Thus, these institutions set policy, and the federal bureaucracy administers them. Yet, it should be obvious that even the lowest level bureaucrat has the potential for being a policy maker. This can occur through his attitudes, which might affect the types of reactions he might obtain to the policies. How he chooses to "interpret" the policy guidelines sent him will determine to a large extent what the policy in reality is. So it cannot be assumed that the bureaucracy and the bureaucrat do not have some policy-making roles to play.[3] They may not be thought of as major roles, but they are essential to an understanding of the importance of the bureaucracy. Because of this, attempts are made to provide the bureaucrat with a guideline or skeleton of what is to be done with the policy and how it should be done, and the prerogatives and decisions left open to him are usually kept to a minimum.

This raises a final point. Given that the bureaucracy does have certain policy-making roles as well as administrative roles, how can the bureaucracy be controlled? One way is to make the legislation as specific as possible. This requires careful detail, and the resulting legislation may be so lengthy that it becomes burdensome. In addition, how can a policy-maker anticipate every possible development and circumstance? Obviously he can not. Another alternative would be to make the bureaucrat accountable if he fails to follow the letter or the spirit of the policy directive. Civil service rules govern proceedings relating to the letter of the law, but the spirit of legislation is much more difficult to uphold. Thus, one is faced with an important and unsolved problem in American democracy, which could continue to grow more difficult as government action becomes more extensive in a wider array of fields.

POLITICAL INTERACTION
AMONG THE FOUR BRANCHES

One of the most widely quoted phrases used to describe American government is "a separation of powers." This means that one branch has a distinctive role to play in one of these areas: legislation (passing the law), execution (enforcing the law), and adjudication (interpreting the law). This works well in theory, but in practice it is often quite difficult to isolate these various roles, as they tend to merge or are so closely interconnected that separation is all but impossible. When the complexities of these three branches are increased by the problems of a bureaucratic system, some real idea of the difficulties of governmental analysis is revealed. The following examples illustrate the complex interrelationships among the various branches.

There has always been a very strong emphasis on religious diversity and freedom in the United States; in fact, the First Amendment guarantees that government will not establish any religion. A long series of court fights has taken place over the interpretation of this constitutional amendment, but none more interesting than the controversy involving a nonsectarian prayer which the New York Board of Regents permitted to be recited in classrooms throughout the public schools of New York State.[4] The controversy began in 1962 when several parents claimed that the prayer, by acknowledging the existence of a supreme being, did in fact violate the constitutional restrictions on the establishment of religion. Eventually the case was heard by the Supreme Court, and its decision, by a split vote, upheld the parents' contention that the prayer, although itself not objectionable, was clearly a violation of constitutional restrictions when used in the classroom. Needless to say, this generated a great deal of controversy.

Public officials denounced the Supreme Court's decision as barring prayer in the United States and encouraging the country to become "godless." The late Everett Dirkson, the powerful Republican senator from Illinois, was adamant in his demands that Congress attempt to guarantee the right to prayer by proposing a constitutional amendment to that effect. In addition, the public's outcry was overwhelmingly against the Court's decision; newspaper editorials and public opinion polls clearly indicated the public's dissatisfaction with the decision. The controversy became so intense that even President Kennedy (whose religious background was Roman Catholic) was asked at a press conference for his reaction to the decision and whether he thought the Court had overstepped its boundaries. In this case, despite the public's reaction and the attempts to change the Court's decision, it stood, and the use of the prayer was discontinued.

This illustrates how decisions made by one branch will usually evoke a response from or involve interaction with the other branches. This is especially true when the issue has a great deal of public interest and can readily be translated into partisan political debate.

The next example indicates that the various branches have their own priorities and feelings of prestige, which they attempt to nurture and protect. In early 1972, President Richard Nixon embarked on an interesting and eventful set of journeys which carried personal diplomacy to two major powers: the Soviet Union and communist China. The announcements of these so-called "summits" were carefully controlled, and few details were made public until all but the final arrangements had been made. President Nixon's advisor on foreign policy, Dr. Henry Kissinger, had spent considerable time and effort arranging both the sites and the details of the meetings. The items discussed on both trips were of utmost importance: the establishment of trade relations with and possible governmental recognition of communist China and increased cultural exchange and possible arms limitation agreements with the Soviet Union. The president's trips received extensive news coverage and were closely followed by most Americans.

Upon his return from both trips, the president briefed the key members of both houses of Congress and attempted to rally Senate support for the arms agreement negotiated with the Soviet Union. While the president and his representatives were able to negotiate with Soviet leaders and agree to the terms of the arms treaty, they were not authorized to make a full and final commitment for the American government. Authorization must await Senate ratification of the treaty. This important restriction is a "check" on the president's action; he clearly understood he could gain Senate approval only if the treaty were within the limits of what Senate members felt was possible.

However, more than formal restrictions were involved. On the trip to communist China, the president was not accompanied by any senators or representatives. Needless to say, some of the more important committee chairmen were a bit "put out" by being ignored. This rekindled competition between the executive and legislative branches for public attention and prestige. As a result, soon after the president's return, several congressional leaders were invited to China and held their own discussions with the top Chinese leaders.

Both of these examples, while not overly significant by themselves, accurately represent the extensive formal and informal interaction among the various participants in and branches of the federal government. Perhaps a general axiom might be that for every action in one branch, there is a reaction in another. Thus, no individual actor in a particular branch, whether he be president, judge, or representative, can ignore the attitudes and powers of the members of the other branches of government. To do so would create substantial problems.

THE FUTURE OF AMERICAN INSTITUTIONS

Rather than an attempt to summarize the preceding three chapters and the past segment on bureaucracy, a brief discussion centering on four major questions will be developed here. They should provide some guidance for considering possible future developments in American institutions.*

(1) Will American society and politics continue to grow more complex? Future technological developments may foster extensive change, and the impact of this change on the social, economic, and political structures of the country is almost certain to result in increasing complexity. Thus, institutions can be expected to grow larger and more intricate in both organization and procedure.

(2) If political problems do become more complex, can existing institutions adequately deal with them, or, more importantly, can present institutions "solve" them? Two things need to be considered in answering this. First, can we ascertain how successfully these institutions have worked in the past? A study of history and your personal values and preferences will determine your position on these questions. If you believe existing institutions have not been successful, what reasons can be offered for their continued failure? Second, how have the institutions solved problems in the past? Most observers would agree that incremental change has dominated American decision-making and that, over an extended period of time, the incremental changes have resulted in comprehensive changes. Whether past procedures and decisions will be suitable for the future is an open question.

(3) What alternatives are available if the institutions, as presently structured and working, are incapable of solving the problems? At least three possibilities can be suggested. The first is to change the persons who occupy the major positions in the institutions. Thus, the composition of the institutions could be changed

by use of the vote or by altering the selection process. A second alternative would be to abolish the existing institutions and replace them with other institutions which supposedly would deal more effectively with the problems. A third possibility would be to ignore these institutions, make no attempt to alter policy within them, and go outside them to effect change, perhaps even by the use of violence.

(4) Finally, these three points bring us squarely into conflict with a basic dilemma which always confronts people concerned with change. Do you change the political institutions, do you change the behavior of the individuals in those institutions, or do you change the behavior of the general public? If the goal is change, decisions must be made as to where and how to bring it about. A difficult and often confusing set of considerations must enter into such calculations. American political institutions and change will be discussed again in the closing chapter.

SUGGESTED READINGS

Bureaucracy: A diverse literature exists on the bureaucracy. Perhaps the best starting point, from a theoretical perspective, would be: H. H. Gerth and C. Wright Mills, *From Max Weber, Essays in Sociology* (New York: Oxford University Press, 1946) and Francis E. Rourke, *Bureaucracy, Politics and Public Policy* (Boston: Little, Brown, 1969). For descriptions of the organization and roles of the American bureaucracy, see: Peter Woll, *American Bureaucracy* (New York: Norton, 1963) and Richard Fenno, *The President's Cabinet* (New York: Vintage Books, 1959). For suggestions on bureaucratic reform, see: *A Report to the Congress by the Commission on Organization of the Executive Branch of the Government* (Washington: Government Printing Office, 1949) and Harvey C. Mansfield, "Federal Executive Reorganization: Thirty Years of Experience," *Public Administration Review*, 29 (July/August 1969).

Politics and the Bureaucracy: The Pendleton Act (1883) established a classified civil service under the administration of the Civil Service Commission. See the Hatch Acts of 1939 and 1940 for the specific restrictions applicable to public employees at the federal level or at the state level if salaries involve federal funds. Other viewpoints on ridding patronage from government can be found in: Luther Gulick, ed., *Improved Personnel in Government Service* (Philadelphia: American Academy of Political and Social Science, 1937); William S. Carpenter, *The Unfinished Business of Civil Service Reform* (Princeton: Princeton University Press, 1952); and Ari Hoogenboom, ed., *Spoilsmen and Reformers* (Chicago: Rand-McNally, 1964).

Future Developments in American Institutions: For an analysis of possible changes in the courts, see: Jerome H. Skolnick, *The Politics of Protest* (New York: Ballantine Books, 1969) and Adda B. Bozeman, *The Future of Law in a Multi-Cultural World* (Princeton: Princeton University Press, 1971). For comments on possible congressional developments, see David B. Truman, ed., *The Congress and America's Future* (Englewood Cliffs, N. J.: Prentice-Hall, 1965).

NOTES

1. *Webster's New Collegiate Dictionary* defines a bureaucrat as follows: "An official of a bureau, esp. one pursuing a narrow and arbitrary routine." *Webster's New Collegiate Dictionary* (Springfield, Mass.: G. & C. Merriam, 1960), p. 111.

2. For an interesting explanation of Jackson's position, see his Annual Message of 1829.

3. For a variety of views on this point, see: Joseph P. Harris, *Congressional Control of Administration* (Washington, D.C.: The Brookings Institution, 1964) and Roger Hilsman, *To Move a Nation* (Garden City, N.Y.: Doubleday, 1967).

4. *Engel* v. *Vitale* (1962).

SECTION III
Subnational Politics

7. *American Federalism*

TWO CONTRASTING VIEWS

During the debate over the constitutional provisions establishing the United States, substantial and heated discussions took place about the relationship between the national and state governments. One group at the Constitutional Convention wanted a complete and specific allocation of duties to the various levels of government and argued that powers not specifically delegated to one level of government be reserved for another.[1] Since the Constitutional Convention, historians and social scientists have disagreed on the factors affecting the relationship between the states and the national government.* Most agree that the United States has a federal form of government—that power is distributed throughout a variety of levels, and that these power relationships may change over time. This is contrasted with a unitary form of government, in which the central or national government has a near monopoly on most aspects of power. If there is general agreement that the United States is a federal system, there is substantial disagreement as to the nature of that federalism. A useful way to view the various schools of thought on this matter is to compare two contending theories which describe American federalism. One has been labeled the "layer cake" theory, the other, the "marble cake" theory. They are depicted in Figure 7-1. An analysis of both is in order.

The layer cake theory has been held by various persons since the days of the drafting of the Constitution. Advocates of this theory

Figure 7-1
Two Contrasting Views of American Federalism

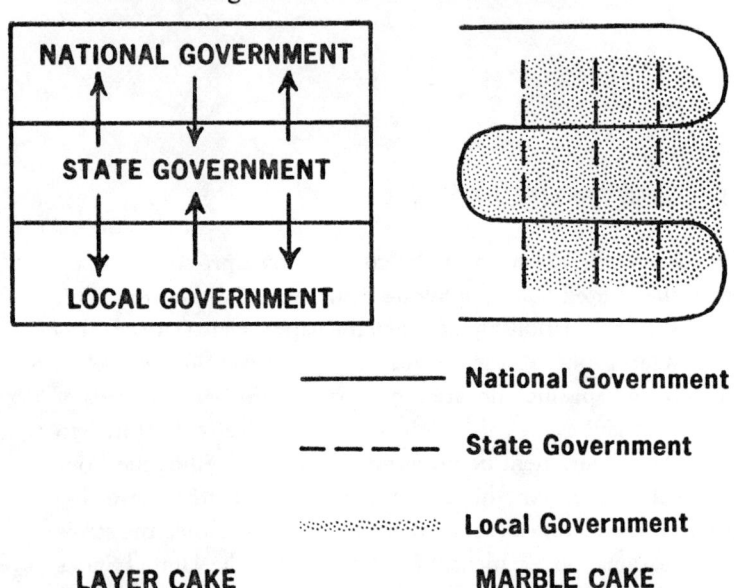

argue that various responsibilities and functions of government clearly belong to either the national or state governments. For instance, those who support the layer cake theory contend that Section 8 of Article 1 of the Constitution (see Appendix) specifically lists the powers which the national legislature has. Section 8 specifies that Congress alone has the right to coin money, to regulate commerce, to declare war, and to perform the other listed responsibilities. In addition, those who support this position cite the Tenth Amendment, which reads as follows, to support their argument: "The powers not delegated to the United States by the Constitution, nor prohibited by it to the states, are reserved to the states respectively, or to the people."

This "reserve clause" is interpreted to mean the national government has only those powers specifically delegated to it by the Constitution. All other powers are reserved for the states or the people. This particular clause is critical to those who support the layer cake theory, because it makes clear which level of government has responsibility in areas not specifically mentioned in the Constitution.

Acceptance of this concept provides a useful means for determining which level of government should do various things. Since the Constitution clearly expresses that the states and the people have the powers not delegated to the national government, there has been considerable debate whenever the national government has acted in areas such as voting qualifications, civil rights, and crime control. Proponents of the layer cake theory maintain that national action in such areas does not reflect the underlying division of powers between the two levels of government. Carried to its extreme, the layer cake concept becomes a powerful rationale for national inaction in various policy areas which the founding fathers failed to anticipate. Environmental quality is an excellent example of an area in which a layer cake advocate would rule out national legislation and favor state or local legislation.

Despite recent evidence that indicates environmental quality was eroding even during the mid 1750s in the United States, there is no mention in the Constitution of which level of government has the power to act to alleviate or control it. Thus, recent legislation which empowered the national government to develop and exercise such control could not be justified if the reserve clause argument were the only consideration. The difficulty with this position is that there are clear examples of environmental quality needs which extend beyond state lines. For instance, what happens to the residents of Indiana and Kentucky if the citizens of Ohio and Pennsylvania fail to control what is dumped into the Ohio River? Or what happens to the residents of Connecticut and New Jersey if New

York fails to control its industrial pollution? Environmental quality is only a contemporary example; there are numerous national priorities which require national action, but which are not specifically delegated in the Constitution to the jurisdiction of the national government.

The courts have used several general provisions set forth in the Constitution to legitimize national legislation when such power was not specifically granted in the Constitution. Among the most frequently used is the "general welfare" clause, which reads as follows: "The Congress shall have power to lay and collect Taxes, Duties, Imposts and Excises, to pay the Debts and provide for the common Defence and general welfare of the United States."

Those who accept the general welfare clause as a legitimate reason for national action usually also accept a second descriptive aspect of American federalism. This is the "marble cake" theory. For the person advocating this concept, cooperation among all levels of government would take precedence over questions of which level has the exclusive power in given activities. According to this theory's proponents, American federalism does not delegate specific duties or responsibilities to the state and national levels. Instead, the relationship between these two levels is a swirled pattern resembling a marble cake. (See Figure 7-1.) In addition, marble cake advocates maintain that local government interacts with the other levels in a similar fashion. Thus, all levels share responsibility.

The marble cake concept stresses two additional points. First, since the pattern is a mixture, it can undergo change. The dynamic quality of this interaction can be viewed historically by looking at various periods throughout the American experience when one level tended to dominate another. Second, the marble cake concept also stresses cooperative interaction between the states and the national government. The advantage of this theory is that instead of concentrating efforts on determining which level of government *should*, according to the Constitution, be doing various things, analysis can deal with what the various levels *are* doing and with the impact of those efforts.

While it may appear unimportant to some whether the American system is best viewed as a layer cake or a marble cake, there has developed a relatively new and expanding, related field of study labeled "intergovernmental relations."* Intergovernmental policy analysis emphasizes the programs and policies in effect at the various levels of government and the specific interaction between policies and programs at the various levels. Since almost all public policy has an intergovernmental aspect, this method of analysis is often quite important. In addition, since decisions are made at various levels of government, analysis of inaction and opposing policy decisions is possible and helpful.

While the various views of American federalism are important, even more important is the realization that the American Constitution ignores an important demographic factor which has had profound influence on American life. The Constitution established a two-tier federalism: national and state governments. It made no provision for urban government in the United States. The result is that each state has been responsible for granting or withholding powers from its urban centers. Recent American history has seen the country become a nation of urban centers which often have no or limited powers granted them by their states' constitutions. The result has been very slow change in the urban centers and, in many cases, no change at all. What this means is that a substantial number of Americans live in areas which receive their political power not as a birthright but as the state legislature sees fit. As the nation becomes increasingly urbanized, this lack of effective constitutional power has limited the urban centers' capacities for dealing adequately with their pressing problems. This question of urban government and the impact of urbanization on the United States will be discussed in the next chapter. The following segment considers American federalism's response to the questions of integration, responsibility, and distribution.

INTEGRATION, RESPONSIBILITY, AND DISTRIBUTION

Any political organization must decide how it plans to organize and perpetuate itself. The unique blend of federalism in the United States has permitted us to cope, with varying degrees of success, with a basic political problem faced by all countries—political integration. Political integration involves the sharing of interests in political needs and institutions; it is basic to the survival and growth of any political system. American federalism is an attempt to reconcile the need for political integration with the desire for local control and autonomy. Theoretically, it works as follows.

The national government is responsible for those things that are either clearly national in scope (defense, international affairs, currency) or which involve the concept of the general "public interest." Public interest is not a readily defined term, and its interpretation will probably vary from person to person; it is an abstract and relative term. Most people would agree that there are certain areas of interest, such as pollution control, which could be classified as in the general public interest. Under the federal system, any policy or decision not noted in the Constitution or in the public interest is resolved by another level of government. In the United States, this means that state and local governments perform a variety of important (education, public safety) and complex (highways) tasks.

Political integration has two aspects deserving particular attention. The first involves the need to integrate policies at the various levels of government, so that they are consistent and not working against each other. For instance, if the state of Massachusetts were involved in allocating large amounts of public education funds to the localities, but the localities were spending those funds on gymnasiums or other noninstructional items, one could argue that the policy application was not very consistent.

An even better example involves school desegregation. In the late 1950s, the federal courts ordered many Southern school districts to desegregate their schools. One result was that state educational laws were utilized to establish "private" schools, which were supposedly beyond the control of the federal government. The implication here is clear: unless there are ways to coordinate and integrate policies, decisions reached at various levels of government may actually work against one another, and the result may be confusion over various public policy choices. But while this need to integrate various public policies reached by different levels of government under a federal system is important, there is a more subtle implication for society.

Consider for a moment the complexities and contradictions which can be found in the United States. The country has changed from an agrarian society to an urban, industrialized giant. The geography of the Great Plains is as different from the geography of the Eastern seaboard as is that of the Southern gulf coast from the Pacific Northwest. Even discounting the tremendous geographical differences, consider the diversity found in the various groups comprising "America." Each ethnic and racial group has contributed its own unique set of characteristics to the American life-style. In essence, the United States is so economically, socially, culturally, and politically diverse that to refer to one "American way of life" is an oversimplification.

Political integration involves more than just coordinating governmental policy; it involves acceptance by the citizenry of the legitimacy and authority of governmental structures to reach decisions. This is not easily accomplished in any society, and indeed some observers argue it has not been done in American society. Political integration does not mean that all segments of a population have the same values, hopes, and wants; instead it means there is a basic underlying consensus that the political system is, at the very least, not keeping them from achieving their goals and, at best, is helping them reach their goals.

Perhaps an example characterizing political integration would be helpful. The United States is a nation of immigrants; in the 1840s, 1880s, and early 1900s, millions of immigrants came to the country from many lands, for many reasons. Once here, they had to be integrated into American society, integrated in a political not a racial or social sense. They had to be convinced that American institutions were open to them and that their efforts to participate would be rewarded.

Because of the several layers of government, the immigrant was able to make contact with and participate in local government. This is the level at which his access and experience enabled him to form impressions about the American political system. By providing this point of access, the American system permitted new immigrant groups to develop a positive orientation toward the political system. This was accomplished by the government's response to the needs and demands of the immigrants. In short, government was responsive; the result was that most of the ethnic groups were integrated into the American political system. They did not give up their customs but simply accepted the "rules of the game"—how American politics were to be played. If the political system had been seen as less than responsive, the resulting behavior would have been interesting to analyze. But in this case, it is important to note that the federal system provided a means, through local governmental participation and action, for successful political integration. Later discussions will consider the success or lack of success of the American political system's attempts to integrate various groups today.

While political integration is important, a closely related problem for most governments involves responsiveness. Few persons would argue that they want their governmental institutions to be unresponsive. The ideal is structured relationships among citizens and their political institutions which permits and encourages responsiveness. One of the benefits often attributed to a federal system is that it permits the various governmental units to be responsive to a wider variety of demands and wants because of the different levels of government. The emphasis is on the supposition that more governmental units should automatically increase responsiveness. While this argument is often cited, it does ignore three factors which are basically unique to and have heavily influenced American federalism.

The first of these involves the rise and dominance of the American political machine.* In this discussion, machine politics means the politics that dominated in many American cities in the late 1800s and early 1900s. Most observers would agree that all but a few of the old machines have disappeared. Mayor Richard Daley's Chicago political organization is often cited as an excellent, but rare, contemporary example of a political machine. What exactly a political machine is and how it operates are two essential questions which deserve our attention.

The word *machine* implies mechanical strength; in the political sense it emphasizes human organization. A machine is a group of individuals which attempts to control the nominating and electoral processes in order to perpetuate themselves in political power. This definition has the advantage of being neutral; the methods used to exercise control may include physical intimidation, violence, vote fraud, graft, and superior political organization. Throughout American history, political machines have been formed by a variety of economic, ethnic, and social groups. The political machine often involved more than merely politics; it was also a vehicle for groups trying to gain economic and social superiority by utilizing their political power to gain such nonpolitical benefits. While the control of political power was an "end," it was also used as a "means" to gain other desirable ends. Too often this fact is overlooked by those who maintain that the machine is a thing of the past. If the conditions responsible for its creation and growth still exist, then the machine may adapt itself. This raises an important point.

Most urban machines in America are associated with Italian and Irish immigrants, who used the machine's political power for economic and social gain. What is the future of the machine, now that many American cities are becoming more highly populated by racial minorities? While each individual city will exhibit unique qualities, some evidence suggests that these racial minorities may even now be developing their own political style and special type of political machine. Needless to say, these new political organizations will reflect the cultural values of the minorities they represent, but the basic form and organization may be the same. In addition, these new political organizations will probably rely on the one essential ingredient which characterized machine politics in the past—limited citizen concern and participation.

Recalling the definition of a machine, which is easier to control: a general election or the nominating process? Does it not make sense to concentrate your resources on determining who gets nominated, since fewer people are likely to be involved in and less public attention focused on the nominating process than the general election? This is exactly the strategy usually followed by a political machine; considerable effort is spent organizing and determining who will be nominated for a particular office. By stressing their patronage power, machine officials are often quite successful in controlling nominations. Once this has been completed, they can withdraw without concern over the election's outcome. Usually few candidates are willing to "buck" the organization and face a primary fight. By concentrating on this level, the machine can use its leadership capabilities quite well. In addition, when there is a contested primary, the machine can call on its usually small, but well-organized membership to vote and actively seek the support of other voters. The end result, in either case, is political power that is reflective of the machine's needs but perhaps not representative of its supposed constituency's needs or desires. When the machine's needs coincide with what the general public desires, there is no problem. When they differ, as is often the case, there can be considerable argument and conflict. Thus, the mere existence of a machine does not mean that public policy will benefit only a few; it does mean that public policy decisions will be made in light of the political considerations affecting the machine.

The second unique feature of American federalism is the general feeling that the states are often the least responsive of the major governmental units. State governments are usually accused of being supporters of the status quo and the well-to-do, and there is some evidence to support this contention.[2] For example, special interests, often representing large economic concerns, normally have easy access to state legislatures. In addition, until recent years, representation in most states' legislative bodies was controlled by largely rural interests.

Another factor contributing to the contention that state governments are unresponsive may be their failure to modernize bureaucratic functions as rapidly as necessary. For instance, the time and trouble it takes most Americans to get a driver's license is ample evidence of the need for reform at the state level. Even more important is the refusal of most states to adopt needed fiscal change. States have not been as responsive to public needs and demands as the proponents of federalism maintain; the existence of a federal system is no guarantee of a responsive political system at the state level. The people staffing the institutions and the institutions themselves determine that degree of responsiveness.

One last point concerning responsiveness should be made. Many Americans argue that the government closest to the people is in the best position to be responsive to their needs and demands. In America, that would be local government; however, consider the following. Even within a medium-size city (200,000 people), there is probably such diversity of feelings and values that no central authority can be completely responsive.[3] In addition, what if the residents of a city lack the resource base necessary to provide the funds or knowledge to solve a particular problem or set of problems? Finally, what if the problem affecting the city (say, it is water quality) is beyond the control of the local authorities because it is outside their jurisdiction? How, in that case, can local government be responsive? These factors may all contribute to a local government which is not responsive. The mere existence of a federal system, with its dual levels of government, does not guarantee responsiveness.

While political integration and responsiveness are important problems, a related consideration affects both of them. This is the problem of fiscal distribution of resources. Table 7-2 indicates the relative percentages of federal, state, and local tax dollars spent on various functions.

Note the emphasis on education at the state level and especially at the local level. Also, note the different demands made on different units of government by their constituents. While Table 7-2 provides an excellent comparison of inter-level expenditures, it does not provide a useful comparison for intra-level expenditures. Tables 7-3 and 7-4 provide selective comparative data on state and local expenditures for various functions.

Note the differences between the various states. While some of the differences can be accounted for by dissimilar costs of living and population sizes (for example, it is reasonable to assume that it costs more to educate a child in New York than in Mississippi), the large differences can not all be attributed to such differentials. In similar fashion, the differences listed in Table 7-4 indicate that some states' localities either have greater resources to tap for public expenditures or are willing to make greater demands on themselves in terms of tax efforts. What all of this means is that the American federal system has considerable fiscal imbalance built into it. Not all states are created equal in terms of revenue potential or the public's willingness to accept tax policies necessary to raise needed

Table 7-2
Functional Distribution of Expenditures by Governmental Levels

FUNCTION	Local	State	National
National Defense			100.0[a]
Education			
Higher education	13.5	86.5	
Local schools	98.9	1.1	
Highways	32.1	67.2	0.7
Public welfare	40.9	44.8	14.3
Health	23.1	20.0	56.9
Hospitals	38.9	41.1	20.0
Police protection	78.3	13.2	8.5
Fire protection	100.0		
Local parks and recreation	100.0		
Natural resources	5.3	17.8	76.9
Housing and urban renewal	59.7	1.2	39.1

SOURCE:

U.S. Department of Commerce, Bureau of the Census, *1967 Census of Governments: Compendium of Government Finances*, p. 30.

a. These figures are percentages of direct general expenditures for the year 1966–1967.

Table 7-3
Selected State Expenditures by Function: 1966–1967

STATE	FUNCTION			
	All Education	Highways	Public Welfare	Parks and Natural Resources
Alabama	212.8[a]	155.9	127.6	22.9
California	876.5	831.2	516.6	535.1
Connecticut	98.1	149.2	98.7	14.4
Illinois	431.3	329.6	313.8	51.3
Kentucky	165.2	253.5	122.5	30.1
Maine	48.8	63.1	31.4	13.9
Michigan	612.4	285.6	234.7	47.0
Missouri	164.5	210.6	168.8	27.8
New Mexico	97.7	82.3	39.8	12.8
North Carolina	179.4	242.2	16.2	31.5
Oregon	151.8	122.5	59.9	36.4
Texas	432.0	570.4	278.5	43.8
Utah	105.9	75.4	31.4	11.1
Wisconsin	353.7	116.9	66.2	39.2

SOURCE:

U.S. Department of Commerce, Bureau of the Census, *1967 Census of Governments: Compendium of Government Finances*, pp. 76, 80, 82, 89, 93, 95, 98, 101, 107, 109, 113, 119, 120, 125.

a. All expenditures are figured in millions of dollars.

Table 7-4
Selected Local Expenditures by Function: 1966–1967

STATE	FUNCTION			
	All Education	Highways	Public Welfare	Parks and Natural Resources
Alabama	347.0[a]	74.0	2.5	10.2
California	3,514.5	505.6	1,110.0	469.0
Connecticut	411.5	48.1	9.6	20.0
Illinois	1,411.3	257.5	80.6	105.1
Kentucky	338.8	18.8	4.4	7.1
Maine	103.9	22.8	3.1	2.4
Michigan	1,452.6	230.0	92.1	78.1
Missouri	612.2	70.3	5.4	28.6
New Mexico	177.3	13.4	.2	10.6
North Carolina	27.4	35.4	103.5	18.6
Oregon	354.6	58.9	3.4	26.2
Texas	1,427.5	217.0	12.1	100.4
Utah	178.4	13.9	.4	8.1
Wisconsin	615.0	257.1	104.8	46.2

SOURCE:

U.S. Department of Commerce, Bureau of the Census, *1967 Census of Government: Compendium of Government Finances*, pp. 76, 80, 82, 89, 93, 95, 98, 101, 107, 109, 113, 119, 120, 125.

a. All expenditures are figured in millions of dollars.

revenues. The resulting descrepancies in revenues played a significant role in the debate over the various types of federal revenue sharing. In revenue sharing, the federal government returns a portion of the revenue it receives from federal income taxes to the states and localities. A variety of revenue sharing plans have been proposed; at least two deserve consideration: one by Congressman Reuss, one by President Nixon.

The first is the concept of federal bloc grants to the states and localities. Sponsored by Congressman Reuss (Democrat) of Wisconsin, this legislation would make bloc grants available to the individual states.[4] Under the original Reuss proposal, HR 11764, five billion dollars would be available the first year, seven and one-half billion dollars the second, and ten billion dollars the third. This money would go directly to the states and could be used for whatever purposes they deemed necessary. Under the Reuss proposal, each state would have to develop and implement a program of modernization for its governmental units in order to qualify for the grants. His proposal makes 50 million dollars available for planning and requires that each state develop a plan every two years.

Once the state plan had been developed, a regional coordinating committee would review it and be sure it would "fit" with the plans being formulated by the other states in the region. A majority vote of this regional committee would be necessary to accept the plan. Also to be acceptable, the state plan would have to include provisions for reform at the local and state levels as well as in the interstate relationships which might develop. Once the regional coordinating committee approves the plan, the president must also approve it. The advantages and disadvantages of the Reuss plan are worth consideration.

Congressman Reuss has maintained that the very simplicity of his proposal is its greatest asset. By eliminating the need for extensive bureaucratic action, Reuss's proposal would speed up the modernization process and provide financial incentives for those states interested in change. In addition, the bloc grants could be spent on priorities the states set, not those imposed by the federal government. Finally, Reuss argues that his proposal of an initial five billion dollars and a final amount of ten billion dollars contains sufficient revenues to encourage states to reform their own tax legislation.

Critics of the Reuss proposal usually concentrate on three aspects of the proposal.[5] First, many argue that Reuss's proposal is fiscally unsound, because it would require a large increase in current tax rates to provide the extra revenue the plan calls for. Second, many opponents of the plan contend that the bloc grant to the states does not guarantee the use of the extra revenue to meet pressing urban problems. In fact, many argue that unless the funds go directly to the cities, they will be of little use in alleviating urban problems, because the state will either use them for other things or will mismanage them. Finally, opponents argue that modernization is unlikely to happen under the Reuss proposal and what modernization does take place will be too political because of the need to gain the approval of the regional committee and the president.

A comparison of the Reuss proposal with President Nixon's revenue sharing plan reveals several interesting points.[6] Under the Nixon proposal, a certain percentage of total personal income, ranging from one-sixth of one percent to one percent by 1975, would be set aside for distribution to the states. The total amount would vary between 500 million and one billion dollars. These funds would be distributed directly to the states, based on their respective percentages of the national population and their tax efforts. Thus, those states which were taxing their citizens at a rate greater than the national average would receive more funds as a reward for their efforts. The states would then have to share a proportion of these funds with the local communities, based on the relative distribution of tax efforts by the state and local levels of government. The only other requirements would be that the state file quarterly reports accounting for its funds and that the states continue their existing level of aid to the localities.

Advantages claimed for this system are several. First, it is relatively simple and permits shared revenues to change as the national economy fluctuates. Second, it is argued that any solution to problems must come from the state level; thus, the reason for making grants directly to the states. Third, by requiring the states to share these funds with the localities, emphasis is placed on rewarding local and state attempts to raise more revenue. Fourth, the administrative requirements are uncomplicated, in order to reduce bureaucratic costs and delays. Finally, the Nixon proposal is justified as a key aspect of the New Federalism, which wants to restore both fiscal and policy strengths at the state level.

Needless to say, the Nixon proposal evoked quite a reaction. Conservatives argued it was unfair and a "giveaway," because it gave considerable autonomy to state officials. Many conservatives felt that the level of government which raises the revenue is also responsible for spending it. On the other side, liberals argued that the Nixon proposal involved too little money and should not include the provision that the revenues go directly to the states. Instead, it was argued, more of the revenues should go directly to the localities. Finally, other adversaries opposed the measure, because its provisions, in their terms, were too uncertain to insure major change at the state level.

While these two plans have similarities and differences, their basic objective is the same: to restructure and strengthen fiscal relationships among the various levels of government. Many argue that if some level of government fails to find an adequate resource base, then that level of government has little or no chance to perform its function, and its power will pass to a more centralized authority. Undoubtedly, the final resolution of these fiscal questions will have a great deal to do with future relationships among the various levels of government. These proposals were the subject of extensive political debate and discussion during the late 1960s and early 1970s. A modification of President Nixon's proposal was passed in 1972 and is presently being implemented. Revenue sharing has become politically involved and enmeshed with the politics of the American federal system.

The examples discussed above indicate the nature of debate concerning American federalism. Power shifts, people and institutions change, and demands are altered, yet most observers would agree that some type of balance among the various levels of government is inevitable. This balance will be dynamic but is also the cornerstone of any understanding of American federalism. After a consideration of state and local governments in the next chapter, the epilogue of this section returns to this aspect of federalism.

SUGGESTED READINGS

American Federalism: For several provocative, theoretical views of the advantages and disadvantages of federalism, see: William H. Riker, *Federalism: Origin, Operation, Significance* (Boston: Little, Brown, 1964); K. C. Wheare, *Federal Government* (London: Oxford University Press, 1953); and Valerie Earle, ed., *Federalism* (Itasca, Ill.: F. E. Peacock, 1968). Literature applicable to the American experience is abundant; for a wide sample and variety of views, see: James Bryce, *The American Commonwealth* (New York: Macmillan, 1916); James A. Maxwell, *The Fiscal Impact of Federalism in the United States* (Cambridge, Mass.: Harvard University Press, 1946); M. J. C. Vile, *The Structure of American Federalism* (London: Oxford University Press, 1961); Daniel J. Elazar, *The American Partnership* (Chicago: University of Chicago Press, 1962); Walter Hartwell Bennett, *American Theories of Federalism* (University, Ala.: University of Alabama Press, 1964); Morton Grodzins, *The American System* (Chicago: Rand-McNally, 1966); Aaron Wildavsky, ed., *American Federalism in Perspective* (Boston: Little, Brown, 1967); and Richard H. Leach, *American Federalism* (New York: W. W. Norton, 1970).

Intergovernmental Relations: For a variety of approaches to this topic, see: James L. Sundquist and David W. Davis, *Making Federalism Work* (Washington: The Brookings Institution, 1969); "Needs and Prospects for Research in Intergovernmental Relations," *Public Administration Review* (May/June, 1970); and Daniel J. Elazar, "Fiscal Questions and Political Answers in Intergovernmental Finance," *Public Administration Review* (September/October, 1972). In addition, a governmental commission and a university center have concentrated their efforts on intergovernmental relations and federalism. See the publications of the Advisory Commission on Intergovernmental Relations (Washington: Government Printing Office, varied dates) and The Center for the Study of Federalism, Temple University, Philadelphia, Pa.

Machine Politics: Two of the more interesting and enlightening descriptions of machine politics in the United States are: Edwin O'Connor, *The Last Hurrah* (Boston: Little, Brown, 1956) and William Riordan, *Plunkitt of Tammany Hall* (New York: E. P. Dutton, 1953). Other historical and social science writings dealing with the urban political machine include: Seymour J. Mandelbaum, *Boss Tweed's New York* (New York: John Wiley and Sons, 1965); Martin Meyerson and Edward C. Banfield, *Politics, Planning, and the Public Interest* (New York: The Free Press, 1955); sections of Oscar Handlin, *The Uprooted* (Boston: Atlantic, 1951); Edward N. Costikyan, *Behind Closed Doors* (New York: Harcourt, Brace and World, 1966); Robert K. Merton, "Latent Functions of the Machine," *Social Theory and Social Structure* (New York: The Free Press, 1957); J. David Greenstone and Paul E. Peterson, "Reformers, Machines, and the War on Poverty," *City Politics and Public Policy*, ed. James Q. Wilson (New York: John Wiley and Sons, 1968).

NOTES

1. For a discussion of the arguments about national/state government, see: Alexander Hamilton, et al., "Federalist #s 5, 6, 7, 8, 9, 10, 14, 27, 28, 44, 45, 46," *The Federalist* (New York: The Modern Library, n.d.).

2. Oliver Garceau and Corinne Silverman, "A Pressure Group and the Pressured: A Case Report," *American Political Science Review* (September, 1954).

3. For pertinent and stimulating comments on size and representation of interests, see Robert A. Dahl, "The City in the Future of Democracy," *American Political Science Review* (December, 1967).

4. Henry S. Reuss, *Revenue-Sharing* (New York: Praeger, 1970).

5. For a discussion of the pros and cons of the Reuss and other revenue sharing proposals, see: "Revenue Sharing: $5.3 Billion for States, Cities," *April 1, 1972 Congressional Quarterly Weekly Report* (Washington, D.C.: Congressional Quarterly, 1972), pp. 739–740; and "General Revenue Sharing: Giveaway or Godsend?," *May 6, 1972 Congressional Quarterly Weekly Report* (Washington, D.C.: Congressional Quarterly, 1972), pp. 1000–1003.

6. Richard M. Nixon, "Special Revenue Sharing Message to Congress," (Washington: The White House, August 13, 1969). For a version of the legislation enacted by Congress, see "Congress Clears Nixon's Revenue-Sharing Plan," *October 14, 1972 Congressional Quarterly Weekly Report* (Washington, D.C.: Congressional Quarterly, 1972), pp. 2701–2703.

8. State and Urban Politics in America: An Overview

INTRODUCTION

Chapter 8 considers the behavioral and institutional roles played by state and local governments in the United States. It offers an overview of the major trends and developments presently occurring within the American federal system as well as suggestions of various strategies for influencing state and local governmental decision-making.

Table 8-1 indicates the locations and potential sizes of the newly enfranchised 18- to 20-year old voters. These new voters will have quite an impact on local and state political life. And, although the role and power of national institutions should not be underestimated, state and local governmental institutions also affect most Americans.

In addition to analyzing the political power the 18- to 20-year old voter will be able to exert at the state and local levels, there is another important reason why a thorough understanding of policies and alternatives at these levels is critical. Consider for a moment the important questions on which most Americans have strong feelings: national security, international affairs, race relations, economic security, education, crime, and personal freedom. While the national government has extensive power in these areas (exclusive power in the first two), state and local governments also have great power to affect these issues. In addition, chances are greater that an individual citizen will have direct contact with and be affected by decisions made in these critical areas by state and local government

Table 8-1
Estimate of 18- to 20-Year-Olds' Vote Potential

STATE	ELIGIBLE NEW VOTERS thousands	% OF TOTAL ELECTORATE
Alabama	198	9
Alaska	19	10
Arizona	107	9
Arkansas	104	8
California	1,130	8
Colorado	145	9
Connecticut	152	7
Delaware	30	8
Florida	358	7
Georgia	277	9
Hawaii	48	9
Idaho	42	9
Illinois	587	8
Indiana	298	8
Iowa	158	8
Kansas	133	9
Kentucky	199	9
Louisiana	224	10
Maine	54	8
Maryland	212	8
Massachusetts	321	8
Michigan	504	9
Minnesota	219	9
Mississippi	135	10
Missouri	258	8
Montana	39	8
Nebraska	87	9

Table 8-1—*Continued*

STATE	ELIGIBLE NEW VOTERS thousands	% OF TOTAL ELECTORATE
Nevada	24	7
New Hampshire	44	8
New Jersey	344	7
New Mexico	58	9
New York	925	7
North Carolina	337	10
North Dakota	37	9
Ohio	586	8
Oklahoma	147	8
Oregon	120	8
Pennsylvania	612	9
Rhode Island	59	9
South Carolina	177	10
South Dakota	40	9
Tennessee	232	9
Texas	678	9
Utah	71	10
Vermont	29	9
Virginia	284	9
Washington	205	9
West Virginia	98	8
Wisconsin	255	9
Wyoming	19	8
District of Columbia	46	9
TOTALS	11,465	8

SOURCE:

U.S. Department of Commerce, Bureau of the Census, *Population Characteristics*, P–20, no. 230, p. 11.

officials. Table 8-2 summarizes the number of governmental units in the United States; note the large number at the state and local levels. For instance, an individual's experience with law enforcement officials will probably be at the state or local level. Personal contact with political leaders is more likely to be at the local level. Unless you are aware of the complexities of the American federal system, you will not be in a position either to understand the forces affecting you or to influence the policy-making process at the state and local levels.

Table 8-2

Governmental Units in the United States

TYPE OF GOVERNMENT	NO. IN YEAR		
	1942[a]	1957[a]	1967[b]
National Governments	1	1	1
State Governments	48	48	50
Local Governments			
Counties	3,050	3,047	3,049
Municipalities	16,220	17,183	18,048
Townships and Towns	18,919	17,198	17,105
School Districts	108,579	50,446	21,782
Special Districts	8,299	14,405	21,269
TOTALS	155,116	102,328	81,304

SOURCES:

a. U.S. Department of Commerce, Bureau of the Census, *Historical Statistics of the United States: Colonial Times to 1957*, p. 694.
b. U.S. Department of Commerce, Bureau of the Census, *1967 Census of Governments*, p. 1.

METROPOLITAN AMERICA

Table 8-3 outlines the urbanization of the United States. Map 8-4 illustrates how it has affected each state.

Not only has there been a shift toward an urban population, but toward an increasingly concentrated urban population.* The

Table 8-3
Rural-to-Urban Population Movement in the U.S.: 1890–1970

YEAR	% OF POPULATION	
	Rural	Urban
1790[a]	94.8	5.2
1810[a]	93.0	7.0
1830[a]	91.5	8.5
1850[a]	84.5	15.5
1870[a]	74.5	25.5
1890[a]	64.8	35.2
1910[b]	54.3	45.7
1930[b]	43.8	56.2
1950[b,c]	40.4	59.6
1970[b,c]	26.5	73.5

SOURCES:

a. Percentages are computed from data in: U.S. Department of Commerce, Bureau of the Census, *Historical Statistics of the United States: Colonial Times to 1957*, pp. 7, 14.
b. Percentages are from: U.S. Department of Commerce, Bureau of the Census, *1971 Statistical Abstract of the United States*, p. 17.
c. A new definition of *urban* is in effect for the 1950 and 1970 figures. For our purposes, this definition includes places having 2,500 or more residents, whether incorporated or unincorporated. Earlier definitions included only incorporated areas.

Map 8-4
Proportions of State Populations in Metropolitan Counties

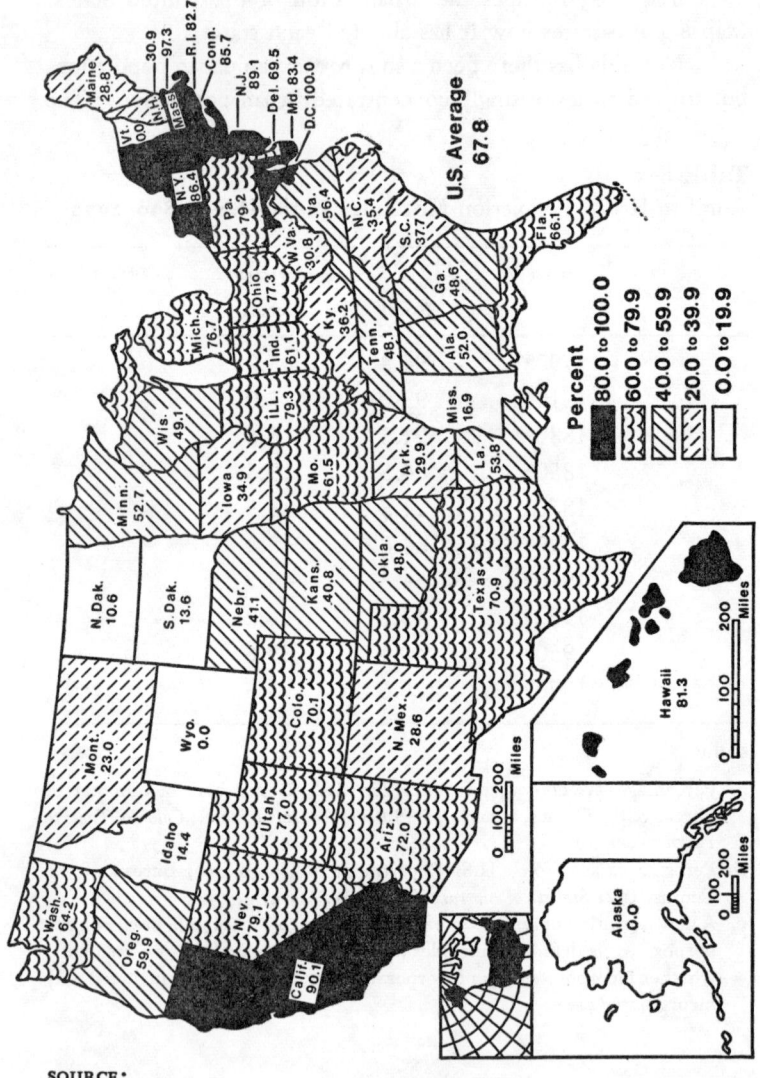

SOURCE:

U.S. Department of Commerce, Bureau of the Census, *Population Estimates and Projections*, P–25, no. 427, p. 4.

growth of Standard Metropolitan Statistical Areas (SMSAs—areas with a population exceeding 50,000) is illustrated in Table 8-5.

While I could go on for quite some time showing how the United States is increasingly becoming a nation of metropolitan centers, a basic point must be made. The resulting economic, social, and political tensions caused by this population shift need to be clearly understood in order to grasp the significance of the absence of nationally constituted authority in the urban population centers. Because of the population concentration in America's metropolitan centers, the important domestic developments and tensions of the 1970s will take place in these areas. For our purposes, four major trends are important.

First, the increased metropolitanization of the American population has resulted in the central city becoming a place of residence for the young and the old. Many younger Americans have been drawn to the major American cities because of the seeming vitality and life there. Many persons on fixed incomes and advanced in age can find no escape from the city. Many middle-age residents, for a variety of economic and social reasons, have left the central city for the suburbs. The great need for services, especially the educational and health facilities required by the young and the old, makes it difficult for the central city to provide these services at a reasonable cost. The demand for basic services is increasing in America's cities, and this increased demand can readily be translated into human costs if the services are inferior or not provided at all.

Second, the central cities of America are increasingly becoming the homes of the upper-middle class and the very poor. A casual stroll through any large American city will confirm the existence of extreme poverty areas next to swank areas. Again, in most cities, members of the middle class have fled the central city whenever possible. The significance is that in many cities the very rich and the very poor have been left to inhabit the urban landscape. This often creates problems when the needs and interests of the members of

Table 8-5
Metropolitan Population Growth in the United States

YEAR	% OF POPULATION RESIDING IN SMSA
1910[a]	37.5
1930[a]	49.7
1950[a]	56.8
1970[b]	62.7

SOURCES:

a. These figures are estimates drawn from data in Donald J. Bogue, *Population Growth in Standard Metropolitan Areas 1900–1950* (Washington: U.S. Government Printing Office, 1953), p. 11.
b. U.S. Department of Commerce, Bureau of the Census, *Metropolitan Area Statistics—1971*, p. 830.

both groups greatly differ. In addition, because of this economic disparity, the central city may lack the fiscal ability to provide the services its population needs and expects.

Third, population shifts have caused considerable business and residential development in areas surrounding the central city. And, in most cases, careful and thoughtful planning has been either ignored or applied too late to insure rational developmental patterns. Consider for a moment the various shopping and housing developments which dominate most American suburban areas; could they have been better, more efficiently planned? Some observers would argue that the single most difficult and ignored aspect of metropolitan growth has been the failure of the metropolitan areas to undertake comprehensive planning which would permit more rational development of these areas. The absence of this type of planning has meant, in most cases, that each suburb has forged its own policies and set its own priorities without any concern for area-wide services or the preservation of desirable environmental conditions.

Fourth, one aspect of the population and economic shifts in metropolitan America has been the continued racial separation of whites and nonwhites. Table 8-6 indicates the proportions of the populations of a number of major metropolitan areas and central

Table 8-6
Population Distribution by Race in SMSAs: 1970

SMSA	SMSA POPULATION % White	SMSA POPULATION % Non-white	CENTRAL CITY POPULATION % White	CENTRAL CITY POPULATION % Non-white	SUBURBAN POPULATION % White	SUBURBAN POPULATION % Non-white
New York	82.0	18.0	76.6	23.4	93.6	6.4
Detroit	81.4	18.6	55.5	44.5	96.0	4.0
St. Louis	83.6	16.4	58.7	41.3	92.5	7.5
Minneapolis St. Paul	97.2	2.8	94.3	5.7	99.2	0.8
Atlanta	77.4	22.6	48.4	51.6	93.6	6.4
Miami	84.5	15.5	76.6	23.4	87.4	12.6
San Jose	94.3	5.7	93.6	6.4	94.8	5.2
Columbus, Ohio	88.0	12.0	81.0	19.0	97.9	2.1
Louisville	87.6	12.4	75.9	24.1	96.6	3.4
Albany Schenectady Troy	96.3	3.7	91.4	8.6	98.9	1.1
Oklahoma City	89.1	10.9	83.9	16.1	95.9	4.1

SOURCE:

U.S. Department of Commerce, Bureau of the Census, *Metropolitan Area Statistics*, pp. 830–833, 850–853, 870–873.

cities which fall into these two categories. These areas are referred to as SMSAs—Standard Metropolitan Statistical Areas.

What has been happening appears to be continuing into the 1970s; the central city is becoming increasingly nonwhite, and the suburbs are, with a few exceptions, maintaining their predominantly white populations. This continuing racial separation may have important consequences for the American political system. In a society where racial integration is often stressed as a desirable and necessary goal, this may seem inconsistent. In its 1968 report, the Kerner Commission concluded: "Our nation is moving toward two societies, one black, one white—separate and unequal."[1] Half a decade later, it appears that this statement may have accurately described the American situation both then and now.

These four trends have important implications for the quality of life in the United States and should be clearly understood by students of the American system. As has been pointed out, the cities of America lack constitutional authority of their own and are creatures of the states. The power and authority they have are directly delegated to them by the states. Since the states have delegated varying degrees of power to the localities, local governmental authority differs too widely to be discussed in depth here. But it can be said, if American federalism is to survive and prosper, the power and authority of local governments must be expanded. Before discussing the various ideas that have been put forth or been attempted to strengthen American federalism, a brief discussion of state politics is in order.

STATE POLITICS

Any attempt to thoroughly understand present state policies and practices must be seen in the perspectives of state political development and the roles the states have played in American

State and Urban Politics in America: An Overview

federalism. A review of American history will not be attempted here; instead, a brief summary of various historical periods will provide the overview that is necessary. The entire topic of the state's position in a federal system has been thoroughly investigated and studied. Interested readers are encouraged to follow this up by pursuing the material listed at the end of the chapter.*

One feature of constitutional development in the United States which is often underemphasized is the central role played by the states. The Constitution itself was written and ratified by delegates from the states to both the Constitutional Convention and the various state ratification conventions. For a variety of reasons, the representatives of the states felt that a national union would meet certain needs and provide a variety of advantages over other cooperative arrangements. That the national government was created by the states should not be overlooked or underemphasized. Understanding this can do a great deal in helping you to understand the complexities of subsequent political development in the United States. Several examples will illustrate this point.

Consider for a moment the complex and complicated series of events leading to the American Civil War. Policy and public decisions from the constitutional days to the outbreak of the violence of the Civil War centered around the powers granted to the states or the national government by the Constitution. The debate had a series of critical historical moments, but the Dred Scott decision in 1857 typifies the intensity and importance of the repeated disagreements.[2] In that case, the United States Supreme Court ruled that the national government did not have the constitutional right to regulate slavery in the states and territories. This decision clearly strengthened the position of those who maintained that the affairs of each state were to be regulated by that state and should not be subject to outside interference. The Dred Scott decision should not be seen as the event that precipitated the American Civil War but as one of many events which contributed to the eventual forced, violent resolution of the question. In this case, the American system, despite its emphasis on conciliation and compromise, was unable to prevent violence. Are there certain issues so volatile and important that the American federal system is incapable of resolving them? Some observers argue that the next example represents such an issue.

In the late 1950s and continuing to the present time, there has been considerable debate and controversy over the role of the federal government in integrating public facilities, especially public educational institutions. This began with the *Plessy* vs. *Ferguson* decision in 1896, which maintained that "dual" public facilities for citizens of different color were constitutional.[3] This decision permitted *de jure* (by law) segregation of public facilities, including educational institutions, if equal facilities were provided. In 1954, in the *Brown* case, the Supreme Court ruled that the "separate-but-equal" doctrine was in fact unconstitutional; the ruling ended de jure segregation of educational facilities.[4]

Twenty years later—the early 1970s—the country still has not resolved this issue in a practical sense. In the 1972 presidential campaign, school bussing was a major issue; President Nixon was concerned enough with the issue to obtain a compromise in Congress to delay the use of federal funds to implement school integration till six months after the 1972 election. Leaving aside the question of civil rights, it is interesting to view this controversy as an extension of the debate over national and state powers within the federal system. The point is that even though we as a nation are approaching our 200th birthday, there is still considerable debate over the powers and responsibilities delegated to the states and the national government in such critical areas.

Despite this lasting controversy, state governments are vital elements in the American federal system. Although often criticized, state governments have not received the careful attention they deserve. State governments have experienced sizable increases in both their expenditures and their number of employees in recent decades.[5] In fact, a great deal of the growth usually attributed to government in general has occurred at the state level. While the states have experienced general governmental growth and development, three common complaints are usually raised about them.

First, it is often argued that the states are organized in an archaic fashion which prevents them from responding to problems which require action. The impression is that the states have undergone very little political modernization in the past 200 years and are unlikely to undergo much change in the future. To support this point, critics usually cite the long and tedious provisions of most state constitutions, the lack of power given to state governors, and the general institutional inertia caused by state decision-making machinery, which is often slow and cumbersome. State legislative bodies are the subject of numerous stories depicting inadequacies and inefficiencies. In short, state government is seen as the main refuge for conservative, nonprogressive political leaders who are only concerned with promoting special interests at the expense of the general public's good.

Second, state governments are often criticized as being not responsive enough to the needs and demands of the citizens of their states. This argument contends that state officials fail to respond in areas that are controversial and which call for forceful action. One of the examples used to support this point is the failure of most states to provide adequate revenue sources to meet their financial needs. This results either in appeals and demands to the federal government for more revenues to assist the state in meeting its problems or in a general reduction in services offered by the state. Many critics contend that this is irresponsible behavior of the worst sort, because state governments are in the position to make many more significant contributions than they do. Since they are, at least in a physical sense, closer to the "people," states are expected to play an active role in providing services and raising revenues to pay for them.

The third common criticism raised about states is that state legislators do not reflect the underlying political allegiances in their states. Stories and anecdotes involving political redistricting and reapportionment are unique to the American states, as exemplified by the congressional district map of Indiana (page 66). In some states, representation is often alleged to be based on the number of cows rather than the number of citizens. In addition, state legislators often hold partisan political positions which affect the legislation they pass. Historically, the rural and farm elements of most American states have been overrepresented in the state legislatures with the result being a general lack of responsiveness to urban needs.

As has been pointed out, the Supreme Court, in a series of decisions, established the concept of "one man—one vote" as the basis for representation in the state legislatures. Prior to these decisions, many states based representation on geographical units instead of on population. Thus, a heavily populated county and a rural county would have equal representation in the legislature, giving more weight to the rural votes. These court decisions resulted in extensive reapportionment in state legislatures, but it is still difficult to assess the results of the reapportionment process. Early indications are that suburban areas in a state may gain more power in state legislatures than the central city. If this is the case, implications for state policy should be most interesting, as it could be expected that the legislatures will become more friendly to suburban interests and needs. The potential results as reflected in state policy are significant.

This chapter has considered the state and urban levels of the American system; the epilogue considers several unresolved problems affecting American federalism. These also deserve careful attention.

SUGGESTED READINGS

Urban Population: Perhaps the best way to divide this literature is into two categories: the first stressing individual reactions and experiences associated with urban living and the second stressing collective information. INDIVIDUAL: Ralph Ellison, *The Invisible Man* (New York: Signet, 1947); Claude Brown, *Manchild in the Promised Land* (New York: Macmillan, 1965); Elliot Liebow, *Tally's Corner* (Boston: Little, Brown, 1967); and Todd Gitlin and Nanci Hollander, *Uptown* (New York: Harper, 1970). COLLECTIVE: Edward C. Banfield and James Q. Wilson, *City Politics* (New York: Vintage, 1966); John C. Bollens and Henry J. Schmandt, *The Metropolis* (New York: Harper and Row, 1965); Robert L. Bish, *The Public Economy of Metropolitan Areas* (Chicago: Markham, 1971); and Robert L. Lineberry and Ira Sharkansky, *Urban Politics and Public Policy* (New York: Harper and Row, 1971).

The States and the Federal System: For a representative sample of this literature, see: Robert A. Goldwin, ed., *A Nation of States* (Chicago: Rand-McNally, 1961); Committee on Federal Grants-in-Aid, *Federal Grants-in-Aid* (Washington: Council of State Governments, 1949); Daniel J. Elazar, *The American Partnership* (Chicago: University of Chicago Press, 1962); Daniel J. Elazar, *American Federalism: A View from the States* (New York: Thomas Y. Crowell, 1966); James W. Fesler, ed., *The 50 States and Their Local Governments* (New York: Alfred A. Knopf, 1967); and Ira Sharkansky, *Spending in the American States* (Chicago: Rand-McNally, 1968).

NOTES

1. *Report of the National Advisory Commission on Civil Disorders* (Washington, D.C.: Government Printing Office, 1968).
2. *Dred Scott* v. *Sandford* (1857).
3. *Plessy* v. *Ferguson* (1896).
4. *Brown* v. *Board of Education* (1954).
5. For varied data on this point, see: *Facts and Figures on Government Finance* (New York: The Tax Foundation, 1969).

EPILOGUE: PERSISTENT AND UNRESOLVED PROBLEMS

While the preceding discussion has attempted to introduce the complexities of American federalism at the state and local levels, this epilogue will argue that any future pattern of political relationships among levels will be based on the resolution of three interrelated problems. The first of these deals with efforts to solve pressing national problems which have great impact at the local level. Two excellent examples are environmental quality and poverty. Each will be briefly discussed.

The early 1970s saw the development of persistent and vocal concern over environmental quality. It soon became obvious that governmental policy regarding environmental quality was not well-formulated. The problem became one of determining which level of government should be responsible for legislation regulating environmental quality, and this created a number of problems, because special interests concerned with environmental legislation wanted access to the decision-makers responsible for that policy. The result was extensive and intensive interaction among the various forces concerned with environmental issues at all levels of government. Thus, various states with strong industrial representation often failed to enact major legislation dealing with air and water quality. Other states, influenced by substantial conservation interests, adopted major land use legislation. The problem was that there was little if any coordination among the states, and quite often there was variation within a given state. The end result was federal legislation which established minimal standards for air and water quality. Many argued that this was usurpation of the states' power by the federal government, but others argued it was necessary if any environmental standards were to be obtained.

The important point is not that there are now minimal federal standards, but that the failure of the states to develop consistent and complementary regulations led the federal government to impose the standards. It will be interesting to follow the relationships which develop regarding environmental quality in the years to come. They will probably reflect underlying political divisions in the United States.

The second example illustrating the problem of which level should deal with a given aspect of public policy concerns the poverty program. In 1964, the Johnson administration launched an ambitious program to "eradicate poverty" in the United States. One aspect of the program included direct citizen participation in community action programs (CAPs). These CAP programs were initially funded directly from Washington by the federal government and in many cases were autonomous political organizations not controlled by local or state political leaders.

Imagine the dismay of the political leader who found a local CAP agency using federal funds to develop political strength to defeat him in the next elections. Needless to say, the vested political interests did not appreciate the possibility, and by 1967 the CAP program was put under more state and local control. The controversy arising from the administrative arrangements in the War on Poverty has been responsible for many excellent accounts of the program's development and actual implementation. Interested readers are encouraged to pursue the suggestions at the end of this segment.* Rather than recount the complexities of the War on Poverty, it is sufficient to point out that it engendered considerable disagreement over the resulting federal relationships. In this sense, it was indicative of the problem of which level of government is responsible for solving or attempting to solve major problems.

The second general problem involves metropolitan decision-making and is related to the first problem of the impact of national concerns on localities. For example, should an entire metropolitan area work together under a unified set of regulations to solve problems, or should each local unit of government be responsible for each set of rules and regulations? Before you answer, consider the following.

First, the metropolitan area is probably composed of racially, ethnically, and politically different groups which have varied interests and needs. The suburbanite who has a reasonable standard of living might be quite interested in controlling pollution, but the marginal factory worker might have to put up with the pollution if he is to have any type of financial security. Thus, different personal values and goals may hinder cooperation.

Second, in a metropolitan area there will be several units performing the same function. For instance, each locality is likely to have its own police, fire, and educational agencies. At what point does it make sense to pool these efforts and to combine the various agencies into one in which economies of scale and greater efficiency might be gained? The argument is made that the combination of service agencies would reduce administrative costs and increase the basic efficiency of the agencies involved. The problem is whether the loss of local control, or at least the reduction of local control, over these agencies offsets the benefits to be gained. For instance, would you favor a metropolitan (central city plus suburbs) school district? Probably so, if you felt the change would better your child's educational opportunities; probably not, if you were convinced the change would reduce the educational opportunities open to your child. The ramifications of changing or broadening areas of governmental control deserve careful consideration.

Finally, what political costs are involved in the decision concerning area size? Who has more to gain—the central city or the suburb? Black political leaders have recently opposed the shift to metropolitan government as an attempt to deny central city residents the opportunity to control their own destinies. In fact, some leaders argue that fear of black or other minority control of the central city has caused the sudden interest in metropolitan government.* Others have argued that the change to metropolitan government would actually benefit the central city, because its residents would receive the added tax base of the suburbs. Needless to say, suburban residents are not too happy with that type of argument. Given these three considerations and arguments, which people or which area should form the basis for decision-making in a metropolitan region?

The third and last problem which deserves consideration is the type of participation open to citizens who want to influence state and local policy. Participation can be a rational process; that is, a person participates only after he has determined that his participation may make a difference. This can be achieved by calculating the costs and benefits of participation. For instance, what is the cost involved in registering to vote and voting in local, state, and national elections? In most cases, the only costs involved are time and a little effort. What are the benefits? Obviously, the fewer votes in an election, the more weight one vote has. That means the significance of a single vote is probably highest at the local level. If policy matters which the local officials decide are of sufficient consequence to offset the costs in time and effort, one would be wise to participate. Thus, American federalism not only provides the individual citizen with multiple access routes to influencing policy but also makes it difficult for this access to result in success. The remaining chapters consider the various ways groups and institutions such as the political party have developed and operated within the context of American federalism.

SUGGESTED READINGS

Poverty Agencies: For an analysis of the legislation establishing the 1964 Economic Opportunity Act, see: Sar A. Levitan, *The Great Society's Poor Law* (Baltimore: The Johns Hopkins Press, 1969); Daniel P. Moynihan, *Maximum Feasible Misunderstanding* (New York: Free Press,

1969); and John C. Donovan, *The Politics of Poverty* (New York: Pegasus, 1967). For detailed discussions of specific poverty and community programs, see: *A Relevant War Against Poverty* (New York: Metropolitan Applied Research Center, 1968); Ralph M. Kramer, *Participation of the Poor* (Englewood Cliffs, N.J.: Prentice-Hall, 1969); and William W. Ellis, *White Ethics and Black Power* (Chicago: Aldine, 1969).

Metropolitan Government: For a discussion of the pros and cons of metropolitan government and a consideration of the instances where it has either been adopted or an attempt was made to adopt it, see: John C. Bollens, ed., *The States and the Metropolitan Problem* (Chicago: Council of State Governments, 1956); Arthur W. Bromase, "Political Representation in Metropolitan Areas," *American Political Science Review* (June 1958); Robert C. Wood, *Suburbia: Its People and Their Politics* (Boston: Houghton Mifflin, 1959); Daniel J. Elazar, *A Case Study of Failure in Attempted Metropolitan Integration* (Chicago: University of Chicago Press, 1961); Henry J. Schmandt, Paul G. Steinbicker, and George D. Wendel, *Metropolitan Reform in St. Louis: A Case Study* (New York: Holt, Rinehart, and Winston, 1961); Scott Greer, *Governing the Metropolis* (New York: John Wiley and Sons, 1962); David A. Booth, *Metropolitics: The Nashville Consolidation* (East Lansing, Mich.: Institute for Community Development and Services, 1963); and David A. Caputo and Richard L. Cole, "Dimensions of Elite Opposition to Metropolitan Consolidation," *Publius* (Fall 1972).

SECTION IV
Group and Party Politics in America

INTRODUCTION

It is difficult to imagine the United States without its diversity of groups. Consider for a moment the wide variety of groups that any individual might belong to on one occasion or another. The list could include fraternal organizations such as Elks, Moose, or college sororities and fraternities; economic associations such as the chamber of commerce, a labor union, a credit bureau; a political organization, perhaps the local Democratic or Republican party or a special group formed for a specific goal, a bloc group, or a voter registration group; and finally service organizations such as Lions, Rotary, or Red Cross. And this listing barely scratches the surface of groups which exist in the United States. The American people have designed and created groups to meet special needs and to provide services which would not otherwise be available.

Consider the American emphasis on groups from another perspective. The groups listed above are largely "formal" groups; that is, they have membership requirements and formal organizations. One "joins" the group either by applying or being selected. One can also leave the group if he desires. Another type of group which deserves our attention is the so-called "informal" group. Such a group is comprised of people who share general characteristics, but this is not a group specifically constituted in a formal sense. For instance, ethnic, economic, and educational backgrounds are characteristics which often place individuals in informal groups. A thorough understanding of the significance of both informal groups and formal groups active in American society is imperative.

Chapters 9 and 10 discuss the basic aspects of groups in the American system and also encourage reflection on the political implications in the group process. These implications will be analyzed and discussed in the section dealing with the American political party system and its role in the public policy process. Nothing is more essential to understanding American politics than a thorough knowledge of the political parties and their roles.

9. Group Politics

Everyone is aware and probably quite fond of the various ethnic jokes which are common in American life. Whether they be concerned with Polish, Italian, Irish, Greek, black, Jewish, or Scotch ancestry, ethnic jokes have become ingrained in American humor. The important point is not the joke itself but that ethnic groups are the subjects of the usually uncomplimentary and even derogatory remarks included in the joke. The very existence of such "humor" suggests at least two features of American life.

First, ethnic humor reflects the fact that this nation is indeed a mixture of immigrants. The only true natives of the American countryside are the American Indians; the rest of the population migrated to this country for a variety of reasons.[1] Consider for a moment Table 9-1, which summarizes by country of origin the migration of people to the United States. Note the pattern: early migration was from Western and Northern Europe; later migration was from Central, Southern, and Eastern Europe.*

Immigrants to the United States were, in most cases, dissatisfied with conditions in their native lands or were forced out by political and economic considerations. The black man, in most cases, was forced to come to the United States as a source of labor; he did not have an option. Reasons for migrating to the United States varied from group to group, and they were important in terms of each group's ultimate settlement. Migration into the United States was highly diversified both as to the countries of origin and the periods of time at which various groups made the transition. Only the adoption of restrictive immigration laws,

Table 9-1
Migration to the United States: A Historical View

YEAR	LEADING 4 COUNTRIES	NO. OF IMMIGRANTS
1820[a]	Ireland	3,614
	Great Britain	2,410
	Germany	968
	Other Northwestern Europe	452
1850	Ireland	164,004
	Germany	78,896
	Great Britain	51,085
	Other Northwestern Europe	11,470
1880	Germany	84,638
	Great Britain	73,273
	Ireland	71,603
	Scandinavia	65,657
1910	Central Europe	258,737
	Italy	215,537
	U.S.S.R. and Baltic States	186,792
	Great Britain	68,941
1940	Germany	21,520
	Other Northwestern Europe	7,743
	Great Britain	6,158
	Italy	5,302
1970[b]	Mexico	44,469
	Phillipines	31,203
	Italy	24,973
	Greece	16,446

SOURCES:

a. 1810–1940 figures from: U.S. Department of Commerce, Bureau of the Census, *Historical Statistics of the United States: Colonial Times to 1957*, pp. 56–57.

b. 1970 figures from: U.S. Bureau of the Census, *Statistical Abstract of the United States: 1972*, p. 93.

especially in the 1920s and later, stemmed this inflow of people.

While the absolute numbers involved are important, even more important is the fact that these immigrant groups brought their own distinctive cultural, social, and historical traditions, and were slow to change. Thus, many American cities and states have distinctive ethnic characteristics, because they were settled by specific ethnic groups: the Scandinavians in Minnesota and the Dakotas; the blacks in the South; the Scotch-Irish in Western Pennsylvania; and the Irish and Italians in the New England states. Regardless of where they settled, the new immigrants usually remained together in their own communities or sections of a state and nurtured their own cultural ties and heritages. This resulted in the continuation of strong ethnic identification. Another result was ethnic rivalry over jobs or other scarce commodities; quite often this led to conflict among the members of various ethnic groups. Thus, distrust and even hatred developed, and continued ethnic competition and conflict today provide the foundation for many of the ethnic jokes already mentioned.

These two factors—the large number of immigrants and the resulting social unrest—force us to consider a critical and interesting problem: what is the current status of ethnicity in the American system? Are ethnic factors playing a lesser or greater role than they did during earlier periods of our history? Basically, one could take either of two opinions in this matter.

The first is that the American social system is made up of highly divergent groups who over the years have been "Americanized." That is to say, they have given up many of the outward identifying symbols of their heritage. Most noticeable to others is the adoption of English and the elimination of the native language as the chief means of communication. Consider for a moment how many persons you know who speak a language other than English which they learned in their homes. Chances are quite good that the number was a great deal higher several years ago.

Those who argue that ethnic groups have been "Americanized" usually claim that the persons involved have been "assimilated" into American society.[2] This means that they have adopted the values and premises of the American life-style and have discarded many values and attitudes which were associated with their native countries. This also applies to dress, social customs, and political activity. In terms of social customs, it means that marriage to someone from a different ethnic group or background would be readily accepted and understood. Consider for a moment whether there are any ethnic groups who still consider marriage as undesirable if the partner is from a different ethnic group. In addition, political assimilation means that the individual votes and supports candidates who are in line with his political preferences and needs, regardless of their ethnic backgrounds. If assimilation takes place, factors such as ethnic identification are supposedly no longer sufficient to warrant one's support for a candidate for office. The common practice of "balancing" a ticket by including candidates from various ethnic groups on the ballot would not be successful or necessary in an assimilated society. Some would argue that this has happened in the American melting pot, that ethnic ties have been effectively reduced and political loyalty is based on other factors.

This position is readily contrasted with a second, which maintains that while ethnic factors may be less visible than they once were, they are no less real in American society today. Thus, while the traditional symbols of various ethnic groups may be less evident, underlying ethnic identification and loyalty remain an important part of the American life-style. In fact, some observers have argued that as various ethnic groups become more middle-class and successful in American life, their ethnic consciousness in political matters increases.[3]

This argument supposes that many immigrants rarely had the time or the predisposition to be involved with politics, because they were too busy adjusting to their new surroundings and attempting to survive physically. As the ethnic group member became more established economically, two things happened. First, he could "afford" to become interested and concerned about politics. Every minute of his life was no longer consumed with the need to make a living; he was free to devote his energies to other things without fearing total economic collapse. Second, as more and more members of the ethnic group gained some measure of economic security, there was an increase in the number of persons from that ethnic group with the financial resources and time required to seek public political office. Thus, more ethnics seek office at a time when there is more interest in politics among others in the group. The result is that ethnic voting *increases* instead of decreases as a particular group becomes more active in American politics. And thus, political identification of the ethnic increases as that person becomes more economically and socially integrated into society. If this is the case, then American society may not be the cultural melting pot that many have contended it is.*

Several examples might help illustrate this conflict. There is a great deal of evidence, summarized in Table 9-2, to show that nonwhite Americans have made economic gains in the last ten years. Assuming that American nonwhites can be considered an ethnic group and that the melting pot theory holds, it is reasonable to conclude that there would be fewer nonwhite political leaders striving for public office and that fewer ethnic demands would be made on the political system today than in the 1960s. Is this the case? Another interesting example is the increased political activism by segments of the Mexican-American and Puerto Rican populations. Does this increased political activism symbolize limited economic progress?

This point becomes especially important if one is interested in understanding the future roles ethnic groups may play in American politics. Keep in mind that the preceding discussion was concerned solely with ethnic groups; our attention is now turned to

Table 9-2
Income Comparisons of White and Nonwhite Americans

INCOME	1947		1960		1968	
	Non-white %	White %	Non-white %	White %	Non-white %	White %
Under $3,000	60	23	40	16	23	9
$3,000 to $4,999	23	28	23	16	22	11
$5,000 to $6,999	9	23	16	21	17	14
$7,000 to $9,999	5	15	13	23	18	24
$10,000 to $14,999	3	11	6	17	15	26
$15,000 and over			2	7	5	16

SOURCE:

U.S. Department of Commerce, Bureau of the Census, *The Social and Economic Status of Negroes in the United States*, 1969, P-23, no. 29, p. 16.

two other types of groups which may have ethnic aspects, but which are primarily socially and economically oriented. They have also been responsible for a great deal of controversy in American politics.

THE "POWERFUL"

One aspect of group development in the United States which is often overlooked is the power the various groups and their members might have. Most Americans are quick to point out that there are numerous people in the United States who are "big shots," who have "connections," or who are able to "get away" with a lot. In short, these people are recognized as being powerful. What is meant when someone refers to another person as powerful? Specific examples of the "powerful" will be offered and their impact on American politics considered. To begin, a consideration of the term *powerful* is necessary.

As the focal point on power in Chapter 1 indicated, when discussing power, the term *powerful* must also be considered in a variety of ways. What makes a person or group powerful? How is that power used? What benefits are obtained by the use of that power? What are the implications of this power for the rest of society? For our purposes, a person is powerful if he or she has an abundance of a scarce resource and if that individual uses that scarce resource to influence political decision-making. Given this imprecise, but workable definition, what can be said about the powerful in American society?

First, economic resources are usually thought of as scarce in American society. Thus, the individual or group which amasses economic resources meets the first part of our definition. In American society, there have historically been and there continue to be large concentrations of wealth under the control of individuals and corporations. Table 9-3 indicates the distribution of family income in the United States in recent years.

Note that the United States has an interesting economic phenomenon—there is a sizable group of families falling between the very rich and the very poor. Thus, the extremes may be somewhat balanced by the presence of a larger middle-income group What are the implications of this for political interaction?

A related and even more important phenomenon unique to American society is the extensive concentration of industrial and financial assets under the control of large corporations. Table 9-4 lists the largest corporations and their assets in 1968.

Note the corporate emphasis on basic industries, such as automobile and steel. Also, these major corporations often have very diverse economic interests which require complex financial

Table 9-3
Family Income Distribution in the United States

INCOME	% OF TOTAL INCOME		
	1950	1960	1970
Under $3,000	42.4	21.7	8.9
$3,000 to $4,999	34.3	20.3	10.4
$5,000 to $6,999	14.2	23.7	11.8
$7,000 to $9,999	5.8	20.0	19.9
$10,000 to $14,999	3.3	10.6	26.7
$15,000 and over		3.7	22.3

SOURCE:
U.S. Department of Commerce, Bureau of the Census, *Consumer Income*, P–60, no. 80 (October 4, 1971), p. 22.

institutions. These institutions have become so highly developed that the independent entrepreneur usually finds it impossible to compete with them.

As the two tables indicate, some individuals and groups (the corporations) do have great economic resources. For instance, if the entire wealth of the United States were conceived of as a pie, the sizes of the slices would vary considerably; all Americans would not have the same size slice. Based on the figures in Table 9-3, what would be a fair estimate of the size of the "piece of pie" for those people earning over $15,000 and under $10,000? Based on this inequality of economic resources, is it also possible to say that those with economic resources are also the "powerful?" Certainly one could argue that they are economically powerful, but judgment on this may be deferred, pending consideration of two other types of scarce resources usually attributed to the powerful.

Table 9-4
Corporate Assets in the United States: 1968

COMPANY	ASSETS × $1,000
Standard Oil (New Jersey)	15,197,439
General Motors	13,273,083
Ford	7,966,800
Texaco	7,162,830
Gulf Oil	6,457,954
Mobil Oil	6,223,861
U.S. Steel	5,606,311
IBM	5,598,670
General Telephone and Electronics	5,430,576
General Electric	5,347,189
Standard Oil (California)	5,309,748

SOURCE:
The Fortune Directory (1968), p. 2.

The first of these is social resources. This means, in popular terms, that a person is born on the "right side of the tracks" and that family and personal connections provide an individual with a unique set of resources. Social resources of this type are usually associated with royalty or aristocracy in nations other than the United States. Since there never was a royal family or formal aristocracy here, can one maintain that social resources do not play an important role in the relations among individuals and groups in American society? Are there not people who are considered "above" or "below" others on a social scale? There are excellent examples of this on the national level, also: do you really think the Rockefellers or the Kennedys are on a social level with the vast numbers of people who vote for them in elections? Probably not!

The point is not that certain people are superior and others inferior because of their social resources but that there is social differentiation in American society, usually at a variety of levels. Now the interesting question is whether the social resources which some have more of than others permit the "haves" to be "powerful."

A third type of scarce resources is political strength. Do all Americans have the same political resources? On the one hand you could argue that since most Americans are eligible to vote, they all have the same basic resource and that the differences which might arise are based on how that resource is used. At the same time, since Mayor Daley of Chicago has one vote in an election and John Doe has one vote, do both have the same political resources?

Most people would probably concede that there is an unequal distribution of political resources, just as there are unequal distributions of social and economic resources. The crucial aspect, however, is how available and open these resources are to others who may wish to gain them. For instance, can an individual acquire any of these scarce resources through his willingness to make sacrifices for them or work for them?

One of the most widely accepted beliefs about American society is that it is an "open" society; that is to say, the individual has the opportunity to gain those scarce resources which he lacks through the widely accepted practices of hard work, self-sacrifice, and dedication. Stories of personal success and achievement are widely distributed and heralded. We are all familiar with Horatio Alger–like success stories, in which an individual overcomes tremendous burdens to achieve major success in American society. But is present American society really open to this type of activity?

First, can a case be made that the economic system is open? Keep in mind the corporate assets listed in Table 9-4. Would not this concentration of economic power make it difficult for a budding entrepreneur to compete? Or, to put it another way, could an individual hope to compete with Ford or General Motors if he had a revolutionary new idea on the manufacturing of internal combustion engines? What would probably, and does, happen is that the new ideas and innovations which in the past resulted in individually owned businesses today would be sold and developed through the corporate structure of the United States. Is this necessarily "bad"? Does it alter the "openness" of the economic system in any substantial way?

Second, can one argue that the American social system is open? There are still widespread taboos on whom one mingles with and great emphasis on his list of social credentials. A brief review of the social pages of a major metropolitan or small-town newspaper quickly illustrates this point. It is apparent that not everyone is given the same amount of attention or publicity when an important social event takes place in their lives. In addition, there are status hierarchies in most communities which clearly differentiate which individuals and families have more social rank than others.[4]

Finally, is the political system open to those who want to increase their political resources? Disagreement exists on this question also. Perhaps the best way to shed light on the subject is to discuss the argument on two levels, one involving local politics and the other involving national politics.

On the local level, there is a great deal of disagreement about the "openness" of the system to those who want increased political power. One position is best represented by the work of Floyd Hunter, who conducted research in Atlanta in the late 1940s and early 1950s.[5] Hunter's argument was that economic resources and those who controlled them determined the social and political resource distributions. Thus, if one wishes to be truly powerful, he must control as many economic resources as possible. Based on them, he can develop and influence social and political events. For Hunter, economic power was essential; it was also concentrated in the hands of a very small number of individuals who used it for their own self-interest. This economic power permitted the covert manipulation of public policy by those the economically powerful selected to govern. For instance, the corporate leaders of Atlanta, according to Hunter, influenced political developments in the city by controlling the elected officials and manipulating policy issues that were being decided. It was not necessary for the economically powerful actually to hold public political office; in fact, their preference was to stay out of the public limelight, to determine policy themselves and then to have the public officials and politicians implement it for them. The emphasis was on covert interaction, the economically powerful quietly deciding policy and then having others gain public acceptance for it.

In Hunter's case study of Atlanta, the ordinary citizen had little access to political resources, since these were controlled by the economically powerful. In essence, social and political resources were controlled by those who had economic control. This is a basic point and one requiring careful attention. How does one gain political power? According to Hunter, political power is secondary to economic power and is unobtainable until economic power is fully realized. The implications of this position are important. Political leaders either lack real power, or they are influenced and controlled by those with economic power. In short, political power is secondary to economic power. A logical conclusion to be drawn from this argument is that if one wants to bring about change in American society, he must do so by altering the economic structure. This position and its logical conclusion can be contrasted with the following.

Hunter's research and findings sparked considerable controversy and debate; the result was research by others who attempted to refute him. Robert Dahl's *Who Governs?*, a study of New Haven, Connecticut, is an inquiry into decision-making in three issue areas (education, redevelopment, and political nominations) of that New England city.[6] Dahl found that decisions were largely made by public officials and politicians operating under a variety of constraints. Furthermore, Dahl found that during various historical periods, different groups (involving both ethnic and social class) exercised and controlled political power in the community.

According to Dahl, economic elites did not dominate New Haven's politics, and more importantly, the general public had a resource which no politician could afford to neglect for too long a period—the vote. Dahl maintained that the private citizen did not have much direct influence in political decision-making, but he did have considerable indirect control through his right to vote. This provided him with a means to influence public policy and control public office holders. Dahl's position was that the ordinary citizen had other resources at his disposal which offset the economic resources open to a few. For Dahl, economic power was not to be ignored, but it was neither the sole nor dominant prerequisite for political power. Dahl discussed other resources, such as time and numbers, and their roles in creating political influence and power. He concluded that New Haven was not dominated by an economic elite and argued that few American cities had characteristics which permitted domination by an economic elite. Needless to say, the differences between Dahl's and Hunter's positions and findings sparked a great deal of controversy and debate, which ultimately resulted in a third major position.

In this position, several observers have argued that while it may be very difficult for a local economic elite to control all decisions, they may be able to control what gets brought up for discussion.[7] Thus, while the elite may not be able to or may not want to control everyone who gains or seeks political office, they may be able to see that certain issues are never raised. In essence, the elite have the power to "set the agenda" and insure that only topics safe for them will be discussed. Thus, issues which could undermine their dominance are never brought up or discussed in the public sector. Are there any issues which the economically powerful might want to avoid at the local level?

Similar arguments and findings have been offered to explain national politics in the United States. C. Wright Mills has maintained that American society is dominated by a "power elite" which determines policy in terms of what is best for its members rather than what is best for the country. If the two are synonymous, then all is well; if not, the country must suffer while the power elite benefits. Others argue that the country is so diverse and complex that no one group can dominate its politics.

The question which needs to be asked is: how open is the political system at the national level? Obviously, this type of question usually draws a prompt response, which varies according to the respondent's value preferences. What is important here is the relative "openness" of the system to new ideas and personalities. In addition, the way issues are raised and resolved is of great importance. One useful and interesting way of considering the "openness" of the American political system is to consider a unique American institution—the political party. A thorough understanding of party politics in the United States provides a clearer perspective on the responsiveness of the system. The next chapter considers the American party system and its important role of introducing new ideas and personalities into American politics.

SUGGESTED READINGS

Ethnic Groups in America: For a variety of perspectives on the customs and experiences of ethnic groups in the United States, see: Oscar Handlin, *The Uprooted* (New York: Grosset and Dunlap, 1951); W. L. Warner and L. Srole, *The Social Systems of American Ethnic*

Groups (New Haven: Yale University Press, 1945); J. A. Hossetler, *Amish Society* (Baltimore: Johns Hopkins University Press, 1963); Herbert Gans, *The Urban Villagers* (New York: The Free Press, 1962); Robert T. Bower, *Voting Behavior of American Ethnic Groups* (New York: Bureau of Applied Social Research, 1944); W. I. Thomas and F. Zananiecki, *The Polish Peasant in Europe and America* (Boston: Badger, 1918–1920); Peter Munch, "Social Adjustments Among Wisconsin Norwegians," *American Sociological Review* 14 (December 1949); William Foote Whyte, *Street Corner Society* (Chicago: University of Chicago Press, 1943); Alphonso Pinkney, *Black Americans* (Englewood Cliffs, N.J.: Prentice-Hall, 1969); and Edgar Litt, *Ethnic Politics in America* (Glencoe, Ill.: Scott, Foresman, 1970).

America as a Melting Pot: For a variety of views on this position, see: Gunnar Myrdal, *An American Dilemma: The Negro Problem and Modern Democracy* (New York: Harper and Row, 1944); Nathan Glazer and Daniel Moynihan, *Beyond the Melting Pot* (Cambridge: Massachusetts Institute of Technology Press, 1963); Oscar Handlin, *Immigration as a Factor in American History* (Englewood Cliffs, N.J.: Prentice-Hall, 1959); Erich Rosenthal, "Acculturation Without Assimilation?," *American Journal of Sociology* (November 1960); Amitai Etzioni, "The Ghetto—A Reevaluation," *Social Forces* (March 1959); and Seymour Martin Lipset, *The First New Nation* (New York: Basic Books, 1963).

NOTES

1. For a consideration of these reasons, see: Oscar Handlin, *The Uprooted* (New York: Grosset and Dunlap, 1951).

2. One of the most intriguing attempts to carefully consider the questions of assimilation and ethnic identification can be found in: Nathan Glazer and Daniel Moynihan, *Beyond the Melting Pot* (Cambridge: Massachusetts Institute of Technology Press, 1963).

3. Raymond E. Wolfinger, "The Development and Persistence of Ethnic Voting," *American Political Science Review* (December 1965).

4. C. Wright Mills, "The Metropolitan 400," *The Power Elite* (New York: Oxford University Press, 1959), pp. 47–70.

5. Floyd Hunter, *Community Power Structure* (Garden City, N.Y.: Doubleday, 1953).

6. Robert A. Dahl, *Who Governs?* (New Haven: Yale University Press, 1961).

7. Peter Bachrach and Morton S. Baratz, "Two Faces of Power," *American Political Science Review* (1962); and "Decisions and Nondecisions: An Analytical Framework," *American Political Science Review* (1963).

10. Political Parties and the 1972 Elections

POLITICAL PARTIES

One of the best examples of group politics in American society is the American political party. Unique in many ways to the American political system, the political party has had a long and varied history in the United States. For our purposes, the definition of a political party will be: an organization which nominates and supports candidates for public office. This definition makes no distinction about the governmental level of the office; thus, local, state, and national offices are included. This should make it clear that any discussion of a political party or party system in the United States must be carefully and cautiously undertaken, because there are a variety of political party organizations at various levels of government in the United States.

As mentioned, the American experience with political parties has been a lengthy one.* In 1796, George Washington warned the nation about the pitfalls of partisan party allegiance when he said:

> *I have already intimated to you the danger of parties in the State, with particular reference to the founding of them on geographical discriminations. Let me . . . warn you in the most solemn manner against the baneful effects of the spirit of party generally . . . It serves always to distract the public councils and enfeeble the public administration. It agitates the community with ill-founded jealousies and false alarms;*

> kindles the animosity of one part against another; foments occasionally riot and insurrection.[1]

Despite this warning, political parties were already forming and by the late 1830s were firmly established in the American political system. Initially, impetus for party organization centered on the question of the relative strength of the federal and state governments. Thus, the Federalist and Anti-Federalist political organizations were founded. From there, it became common practice to include other issues and personalities, with the final result being the establishment of the contemporary two-party system.

Although this question will be considered again later, it also deserves our attention now. Why, given the cultural, economic, and political diversity that has characterized the United States, have there been just two major political parties in existence for most of its history?

Probably the single most important reason is the electoral law used in the United States. All major offices in the United States are based on a winner-take-all system, with a simple plurality needed to win. What this does is make it very difficult for a candidate not from one of the major parties to win. There are exceptions, but not at the national level. For instance, in 1968 there was little chance that Governor George C. Wallace of Alabama, running on the American Independent Party ticket, could be elected president. There was, however, an excellent opportunity that his candidacy might keep either of the other candidates (Humphrey, D. and Nixon, R.) from the necessary majority of votes needed in the electoral college to gain the presidency. As Table 5-1 (page 90) indicated, the electoral college system magnifies margins of victory and penalizes the candidate who has run a strong second or third place finish. No other major office is determined by the electoral college system; they are all based on the need for a simple plurality of votes to win.

In addition to the electoral mechanics, which make it difficult for other than a major party candidate to gain victory, the group basis of American politics and other institutional forces results in the strong personal identification most Americans have with either the Republican or Democratic party. The reasons for this identification will be explored later, but the important point is that the American two-party system has survived for quite some time and shows few signs of not continuing into the future. This has important implications if you are interested in using the political party as a means of accelerating change; this aspect will be considered when the future of American politics is discussed in the closing chapter.

Perhaps the best way to consider what a political party actually does would be to view a national party as a loosely knit confederation of state and local parties, each of these units having its own organization and autonomy, plus control over its activities. This describes the decentralized nature of American party politics. For instance, if each unit of the Democratic or Republican parties were expected to hold the same views or adopt the same policies, how could the Democrats of Mississippi and California or the Republicans of Arizona and New York reach agreement and work together? Obviously they couldn't in many cases, but fortunately in most cases they don't have to. The result is often disorganization, but with an underlying concensus on party principles and goals. Because of the lack of ideological consistency at all levels, American political parties are able to perform a variety of tasks. Three important roles will be discussed and several other functions described.

First, any political system requires some method of expressing public preferences. This is usually referred to by the social scientist as "interest articulation"; what it means is that some institution or person is capable of raising issues which are important to the citizenry or which need to be resolved by that political system.[2] In the American system, political party members usually perform this task. For instance, the furor over school bussing for racial integration was begun when political party leaders and publicly elected officials, with various party identifications, began to question the utility and constitutionality of such measures. Thus, the political party becomes a mechanism for introducing such issues into the political forum to be discussed and, it is hoped, resolved.

Related to this interest articulation role is the role of organization in the political process. Consider a local decision-making body, such as a city council. Normally, political party affiliations will be a key factor in who supports which measures and why. The same is true of state legislatures and the national Congress. Party affiliation is especially important in organizing debate and subsequent action on any major issue.[3] Usually, party affiliation is an excellent predictor of a person's behavior on many issues. Political parties provide the basic nucleus for organizational development and are a shorthand way for the general public to determine a political leader's position on a particular issue. Yet the lack of rigid ideology in both major American political parties often makes it difficult for the public to determine a person's position based solely on his party affiliation. For instance, the position of a Democratic legislator from Rhode Island on school integration is likely to differ from that of his Democratic colleague from Louisiana. In similar fashion, a Republican senator from New York will probably hold positions on many issues which are different from those of his Republican counterpart from Arizona.

Finally, political parties perform a very necessary but often overlooked role. Usually, political parties and those who belong to them act as conflict resolvers in the American system. That is to say, they bring about compromise and discussion on an issue, which often diffuses its potential disruptive tendencies. Studies have indicated that political party leaders in the United States hold more moderate and less extreme views on most issues than most Americans.[4] The implication is that political party leaders are often willing to compromise or moderate their views on many issues. Thus, many potentially disruptive issues are resolved because of the moderating effects of the two-party system. If one wished an issue to remain divisive, his view of the conflict resolution role of the political party would be negative.

In addition to these three important roles, the political party performs several other functions. Probably the most important of these is the opportunity for political participation a political party provides the citizen. Although only three to five percent of the American voting population is active in political parties, most party organizations encourage and actively seek participation by individual citizens. What this does is socialize the participant with the norms and values of the American party system.[5] It permits the evolution of new leaders who have been part of this socialization process and who have accepted the "rules of the game." In short, party participation stresses fundamental values, which are then carried by the individual into the political arena as he or she undertakes a more active role.

Finally, the party performs a very distinct social function. By giving the citizen access to public officeholders, the political party stresses the fulfillment of needs for those who participate. The party also provides an outlet for those who want to get into politics, but who do not seek office for themselves.

One could continue listing the various contributions political parties make to the American system, but there is a need to consider another aspect here: are these contributions worthwhile, and what do they add to the American system? For instance, is it advantageous to have the political party serve as the main interest articulator for the American political system? Also, have the parties adequately served over the years as conflict resolvers? These types of questions lead to the basic criticism that the American two-party system is too status-quo oriented and not capable of permitting basic change to occur. The result is the charge that the political parties are unrepresentative of many American voters. This, according to the argument, leads to frustration, apathy, and finally alienation on the part of the American public.[6] Thus, the low percentage of Americans who actively participate in politics is not due to lack of interest, rather to the realization that the present two-party system offers little alternative and that no major change will result as long as both parties attempt to moderate and gain control of the center.

In order to consider this point about each party moving towards the center, the nature of the American electorate needs to be explored and recent developments within each party evaluated. Table 10-1 summarizes survey results in recent years of the American electorate's party preferences.

Table 10-1
Party Preferences of the American Electorate

QUESTION: IN POLITICS TODAY, DO YOU CONSIDER YOURSELF A REPUBLICAN, DEMOCRAT, OR INDEPENDENT?

Date	Republican %	Democrat %	Independent %
August 1971[a]	25	44	31
August 1970[b]	29	44	27
July 1969[c]	28	42	30
July 1968[d]	27	46	27
September 1967[e]	27	42	31
June 1966[f]	26	48	26
August 1965[g]	27	50	23

SOURCES:
a. *Gallup Opinion Index* (October 1971), p. 22.
b. *Ibid.* (August 1970), p. 3.
c. *Ibid.* (August 1969), p. 8.
d. *Ibid.* (August 1968), p. 2.
e. *Ibid.* (October 1967), p. 6.
f. *Ibid.* (August 1966), p. 7.
g. *Ibid.* (August 1965), p. 9.

Note the advantages the Democrats have experienced; nearly half of the electorate has identified in recent years with that party, while the Republicans have had significantly fewer identifiers. The result is that the Democrats have an advantage in any presidential election, since they start with a larger number of party identifiers than do the Republicans. Another conclusion can be drawn from Table 10-1. If many Americans are dissatisfied with the two major parties, would it not be reasonable to expect an increase in Independents?

Scholars are agreed on one point—party identification is an important stabilizing factor in American elections.* Research has indicated that party allegiance or identification is the best predictor of an individual voter's behavior.[7] That is to say, the candidate's positions on key issues are less important than if he belongs to the political party with which the voter identifies. The significance of this should not be underestimated. Rather than finding fault with the party system as supporting the status quo, one might concern himself with changing the party identification of the electorate. In other words, rather than attempting to change the parties, why not influence the voters to put aside party identifications and vote for the candidates who support their desired policy positions on specific issues?

Research indicates that party identification is often set early in the lives of Americans and that it is apt to be affected only by major social and political change.[8] One such change was the Great Depression of the 1930s, to which many observers attribute the present prevailing tendency to identify with the Democratic party. If party identification is subject to shifts when major social, economic, and political controversy confronts the nation, are there any such events which could affect the party identification and subsequent political behavior of the current generation? Many maintain that the general distrust and alienation brought about by the Vietnam War will result in major shifts in party identification.

Other issues, such as environmental concerns; underemployment and continued inflation; increasing possibilities of conflict among races, classes, age groups; and the entire nature of a large-scale technocratic, bureaucratically controlled urban society, may also contribute to realignment or even disruption of the party system.

Finally, perhaps the best way to illustrate the ways a political party may bring about internal change is to discuss briefly the reforms undertaken by the Democratic party in 1972. Few Americans will forget the violence and disarray which characterized the 1968 Democratic National Convention. The Chicago police and demonstrators clashed outside, while inside the delegates to the convention were engaged in bitter fighting for party control and the presidential nomination. Many still assert the Democrats lost that presidential race in Chicago rather than to Richard M. Nixon during the subsequent campaign.

The turbulence in Chicago prompted party leaders to consider full and complete reform of the party. A study group was formed, known first for its original chairman, George McGovern, and then for Donald Fraser, his replacement. The McGovern-Fraser Commission, after several years of discussion and consideration, drew up a set of recommendations which the party's national committee approved.[9] Included in these reforms were provisions which stipulated how delegates to the party convention were to be chosen and the composition of the various convention committees. Results were slow to materialize, but the 1972 Democratic Convention indicated just how far the party had reformed itself. Long-time politicians were a minority at the convention; larger numbers of young, black, and female delegates were common. In addition, the convention was to most observers an "open" convention, in that views ranging from those of Governor Wallace to those of pro-abortionists were offered and considered. The result was a sense of relief on the part of the Democrats who had developed the reforms to bring about change. The interesting question is whether the party reforms will result in an open and responsive party or whether they will permit the replacement of one small and usually unrepresentative group which dominates the party with another. Only time will tell. This example is significant in that it illustrates an attempt by a major political party to reform itself. With this point in mind, let us turn our attention to the 1972 presidential race and the strategies pursued by each candidate and political party.

THE 1972 ELECTIONS

The 1972 elections were among the more interesting yet confusing of recent American elections.* The presidential election will receive most of our attention, but the other contests cannot be ignored and their results will be discussed. As has been pointed out, there are a variety of steps in a successful election campaign; probably the most important is receiving the nomination of a party. A few comments on that are in order.

Richard Nixon, as the incumbent president, faced minor dissension within the ranks of the Republican Party. Conservative elements in the party, while publicly annoyed at his trips to China and the Soviet Union, did little to influence his political actions. Congressman John Ashbrook of Ohio challenged the president in several primaries but failed to receive significant popular support. Liberal elements in the party, led by Congressman Robert McCloskey of California, challenged the president on both his policy in Vietnam and domestic issues. The result was that McCloskey decided to enter several of the early primaries in the hope of generating substantial anti-Nixon sentiments within the Republican Party. Keep in mind that Ashbrook's and McCloskey's strategies were similar to the strategy followed by Senator Eugene McCarthy when he entered and ran well against the then incumbent president, Lyndon Johnson, in the New Hampshire primary in 1968. In McCloskey's case, the strategy failed, and President Nixon emerged from the primaries unscathed.

The lack of conflict in the Republican primaries is readily contrasted with the considerable clamor and debate on the parts of the pursuers of the Democratic nomination. To begin with, Senator Edmund Muskie had emerged from the 1968 campaign, in which he was the vice-presidential candidate, as a leading presidential contender in 1972. Many observers felt the nomination was his. Hubert Humphrey, reelected to the Senate in 1970 from Minnesota after his narrow defeat by Richard Nixon in 1968, was still a power to be reckoned with, but many argued that his apparently vacillating position on the Vietnam War would make him less attractive. Then there were others: Senator George McGovern of South Dakota announced he would seek the nomination, as did Senator Henry Jackson of Washington. Congresswoman Shirley Chisholm announced she would seek the nomination, as did Los Angeles Mayor Sam Yorty. In short, the Democratic presidential nominating contest was seen as wide-open and obtainable by any one of several people. Some of the candidates hoped they would receive enough support to be in a bargaining position at the convention. What happened from the New Hampshire primary in February 1972 through election day is an interesting chapter in American history and will be the subject of a great many writers.

The Primaries

Presidential primaries are important, but vary so greatly from state to state that little overall order is possible. Basically, a presidential primary is a statewide election in which the voters of that state vote for the various candidates and/or for delegates to the nominating convention who are pledged to particular candidates. In some states, any voter can vote for any candidate despite party allegiance; thus, registered Republicans can vote for Democratic candidates if they wish, and vice versa. The result of these various possibilities and situations may be that a candidate who has a small, but dedicated group of supporters is successful in primaries in various states. But can the winners of the Florida or Wisconsin presidential primaries claim their victories to mean similar support on the national level? Table 10-2 summarizes the dates of selected primaries and how the major candidates did in them.

Given the complexities and uniqueness of each of the various primary states, the Democratic candidates followed varying practices. Senator Muskie vowed he would run campaigns in all of the primaries; Senator McGovern announced he would be selective, and Senator Humphrey did likewise. As Table 10-2 indicates, the results were interesting. Muskie was forced to stretch his limited resources of time and money to the breaking point and fared poorly in the primaries. This vice-presidential candidate of 1968, who seemed to embody personal strength, integrity, and leadership, was viewed in 1972 as a weak, contradictory, and emotional candidate by many voters. Muskie's primary performance caused many of his backers to reconsider their support, and he was never able to get his campaign off the ground. Hubert Humphrey stressed the traditional values of the Democratic Party and in most instances ran well enough to establish his credibility as a contender. Other candidates usually gathered from four to ten percent of the vote, with the exception of two other contenders.

Alabama Governor George Wallace, who had sought election as a third-party candidate in 1968, entered presidential primaries in a number of states in order to influence or even receive the Democratic nomination. He ran well and was a force to be contended with at the convention. The election may have been different if George Wallace had not been paralyzed by an attacker, Arthur Bremmer. Wallace made an effort to continue the campaign, but his paralysis forced him to abandon his efforts to either influence the Democratic nomination or run again as a third-party candidate. His

Table 10-2
Selected 1972 Democratic Presidential Primary Outcomes

DATE/STATE	HUMPHREY	MCGOVERN	MUSKIE	WALLACE	OTHERS
			% of total vote		
March 7, New Hampshire	NE[a]	37.2	46.4	NE	16.4
March 14, Florida	18.6	6.2	8.9	41.6	24.7
April 4, Wisconsin	20.7	29.6	10.3	22.1	17.3
April 25, Pennsylvania	35.1	20.4	20.4	21.2	2.9
May 2, Indiana	46.8	NE	11.6	41.6	NE
May 4, Tennessee	15.9	7.2	2.0	68.0	6.9
May 16, Michigan	15.7	26.8	2.4	51.0	4.1
May 23, Oregon	12.5	50.3	2.5	20.1	14.6
June 6, California	39.2	44.3	2.1	6.0	8.4

SOURCE:
Congressional Quarterly Weekly Report (July 8, 1972), p. 1655.

a. NE = not entered.

withdrawal left conservative Democrats with only Senator Jackson and Mayor Yorty to support; the result was that many conservative Democrats came to feel isolated from their party and its leaders.

The other contender who fared well was Senator George McGovern. The Florida and Wisconsin primaries were of special importance to him, and he steadily increased his lead in other primaries. His persistent fight led to the showdown primary in California, where, because of the state's diversity and electoral strength, the winner stood an excellent chance to capture the presidential nomination. When McGovern captured the California primary, there was little doubt left that he would receive the nomination.

Throughout the preconvention and the convention period, Senator Ted Kennedy's name constantly appeared as a possible presidential candidate. Kennedy denied being interested in the nomination and made it clear he would not accept a draft. Despite this disclaimer, many Democrats felt he was their logical candidate and tried to persuade him to run. Kennedy remained aloof from the convention; some felt his actions were calculated to gain publicity and prepare the way for his nomination in 1976. Only time will reveal if that was the case.

Conventions

The two presidential conventions were interesting contrasts in style and substance. The Republicans, due to the dominance of President Nixon and his decision to renominate Spiro Agnew as his vice-presidential candidate, had a short and restrained convention dedicated to launching a successful and positive campaign to reelect the president. Speeches were punctual, rules were obeyed, and general decorum prevailed. Whenever conflict threatened to break out openly, immediate attempts were made to reconcile the differences in private. This provided a very definite contrast to the

Democratic Convention, which had been held earlier and which had produced interesting compromises and substantial conflict.

In the first place, Senator McGovern was seen by his supporters as a true reformer; his opponents saw him as a person who wanted reform only to advance his own candidacy. Thus, the 1972 Democratic Convention spent considerable time and energy deciding whether the "unit rule" and other practices of the past were to be changed for the 1972 or 1976 conventions.[10] Senator McGovern, with the fight over the California delegation being most critical, won the important early votes in the convention and went on to an easy and convincing first-ballot nomination. Although the Democrats had chosen a presidential nominee, the convention did much more.

The reforms advocated by the McGovern-Fraser Commission were adopted. This set the stage for continued reform in the party and the possibility of future conflict, due to the diversity of groups in the Democratic Party. In addition, the McGovern forces left the convention with a splintered party: Mayor Daley of Chicago, although he was later to support the Democratic ticket, lost a key vote to the McGovern forces and threatened reprisals; the forces of Hubert Humphrey, Henry Jackson, and Edmund Muskie felt they were ridden over roughshod and publicly voiced their dislike of McGovern's tactics; finally, the Wallace supporters, although many felt he was treated with dignity and respect when he addressed the convention, could not accept several of the key passages of the Democratic platform which dealt with the Vietnam War and domestic welfare policies. In these respects, the McGovern victory left the party in disarray and disunited. Traditionally, the presidential nominee attempts to unite the party by his selection of a running mate, and Senator McGovern made the same attempt.

McGovern's dilemma was obvious; he needed a vice-presidential running mate who would unite the party and enhance the ticket on the national level. After considerable efforts to draft people and after apparent refusals by Senators Muskie and Ribicoff, Senator Thomas Eagleton was selected. Eagleton was from an important electoral state, Missouri, and had the benefit of being an "unknown" and hence not liable to alienate party regulars. In subsequent weeks, there was little doubt that Eagleton's selection was one of the most, if not the most, controversial decisions reached by McGovern and his staff.

The important point is that the Democrats left their convention divided and angry with one another. In addition, they had once again created an image, due to the extensive media coverage and their own lack of planning, of being disorganized and poor planners. The Republicans provided a contrasting picture, and thus the stage was set for the campaign.

Campaign Strategies

George McGovern, with the strains of the national convention barely behind him, was forced to deal with an issue on which, no matter what his decision, he was bound to lose some support. This happened after several enterprising journalists secured information pertaining to vice-presidential nominee Thomas Eagleton's medical history. The records indicated he had undergone electric shock treatment on several occasions for fatigue and depression. McGovern and his staff maintained that this information was not known to them at the time of the selection and that Eagleton should have provided more information concerning it.

The result, after a series of statements supporting Eagleton, was that McGovern asked him to withdraw. Eagleton apparently did not want to but responded favorably to McGovern's request. McGovern and the Democratic National Committee then had to select another nominee. After considerable searching, Sargent Shriver was nominated. To many of the anti-Kennedy forces in the Democratic Party, this was tantamount to a sellout to the Kennedys by McGovern. To some members of the party, the decision not to continue with Eagleton was unpardonable, and they pledged not to work for the new ticket as a result of the decision. The end result was that McGovern had to deal with more interparty strife just at the time his own campaign was being developed. This did little to help him.

A quick review of Table 10-1 (page 186) shows the advantage McGovern had in party identification. His strategy was to build a liberal coalition of intellectuals, blacks, Spanish minorities, and members of the working class who were expected to be dissatisfied with the Nixon stand on the Vietnam War and domestic issues. As key campaign issues, McGovern stressed the Nixon policy in Vietnam and the special emphasis given to large economic interests at home. In addition, McGovern attempted to show that the Nixon administration was corrupt. The "bugging" of the Democratic headquarters was used as a justification for this position.

President Nixon countered this strategy with an interesting and unusual one of his own. During the early days of the campaign, cabinet officials and others answered the charges made by the McGovern-Shriver team; in the later stages, President Nixon himself campaigned in a number of crucial states where the contest was felt to be close. In addition, Nixon and his main campaign organization, the Committee to Reelect the President, decided to concentrate on his reelection alone; little attempt was made to help other Republican office seekers. Thus, the president dismissed the idea of trying to increase the length of his "coattails." One other strategy was used by the president, and it provided returns. An organization entitled Democrats for Nixon was set up and headed by former Texas Governor John Connolly. Its main purpose was to encourage dissident Democrats to support President Nixon; the rationale was that many Democrats could be wooed from their party if proper encouragement were given them. The advertising campaign of this group was aimed at the working class voter who traditionally voted

Democratic but might be opposed to McGovern on the basis of his position on Vietnam and certain domestic issues.

Despite the differing audiences, both candidates stressed a media-oriented campaign. Both used spot and regular television advertisements. In states such as Wisconsin, Illinois, California, Ohio, and New York, where the race was expected to be close, both sides concentrated a large amount of their financial resources. In short, the McGovern strategy was to remobilize the Democratic coalition, while the Nixon strategy was to keep the traditional Republican vote and gain support from traditionally independent and Democratic voters. Both candidates, through their organizations as well as their personal appearances, tried to gain the youth vote. Republicans and Democrats realized the importance and potential of the new voters and attempted to gain their support.

THE OUTCOME

There is no doubt that the 1972 election was the most lopsided victory for a Republican presidential candidate in American history. President Nixon received over 61 percent of the popular vote; McGovern's 38 percent was the lowest ever received by a Democratic presidential candidate. Table 10-3 compares the results of this election in California, Illinois, Michigan, Missouri, New York, Ohio, Pennsylvania, Texas, and nationally with the presidential elections of 1960, 1964, and 1968. Note the wide differences.

Despite this massive victory for Nixon and Agnew, the Democrats did not fare poorly at other levels. They gained two seats in the Senate, lost twelve seats in the House, and gained one gubernatorial office.

These results lead to several interesting conclusions and pose a number of perplexing questions, among them: Why didn't the Republican landslide at the presidential level filter down to other

Table 10-3
Comparisons of Recent Presidential Elections

STATE	1960[a,e]		1964[b,e]		1968[c,e]			1972[d,f]	
	D%	R%	D%	R%	D%	R%	AIP%[g]	D%	R%
California	49.6	50.1	59.1	40.8	44.7	47.8	6.7	43.0	57.0
Illinois	50.0	49.8	59.5	40.5	44.2	47.1	8.5	41.0	59.0
Michigan	50.9	48.8	66.7	33.1	48.2	41.5	10.0	44.0	56.0
Missouri	50.3	49.7	64.0	36.0	43.7	44.9	11.4	38.0	62.0
New York	52.5	47.3	68.6	31.3	49.7	44.3	5.3	41.0	59.0
Ohio	46.7	53.3	62.9	37.1	42.9	45.2	11.8	31.0	69.0
Pennsylvania	51.1	48.7	64.9	34.7	47.6	44.0	8.0	40.0	60.0
Texas	50.5	48.5	63.3	36.5	41.1	39.9	19.0	34.0	66.0
NATIONAL	49.7	49.5	61.1	38.5	42.7	43.4	13.5	38.0	62.0

SOURCES:

a. *America Votes 4* (Pittsburgh: University of Pittsburgh Press, 1962), p. 1.
b. *America Votes 6* (Washington, D.C.: Governmental Affairs Institute, 1966), p. 1.
c. *America Votes 8* (Washington, D.C.: Governmental Affairs Institute, 1970), p. 1.
d. News Election Service figures as reported by the Associated Press.
e. Figures are percentages of the total vote.
f. Figures represent percentages of the major party vote.
g. AIP = American Independent Party, Wallace's party in the 1968 election.

offices? One explanation is that the presidential voting was either a pro-Nixon or an anti-McGovern phenomenon. Another is that the president and his campaign strategists either failed to realize the importance of actively campaigning for other candidates or felt the president's campaigning would not significantly alter the outcome in these races. A third and probably the most logical explanation is that the American public decided its votes for various political offices for different reasons. Thus, one could vote for Nixon for president while still casting a vote for Democratic candidates at other levels. In short, the decentralized aspect of American politics seems to have dominated, and local issues and personalities had a marked effect on national voting patterns. In any case, the 1972 results are cause for thought.

Secondly, what effect will 1972 have on American politics? If one accepts the "ebb-and-flow" theory of American politics, does it signal the beginning of a Republican dominance of the presidency, or can it be explained by the personal magnetism of Richard Nixon?[11] Is the Republican Party becoming the majority party despite what the party identification results indicate? Will the conflict and anger generated in 1972 force the Democrats to reunite in the future, or will it cause the party to splinter further? Is it possible for the Democrats to rebuild their coalition and find a candidate who can unite the party?

Finally, what does the fact that only 55 percent of those eligible actually voted in 1972 mean for the future? Is this low turnout a result of disinterest in this particular election or of a general disinterest in candidates or elections? If it is general disinterest, what are the implications for the future?

SUGGESTED READINGS

Political Parties and the American Experience: If you are interested in the history of political parties, see: Charles A. Beard, *The American Party Battle* (New York: Macmillan, 1928); E. E. Schattschnider,

Party Government (New York: Farrar and Rinehart, 1942); Wilfred E. Binkley, *American Political Parties* (New York: Alfred A. Knopf, 1943); Charles E. Merriam and Harold F. Gosnell, *The American Party System* (New York: Macmillan, 1949); William Goodman, *The Two-Party System in the United States* (Princeton: Van Nostrand, 1962); Charles O. Jones, *The Republican Party in American Politics* (New York: Macmillan, 1963); and Hugh A. Bone, *American Politics and the Party System* (New York: McGraw-Hill, 1969). For an emphasis on the behavioral implications and aspects of American political parties, see: V. O. Key, Jr., *Parties, Politics and Pressure Groups* (New York: Thomas Y. Crowell, 1964); Frank J. Sorauf, *Political Parties in the American System* (Boston: Little, Brown, 1964); Samuel J. Eldersveld, *Political Parties: A Behavioral Analysis* (Skokie, Ill.: Rand-McNally, 1964); and sections of Donald R. Matthews and James W. Prothro, *Negroes and the New Southern Politics* (New York: Harcourt Brace Jovanovich, 1966).

Party Stability: On the points of party identification and stability, see: Angus Campbell, Philip E. Converse, Warren E. Miller, and Donald E. Stokes, *The American Voter* (New York: John Wiley and Sons, 1960); and Angus Campbell, et al., *Elections and the Political Order* (New York: John Wiley and Sons, 1966). For two differing, but important interpretations of these points, see: Philip E. Converse, "The Nature of Belief Systems in Mass Publics," and V. O. Key, Jr. and Frank Munger, "Social Determinism and Electoral Decisions: The Case of Indiana," both in William J. Crotty, ed., *Public Opinion and Politics: A Reader* (New York: Holt, Rinehart and Winston, 1970).

Electoral Strategy: Undoubtedly several excellent accounts of the 1972 election will soon be available. In the meantime, the reader may want to review what several observers predicted would happen if certain strategies were followed. Several excellent choices are available: Samuel Lubell, *The Hidden Crisis in American Politics* (New York: W. W. Norton, 1970); Kevin Phillips, *The Emerging Republican Majority* (Garden City, N.Y.: Doubleday, 1970); and Richard M. Scammon and Ben J. Wattenberg, *The Real Majority* (New York: Coward, McCann & Geoghegan, 1970). Theodore White's works concerning the presidential elections since 1960 are well known and deserve special attention. Hopefully his account of the 1972 election will be as well done as the 1960 recounting. See: Theodore H. White, *The Making of the President 1960* (New York: Atheneum House, 1961).

NOTES

1. Henry S. Commager, ed., *Documents of American History* (New York: Appleton-Century Crofts, 1962), p. 172.
2. Gabriel Almond, *The Politics of the Developing Areas* (Princeton: Princeton University Press, 1960), pp. 33–45.
3. V. O. Key, Jr., *Politics, Parties and Pressure Groups* (New York: Thomas Y. Crowell, 1964), pp. 199–227.
4. For an intriguing analysis of the attitudes of political party leaders and members, see: Herbert McClosky, Paul J. Hoffman, and Rosemary O'Hara, "Issue Conflict and Consensus Among Party Leaders and Followers," *American Political Science Review*, 54 (June 1960).
5. Frank J. Sorauf, *Political Parties in the American System* (Boston: Little, Brown, 1964), p. 3.
6. Periodically there are demands for party reform in the United States. As examples, see: *Toward a More Responsible Two-Party System* (New York: Holt, Rinehart and Winston, 1950); and Austin Ranney, *The Doctrine of Responsible Party Government* (Urbana, Ill.: University of Illinois Press, 1954).
7. To support this point, see: Angus Campbell, Philip E. Converse, Warren E. Miller, and Donald E. Stokes, *The American Voter* (New York: John Wiley and Sons, 1960), pp. 136–145.
8. *Ibid.*, pp. 146–167.
9. See: "18 Rules Created by McGovern-Fraser Commission," *Congressional Quarterly Weekly Report* (August 29, 1972), p. 945.
10. The unit rule controversy centered on whether a state with a contested primary should have 100 percent of its delegates pledged to the primary winner or just the same percentage as he had earned in the primary. In the latter case, each of the candidates would receive a proportionate number of delegates as they had votes. Rather than

magnify the winner's margin, the abolition of the unit rule makes delegate representation more consistent with electoral choice. It also makes it more difficult for a candidate to gain large numbers of delegates.

11. For insights into this, see the following selections: "The Concept of a Normal Vote," "A Classification of the Presidential Elections," and "Loyalty and the Likelihood of Deviating Elections," all from Angus Campbell, et al., *Elections and the Political Order* (New York: John Wiley and Sons, 1966), pp. 9–39; 63–77; 125–135.

SECTION V
Public Policy

11. *Public Policy: Importance and Implications*

INTRODUCTION

As the preceding pages have indicated, the American political process is indeed complex and often confusing. While observers and students have searched for simple descriptive terms to explain the intricacies of the process, the system has undergone numerous technological and political changes. Obviously, the United States in 1789 was not the same as it is presently; neither are the political institutions and processes of today the same as they were then. This chapter will consider the American political system from a public policy perspective; that is to say, how are decisions made, and who benefits and loses from those decisions in the contemporary reality of late 20th-century America? Thus, a short introduction to public policy analysis is required if one is to understand the important public policy choices confronting society today.

Social scientists in general and political scientists in particular have attempted to become more rigorous and scientific in their analysis and work.[1] Two of the ways this has been attempted are: using models to describe the political aspects of the "real" world and developing statistical and mathematical tools which permit the observer to base his statements on empirical and factual material rather than having to rely on moral and philosophical positions.

One of the more widely used models is "systems analysis."* Using systems analysis, the observer includes as many variables as possible which might influence various participants in institutions. The goal is to view the political system in its entirety and

Public Policy

Figure 11-1
A "Systems" Model for Political Analysis

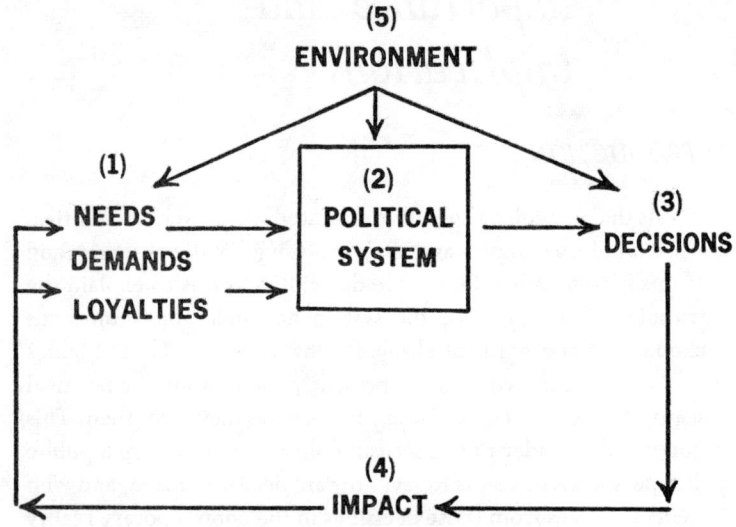

complexity. For example, Figure 11-1 illustrates one possible way of schematically viewing a political system.

As Figure 11-1 indicates, the various components are quite general, but still specific enough to provide a comprehensive overview of any political system and a comparison of different political systems. For instance, consider each of the numbered components: (1) represents the variables which influence any political system. People have needs which political systems often try to meet. One such need might be protection from foreign military aggression. Another might be relief from hunger. An example of the second variable, "demands," would be a specific grievance or suggestion the citizens of any political system might make to their political leaders by working through the political system. Some have chosen to interpret the violence which occurred in America's inner cities in the mid and late 1960s as demands for more government action in specific areas. Another type of demand was the political furor which erupted in the summer of 1972 when flood victims in the Northeast accused the federal government of insensitivity to their plight. Can you think of other possible demands? The last variable included in component (1), "loyalties," deserves careful consideration. It reflects the degree of allegiance people perceive they owe to public authority and the amount of satisfaction an individual or group of individuals might have with a particular political system. Since this is subject to change, as are the other factors, its use and study provide a dynamic aspect to the model. Thus, if loyalties were high, one might expect a different type of political behavior than if they were low. During times of extreme needs and demands, loyalties might decrease, and, therefore, different types of political activity might be forthcoming.

In general, these three variables included in (1) can be used to characterize and describe both the individual in and composite population of any political system. Thus, the observer, after having studied both individual and group characteristics, should be in an excellent position to understand what factors are affecting the political system.

Component (2) consists of the people and institutions which make the basic political decisions in a society. In American society, the institutions and processes discussed in previous chapters comprise this component. If properly analyzed and studied, predictions on how various needs and demands might be processed or handled by the political system would be possible. This is one of the basic objectives of the systems approach; the development of predictive reliability is a much sought goal in the social sciences. If ever achieved, it would broaden the claim that political inquiry can be scientific and that political behavior can be described by a general set of propositions which have a theoretical content that has been proven by the tests of experience. Consider the implications of this for man and his political world.

The dynamics of the decision-making process within the American political system is a critical aspect which deserves considerable attention. This is what the political scientist is primarily concerned with; once the inner workings of the political system are understood, it should be possible to predict with accuracy how various issues and problems can be resolved. Unfortunately or fortunately, depending upon one's broader perspective, political scientists have not achieved predictive ability on major policy questions or on most of the other significant aspects of political behavior.

Component (3), decisions, is simply those policies which are enacted by the political system as a result of the interplay of needs, demands, and loyalties with the people, institutions, and other factors which affect the system. For instance, present governmental policy on domestic economic matters resulted from decisions by the political system. These decisions are represented by (3) and are the tangible results which can be studied and measured. An example would be American troop strength in Vietnam; the rise and fall of that troop strength is the result of the various interactions which have taken place between components (1) and (2).

Component (3) has another aspect which deserves consideration. The chapters on state and local policy (8 and 9) include brief discussions about the power often attributed to some people capable of keeping certain questions from ever coming up for decision. This concept could also apply here if the political system simply chose to ignore various needs and demands made upon it. Thus, despite the pressures which might develop, the political system could simply ignore demands and needs. The interesting questions are the how and the why of such action. Are there specific issues which might be ignored by the political system? Why would they be ignored? Finally, what would the consequences be for the stability of the political system if those needs and demands are continually ignored?

Components (4) and (5) of Figure 11-1 are no more complex than the other components, but they are more difficult to separate from the others. Component (4) represents the impact a decision (or lack of one) might have on the variables in component (1). For instance, it is conceivable that a decision on domestic economic policy could lower needs and demands and increase loyalties. At the same time, a poverty program may lower the demands of the poor, but might increase the demands of the other members of society who are opposed to such government action. The important thing about (4) is that it provides the model with another dynamic feature; this means the model is not static, but capable of analyzing a political system over a protracted period of time. It permits the observer to view the system in a variety of stages and as various developments occur. In short, the model is capable of incorporating change over time into its explanatory capacity.

What happens when loyalties drop but needs and demands rise? It is conceivable that the political system may find it difficult to continue to function, and the resulting pressures might lead to major change. For instance, those individuals serving the political system might be removed from political office by a variety of means, or, even more importantly, the political system itself may be drastically altered or replaced with an alternative system which may or may not lower needs and demands and raise loyalties. The point here is that components (1) to (4) permit the observer to view and attempt to explain changes in the political system. They are very powerful analytical tools which permit analysis over the long run.

Finally, component (5) deserves consideration. Component (5) represents the so-called "environment" or the setting in which components (1) to (4) find themselves. It is important, because it may have both an indirect and a direct influence on each of the other components. For example, consider the devastating floods which affected South Dakota and the Northeastern section of the United States in 1972. These natural catastrophies resulted in extensive needs and demands on the political system and subsequent decisions. Yet the floods were weather misfortunes beyond the control of man. To ignore such environmental factors would be to ignore crucial components affecting, but not part of, the total system.

One other point about the environment should be made. Few would disagree with the proposition that the United States is a technologically advanced society. Yet, what is the relationship between technological advance and the political system? Is such advance merely part of the environment in which the political system operates, or is it much more important than that, because it may have a major role to play in affecting the various components? For instance, consider the political implications of such technological and scientific advances as the automobile, family planning, or genetic alteration. What impact have these had or might they have in the future? Does the political system affect them, or do they affect the political system? Or is the action and reaction reciprocal?

The systems approach described in this section will now be used to analyze several specific examples of public policy in order to illustrate its uses and limitations. The examples are illustrative and can be replaced with other examples which more directly affect you.

CIVIL DISTURBANCES

Few Americans are willing to face the realization that their nation has a long history of violence and conflict. Such violence often erupts in unexpected places. This was the case during the mid and late 1960s, when the United States experienced unprecedented urban civil disturbances.* These were concentrated, in the main, in the black areas of many American cities. In fact, during the first nine months of 1967, as the Kerner Commission Report (the official report of the federal government concerning the disturbances) points out, there were 164 such disturbances. The tragedies of Harlem (1965), Watts (1965), Detroit (1967), Newark (1967), and Washington, D.C. (1968) need to be briefly described in order to understand what was involved.

These disturbances were unique in that they were marked by much property loss and extensive personal injury.[2] In short, they were violent confrontations. Table 11-2 summarizes four disturbances which took place during 1967 and 1968 and the estimates of property losses and casualties associated with each disturbance. In most cases, the disturbances could be studied by dividing the events which took place into a number of distinct steps. For instance, a "precipitating" or "spark" event which triggered each conflict could be identified. In the case of Washington, D.C. (1968)

Table 11-2
Civil Disturbances and Their Effects

CITY/DATE	ARRESTED	KILLED	INJURED	DAMAGE $ millions
Cincinnati, 1967[a]	404	1	63	1 +
Detroit, 1967[a]	7,200+	43	324	40.5+
Newark, 1967[a]	1,510	25	725	10.3
Washington, D.C., 1968[b]	7,600	12	1,190	24

SOURCES:

a. *Report of the National Advisory Commission on Civil Disorders*, pp. 28, 38, 59–61, 184, 325.
b. Ben W. Gilbert, *Ten Blocks from the White House* (New York: Praeger, 1968), pp. 119, 178, 224.

it was the assassination of Dr. Martin Luther King in Memphis. In Watts (1965) and Newark (1967), it was the alleged mistreatment of citizens by local law enforcement officials which seemed to "trigger" the outbursts.

In addition, the conditions which provided the basis for the conflict and the resulting strategies and tactics used by the participants during the disturbances can be isolated and studied. Several useful and revealing case studies of the events which took place in several of the cities are worth pursuing, as they attempt to explain and describe the disturbances; these are described in the supplementary reading suggestions. Interestingly enough, many observers disagree on what the disturbances meant, why they occurred, and the results obtained by them.[3] Nevertheless, many observers do agree on some descriptive aspects pertaining to them. These descriptive aspects do a great deal to shatter the myths that many Americans still hold about the events of the 1960s. The following list summarizes the major points.

(1) The disturbances were not the result of an organized and conspiratorial group which efficiently planned each of the disturbances. In fact, most observers feel that disorganization and lack of group cohesion were the dominant characteristics of the disturbances. This point dismisses the possibility that the disturbances might have been fomented by foreign agents or any domestic group dedicated to violent change. In short, the disturbances were not systematic acts of revolutionary violence.

(2) The disturbances were almost exclusively in predominantly black areas. Washington, D.C. was an exception in that there was extensive damage in the commercial downtown area. In no case were there "invasions" by blacks into white residential areas which resulted in personal injuries or deaths. The disturbances were not marked by well coordinated and carefully planned attacks by blacks on whites. This is important, because it prevents the "race riot" label from applying to these disturbances. They were

more than racial clashes between various groups; thus they deserve more attention.

(3) The disturbances resulted in extensive arson and looting; property damage was nearly impossible to estimate in dollars, but it was extensive. Looting, primarily for consumer goods, was a major characteristic of the disturbances.

(4) The majority of residents in the areas where the disturbances took place did not participate. Those that participated tended to be younger and better educated than the average residents in the disturbance area. The participants also tended to have longer periods of residency in the area than the other residents.

(5) The disturbances did not result in any attempt by the participants to gain political control over any of the territory in which the disturbances occurred. It is true that the participants did control various amounts of "turf" at different points, but they made no efforts to establish separate forms of government or control. This is additional support for the theory of the nonrevolutionary nature of these disturbances.

(6) The disturbances were ended only by massive use of counterforce by official law enforcement agencies. This meant the extensive deployment of local police, national guard troops, and, in some cases, federal troops. It was during this phase that a large proportion of the deaths and injuries took place. The vast majority of the deaths and injuries occurred among the participants rather than among the law enforcement officials.

These six points should be kept in mind for a number of reasons. The most important is the link they provide to a perplexing era of American life. Were the disturbances of the 1960s unique events caused by a combination of unforeseen occurrences, or were they merely a continuation of the political violence which has come to characterize American society? This question can be investigated by using the systems model (Figure 11-1) discussed earlier in the chapter.

What were the demands, loyalties, and needs of the black urban dweller at that point in time? Keep in mind that the 1960s saw a marked rise in the consciousness of the black man. Leaders such as the Reverend King and Malcolm X rallied support for their positions, which opposed white supremacy and called for an end to white racism which, according to their views, resulted in economic and political control by the white race.[4] In addition, the 1960s saw increases in demands made by the poor, particularly the urban poor. After his experience in West Virginia in 1960, President Kennedy became more interested in poverty alternatives and involved the federal government in new attempts to alleviate poverty.[5]

In addition, the needs of the urban dweller were increasing in both absolute and relative terms. In absolute terms, conditions in America's urban centers were worsening and, to many, becoming intolerable. Transportation and housing problems were common. In addition, black unemployment was high. In relative terms, both the black laborer and the educated black person received proportionately less for their efforts than their white counterparts. The conclusion was inevitable; in terms of needs and demands, the American political system was experiencing a dramatic increase. In terms of loyalties, many people were no longer content to wait for government action, they were now attempting to prompt and promote it. In essence, they were less sure the government would take such action without intensive pressure on their part.

This activity and change in the area of demands, loyalties, and needs must be placed in a clear environmental perspective. Keep in mind that "environment" includes the events and conditions affecting the political system. The United States was beginning to prosper after the economic setbacks of the late 1950s; in essence, more Americans could consider the problems of poverty, because they were no longer personally poor and did not think poverty would be a problem for them in the future. In addition, public leadership became more aware of the problems and stressed the need for governmental action. Finally, some political leaders, especially in the South, adopted harsh and unyielding tactics against those who peacefully protested; the result was a general increase in sympathy and support for those advocating change. The point is that the environmental conditions during the 1960s were such that the demands made for change were falling on receptive ears.

In terms of government programs and decisions, the most important was the War on Poverty, which was adopted in 1964. Its provisions are less important than its intent—to eradicate poverty in America. Federal revenues for housing and other urban improvements increased. So, again, there were signs of positive support or response by the government through its programs. Now comes the interesting part of the analysis.

Observers differ in assessing the "impact" created by these programs and policies. One group argues that the programs were totally meaningless, little more than tokenism. Their argument is that the urban residents, especially the urban blacks, soon realized this and were left with only one alternative. That was to rise against the society which was keeping them disadvantaged. In essence, this position contends that the urban disturbances were simply demands being placed on the political system through the use of violent means,[6] that the demands were the result of constant failure of the political system to respond to the conditions of the poor and were a signal to the system and its leaders that more beneficial and appropriate policies must be forthcoming if the violence were to stop and not reoccur in the future.

A second position dealing with the question of impact is quite different. In this case, observers maintain that the civil disturbances which they often refer to as rioting, were the result of excessive energy, the desire for short-range economic gains, or the wish to follow the socially accepted thing to do.[7] In other words, the civil disturbances were not political expressions of demands but simply violent attempts to gain short-range material benefits.

Thus, they had little, if any, consequences for the political system.

While considering these two positions, a third point of view might be offered. Tom Hayden, who was a community worker in Newark, has maintained that the disturbances were largely caused, created, and perpetuated by the official authorities as a means of limiting or ending the rise of unity and consciousness among America's disenchanted. Hayden argues that Newark was largely a "police" riot and was a direct response to the increased demands and needs of the Newark black population.[8] It was a "warning" by white society to the poor black not to demand too much from the racist system.

Obviously the three positions just discussed are not mutually compatible. Which of the three you accept and why are personal decisions and worthy of careful consideration. Before concluding this section, several additional points deserve attention.

First, the systems model is capable of analyzing other than supposedly "normal" events. In this case, it is a useful device for appraising the problem of violence in the political system. In fact, the utility of the approach becomes obvious when a specific civil disturbance such as Watts, Detroit, or Newark is carefully studied within the framework provided by the model. The model permits an analysis of the participants, their actions, and the possibility that such events might take place again.

Second, the systems model, in this case, may offer some interesting and important conclusions for the future. For instance, why have the disturbances not continued into the 1970s? What contributing factors have changed and why? Are the feedback channels (impact) closed, or are the demands and needs of the urban population different from what they were in the 1960s? The answers to these questions may reveal a great deal about future potential for stability or instability. If one is interested in questions about future development, the systems model may be of great help in developing predictive abilities.

Finally, does the apparent simplicity of the model really mask a much more fundamental complexity? For instance, are demands and needs so neatly tied together? Does feedback take place as depicted and influence loyalties, demands, and needs in such a simple and direct fashion? In other words, does the model assume too much about complicated social and political relationships? Is it too simplistic to say that because economic conditions in the 1960s were generally good, more people became more interested in the poor? Or does the model need to supply more overt "linkages" between one variable and another? These questions will be reconsidered in the closing segment of this chapter but also deserve consideration while the specific points about civil disturbances are fresh in your mind.

SOUTHEAST ASIA

Americans, regardless of their political persuasions or opinions, have been preoccupied with the events surrounding the war in Southeast Asia since the early 1960s. Daily battle reports and reports of new peace initiatives have brought the war to the American public and made it a crucial and constant aspect of American politics. As the 1972 presidential campaign indicated, issues and views on the war are complicated and often difficult to clarify. In fact, few subjects seem more complicated than the whys and wherefores of American involvement in Southeast Asia. In order to clarify the events related to the war and to illustrate the utility of the systems approach in studying complex social phenomena, a brief discussion of each component of the model presented previously will again be undertaken. The complexity and variation which the example reflects is affected by the fact that it represents a considerable period of recent American history.

If the analysis is confined to the period from 1960 to 1972, the differences which took place over the years become clearer. Table 11-3 summarizes the American military commitment in South Vietnam for selected years during that period. As the table indicates, American military involvement has fluctuated. Note the rise in combat personnel from 1960 to 1968 and then the decrease from 1969 to 1972. This represents an obvious shift in American policy; by using the systems model, a clearer understanding of the decision-making involved is possible.

First, consider the situation from 1960 to 1964, when American combat troop commitment stayed relatively the same. This was a period of steady economic growth and prosperity in the United States; economic needs of the majority of Americans were being met. The demands that were being made were for increased civil rights for racial minorities and increased American involvement in foreign matters around the world which were thought crucial to our national security. In general, the early 1960s saw peaceful protest and orderly change dominate; the war was far away and not central to most people's concerns. The environment, component (5) of the model, was generally favorable to the United States. Our allies did not disagree with our stated policy that South Vietnam's collapse would result in all of Southeast Asia falling under Communist domination. Many people easily accepted the "domino" theory. In fact, the decisions being reached by the political leaders of the time were indeed basic decisions with far-reaching consequences, for they served to "lock" the United States into a position of supporting a constituted authority in South Vietnam which was basically unpopular and largely undemocratic. In this case, component (4) of the model was also quite important; decisions reached during this time were to have an effect on subsequent policy alternatives. Different strategies and decisions during the early 1960s would have permitted different decisions in later years.

Table 11-3
American Combat Troops in Vietnam: 1960–1972

YEAR	TOTAL	ARMY	NAVY	MARINES	AIR FORCE	COAST GUARD
1960–1963	an average of 650 advisory troops					
1964	23,300	14,700	1,100	900	6,600	—
1965	74,300	6,800	8,400	38,200	20,600	300
1966	385,300	239,400	23,300	69,200	52,900	500
1967	485,600	319,500	31,700	78,000	55,900	500
1968	536,100	359,800	36,100	81,400	58,400	400
1969	475,200	331,100	30,200	55,100	58,400	400
1970	334,600	249,600	16,700	25,100	43,100	100
1971	157,800	119,700	7,600	600	29,800	100
June 1972	95,600	69,400	5,100	400	20,600	100

SOURCE:
Statistical Abstract of the United States: 1972 (Washington, D.C.: Government Printing Office, 1972), p. 260.

The next phase, from 1964 to 1968, was marked by rapidly increased American involvement in the war and controversy over the war and its conduct. At that point, the decision-makers in component (3) were subject to a much wider array of demands, needs, and loyalties. For instance, many Americans felt it was vital to America's national security for us to be involved in Southeast Asia. In essence, concern over our own national security became a need widely shared by large segments of the populace. On the other hand, other segments of the population began to feel a need to lessen American involvement and put greater emphasis on domestic problems. This underlying contradiction of needs soon led to a contradiction of demands. Some argued that American military power should be unrestricted so that the war could be concluded. Others wanted the American military force expanded so that North Vietnam and China would be directly involved. Yet others demanded an immediate cessation of American military activity and active withdrawal. The period from 1964 to 1968 was characterized by extensive peaceful antiwar activity and demands. People marched and demonstrated, for the most part peacefully. While these two opposing needs were changing and coming into conflict with one another, loyalties did not seem to sway a great deal. The emphasis was on attempting to convince those in power to take a certain course of action rather than on removing them from office through the ballot or by way of the bullet. There was a general feeling that the federal government would "respond" to the demands made upon it.

Meanwhile, American policy in Vietnam allowed American military forces to take over a major part of the combat activity. American units were used in both offensive and defensive roles. It became clear that American military power was going to be used to whatever extent necessary to support the South Vietnamese and prevent a military collapse of the Saigon government. During this period, general world opinion became more mixed toward American involvement; questions were asked and many reservations expressed.

By 1968, as a brief review of each of the systems model's components would illustrate, the situation had drastically changed. On the one hand, the demands and needs of the American public became more polarized. Some Americans argued and pressed for an end to the war by pointing out the need for increased domestic spending; others pointed out the general destruction and havoc brought about by the civil disturbances and maintained that domestic peace and a re-ordering of national priorities should take precedence over military commitments. At the same time, those favoring a "hard" line in Southeast Asia became more and more convinced that American military policy was too "soft" and sparing of the enemy. The result was tremendous domestic tension which received a jolt from one event and undoubtedly helped another to occur.

In February of 1968, the Vietcong and North Vietnamese forces in South Vietnam lauched an offensive that surprised both the American military and the American public with its scope and intensity. Even the American embassy in Saigon was threatened, and news coverage of the "Tet Offensive" brought the war home once and for all. The savagery of the fighting and the drain on American lives could no longer be ignored by the public. The reaction tended to be one of calling for either increased involvement or a decline in involvement. Again, the needs and demands of the populace lacked consistency and created difficulty for the political decision-makers.

The second event which had historical implications was the decision by the incumbent Democratic President, Lyndon B. Johnson, not to seek reelection. This happened after a strong antiwar showing in the primaries by Senator Eugene McCarthy reflected the split within the Democratic Party concerning Vietnam policy. The result of Johnson's decision not to seek reelection, an apparent tacit admission of error in his war policy, and of the success of the

Tet Offensive was that demands on the political system drastically increased. In essence, the country became sharply divided, and the presidential campaign of 1968 reflected this division and deep hostility within the American system. People opposed one another on the war, and immediately questions of loyalty and allegiance entered. One was quickly stereotyped on a number of issues, based on his position on the war. Some dissidents turned to violent acts to show their disavowal and lack of faith in the system.

By election time, two other series of events had profoundly affected America. The first involved the growing international sentiment against American policy: our allies were less supportive, and nations which had remained silent in the past had begun to denounce "American aggression." Coupled with this was a growing personal identity with the war on the part of the Americans. Table 11-4 illustrates the casualties related to the war over a 12 year period.

By 1968, most Americans knew of a friend or relative who had been affected by the war, someone who had served, was about to serve, or was a casualty of the war. In essence, the war became more personal. Americans began to ask more questions about the war, and it became an even more important issue. The presidential aspirant Richard Nixon campaigned, saying he would end the war if elected. The point is that by 1968 the nation had become sharply divided on and by the war issue, and attempts at reconciliation were difficult. Again, the political system was faced with the difficult task of reconciling the conflicting elements and maintaining some semblance of order.

The period from 1968 to 1972 represents an important and interesting period in modern America. As Tables 11-3 and 11-4 indicate, both American involvement and casualties decreased, yet American concern over the war became more marked. In this case, college campuses often became armed battlefields over elements of American policy. Kent State and the shootings which took place

Table 11-4
American Casualties in Vietnam

YEAR	BATTLE DEATHS	WOUNDED	MISSING	CAPTURED
1964	267	783	4	3
1965	1,369	3,308	54	74
1966	5,008	16,526	204	97
1967	9,378	32,371	226	179
1968	14,592	46,799	294	95
1969	9,414	32,940	176	13
1970	4,221	15,211	85	12
1971	1,380	4,817	79	11
June 1972	53	198	121	29
TOTALS	45,682	152,953	1,243	513

SOURCE:

Statistical Abstract of the United States: 1972 (Washington, D.C.: Government Printing Office, 1972), p. 260.

there are symbolic of the general mistrust and tension which characterized certain segments of the American people in the 1967–1971 period. Acts of political terrorism and rapid and stern governmental responses became more prevalent and widespread. While our troop strength declined, American bombing of North Vietnam began anew and was characterized by greater intensity and frequency than at any other point during the war. All of these factors contributed to the tumultuous campaign of 1972 and the continuation of the debate and conflict. Several important points should be drawn from this discussion.

(1) Despite the utility of the systems approach, it does not eliminate the complexity and often the confusion which dominate the various aspects of a political system. The demands of the American public, although capable of being described in general terms, cannot be specifically detailed and are often contradictory. The same goes for the decision component. An excellent example is the contradiction evident in Nixon's decision to end American ground combat involvement while expanding and increasing the intensity of American air and naval involvement.

(2) The systems model is useful in exploring the links between overt decisions and subsequent needs, demands, and loyalties. The problem, however, is to be able to show that a particular policy decision actually caused a change in one of the variables contained in component (1). This is a very difficult task.

(3) The systems model presents the observer with an opportunity to observe more efficiently the events which develop over time. The benefit is a richness and depth of understanding which would be limited without the approach.

(5) Finally, consider the predictive abilities of the model. Based on prior events and analysis, what would the future hold for American involvement and debate over Southeast Asia? Using the systems model, can the needs, demands, and loyalties of the American people be surmised? If so, for what period of time and with what effect? What about subsequent decisions and their dynamic relationships to the various components? The next section considers the implications of these case studies.

IMPLICATIONS

The two preceding examples are indicative of the analytical power and utility of the systems model and approaches. Based on these examples, several general but important implications should be considered.

Public Policy: Importance and Implications 225

First, the systems approach provides the social scientist with a unique opportunity to investigate the complex social and political relationships which characterize human society. By dividing the social system into distinctive components and by realizing the dynamic aspects of politics, the social scientist may gain a more comprehensive view of the system.

Although extensive claims are made for the utility of systems models, two important limitations must be pointed out. First, by taking so comprehensive a view, the investigator is forced to become immersed in many facets of political developments and nonpolitical variables; in fact, such involvement may detract from the investigator's ability to understand anything because of the complex relationships which demand such mastery. In short, the social sciences, by stressing the systems approach, may have made it impossible for the single researcher to learn much of anything because of the knowledge and training required of him. The result has been extensive use of computers and other statistical devices to study large-scale and multifaceted political systems. For this reason, some social scientists have been accused of "ignoring" the personal, spiritual side of human existence by stressing the need for objective data. Obviously this becomes an important point if one feels that society needs to stress humanistic values and not strictly behavior-oriented standards. The problem is in reconciling the two needs.

The second limitation of the systems model is that very careful attention must be paid to linking the various components together. This needs explanation. Recall the emphasis placed on loyalties in component (1) and the stress on how this variable could change. As an example, let us postulate that the social scientist finds that the loyalties of a particular group are declining. Assuming that observation is correct, the next questions would probably be: "why are the loyalties declining, and what effect will this have on the political system?" The systems approach complicates matters where it requires linkages; that is to say, one cannot assume that simply because loyalties are dropping and the unemployment rate is increasing that unemployment causes disloyalty. This is a logical conclusion, but it must be more vigorously and carefully investigated if it is to be accepted as an explanation. Thus, the systems model does provide comprehensiveness, but it creates problems when trying to link one variable with another. How might one go about linking an event with a subsequent event? What does this do for sophisticated analysis?

A second general implication that can be drawn from the systems model approach is that despite its complexity it has a great deal to offer any reasonably intelligent person who is interested in a better understanding of the society about him. By systematically looking at more than one variable and by attempting to consider the interrelationships among them, the individual observer is forced to do away with simplistic notions and concepts of "good" or "bad." The political world becomes more complicated, and the individual becomes more capable of discerning who is "telling it as it is" and who is misrepresenting things. Granted, the complexity of the system may make it difficult for the individual to accept his own personal role in the system, but it is important that he realizes the limitations of his actions rather than assumes he has unlimited ability to influence society. This leads to a related and crucial point.

How does the individual know which person or position to believe when confronted with conflicting statements? In the political world, the use of the systems model would be of considerable utility for the individual citizen. By using such a model, in his own less complicated fashion, the observer should be in a better position to assess who was responsible for what. Thus, if candidate A says his actions caused events B and C to take place, the observer should be able to decide if that might be true or whether it is impossible, given the constraints of the systems model.

The systems model, then, is a very powerful tool for evaluation; it provides the individual with a systematic way to evaluate the various actions and statements which might be forthcoming from participants in the political system. The value of this evaluation does not stop here; it can also be used to provide the individual with a way to make more rational participatory decisions.

How, as a voter, do you decide which of the candidates for a prospective office you should support? The systems model provides you with a very useful way to analyze the various positions, but it does more than that; it even indicates whether you should participate or not. Assuming that most people do not want to waste one of their scarcest resources, time, they must reach a decision on how, where, and on what they are willing to spend time. By utilizing the systems model, an individual can decide whether or not his participation is justified. Figure 11-5 indicates the various possibilities for participation.*

If an individual felt intensely about any particular issue, it would make sense for him to participate in any way possible, regardless of his chances for success. This is represented by the As in

Figure 11-5
Participation Justification: A Schematic View

INDIVIDUAL FEELING TOWARD DECISION	INDIVIDUAL CHANCE OF AFFECTING OUTCOME OF DECISION			
	Not determined	Low	Moderate	High
Intense	A	A	A	A
Moderate	B	B	A	A
Passive	C	C	C	B

LETTER KEY:
A: Cases in which individual would participate.
B: Cases in which individual would be undecided.
C: Cases in which individual would probably not participate.

Figure 11-5. The Cs represent cases where the passive feelings of an individual indicate that he probably should not invest any resources in participation unless he were almost assured of the outcome. The person who has the most difficult decision to make concerning participation is the one represented by the Bs; he is in the position of having the most uncertainty. In order to illustrate the utility of this chart, a specific example is in order.

It is the summer of 1976, and the two political parties have just nominated their presidential candidates. How will you make a decision on the amount and type of participation you will engage in? By using the systems model described earlier, you might be able to determine your individual chances of affecting outcomes. Once this has been determined, you are then in the position to measure the intensity of your feelings, which is a highly individual and personal matter, and decide whether you will participate or not. By using the participation justification chart to assess your chances of affecting the outcome, a more rational component has been introduced. Remember, the rationality of the systems model will appear more desirable the less strongly you feel about a particular issue or plan of action. An individual is less likely to be drawn into participation when his actions have little or marginal effect. This increased rationality may heighten political consciousness and increase the effectiveness of political participation. If this is the case, then the systems model has made an important contribution.

The final implication of the systems approach which must be discussed concerns the meaning it has for society. In the first place, complexity is the rule, not the exception. Social and political systems become complicated and multifaceted; the implication, then is that change in a political system is neither simplistic nor rapid. If that premise is accepted, the implication becomes much more interesting to study. In the case of the systems model, one position might be that society, whether it be defined as a political or social system, is too complicated and nothing can be done to alter it.

Therefore, one abandons any form of activity and simply responds to the system. On the other hand, one might decide that the system is so complicated and complex that a little tinkering here and there may bring about tremendous change because of the delicate balances involved. Both positions may be valid, but the point is that change in a complicated system also comes about in complicated ways. Given this, the person interested in effective change should be investigating the political process and political system to see where participation in other activities might have some very real impact. Thus, the critical points at which participation might bring about change are sought; if discovered, the political system itself might be altered. These implications should be carefully considered, since they point out both the limitations and promises of the systems approach. If properly understood, these implications can expand an individual's awareness of the society about him. In addition, they offer insights into the possible "scenarios" describing the future of American politics, which are considered in the concluding chapter.

SUGGESTED READINGS

Systems Analysis: See: Gabriel Almond, *The Politics of the Developing Areas* (Princeton: Princeton University Press, 1960); David Easton, *The Political System: An Inquiry into the State of Political Science* (New York: Knopf, 1953); D. M. Martindale, ed., *Functionalism in the Social Sciences*, Monograph 5, American Academy of Political and Social Science (February 1965); James C. Charlesworth, ed., *A Design for Political Science: Scope, Objectives, and Methods*, Monograph 6, American Academy of Political and Social Science (December 1966); Gabriel Almond, "A Developmental Approach to Political Systems," *World Politics* (January 1965); and Karl Deutsch, *The Nerves of Government* (New York: The Free Press, 1963).

Urban Civil Disturbances: For a summary report of the 1965–1967 period, see: *Report of the National Advisory Commission on Civil*

Disorders (Washington: Government Printing Office, 1968). The following are specific accounts of various disturbances: Robert Conot, *Rivers of Blood, Years of Darkness* (New York: Bantam, 1967) on Los Angeles; Thomas Hayden, *Rebellion in Newark* (New York: Vintage Press, 1967) on Newark; Ben Gilbert, *Ten Blocks from the White House* (New York: Praeger, 1968) on Washington, D.C. For general comments on the disturbances, see: Peter A. Lupsha, "On Theories of Urban Violence," *Urban Affairs Quarterly* (March 1969); Peter H. Rossi, ed., *Ghetto Revolts* (Chicago: Aldine, 1970); and Edward C. Banfield, "Rioting Mainly for Fun and Profit," in James Q. Wilson, ed., *The Metropolitan Enigma* (Garden City, N.Y.: Doubleday, Anchor, 1970), pp. 312–341.

Citizen Participation: For both descriptive and prescriptive aspects of participation, see: Lester Milbrath, *Political Participation* (Skokie, Ill.: Rand-McNally, 1965); William C. Mitchell, *Why Vote?* (Chicago: Markham, 1971); Joseph F. Zimmerman, *The Federated City* (New York: St. Martin's Press, 1972); and Milton Kotler, *Neighborhood Government* (Indianapolis: Bobbs-Merrill, 1969). For a comparative view of participation, see: Gabriel Almond and Sidney Verba, *The Civic Culture* (Princeton: Princeton University Press, 1963).

NOTES

1. As examples, see: Harold D. Lasswell, *Politics: Who Gets What, When and How* (New York: McGraw-Hill, 1936); and David Easton, *The Political System, An Inquiry into the State of Political Science* (New York: Knopf, 1953).

2. *Report of The National Advisory Commission on Civil Disorders* (Washington, D.C.: Government Printing Office, 1968), pp. 19–61; and Ben Gilbert, *Ten Blocks from the White House* (New York: Praeger, 1968), pp. 119, 178, 228.

3. See: Peter A. Lupsha, "On Theories of Urban Violence," *Urban Affairs Quarterly* (March 1969); Peter H. Rossi, ed., *Ghetto Revolts* (Chicago: Aldine, 1970); and Robert M. Fogelson and Robert B. Hill, "Who Riots? A Study of Participation in the 1967 Riots," *Supplemental*

Studies for The National Advisory Commission on Civil Disorders (Washington, D.C.: Government Printing Office, 1968).

4. See: *The Autobiography of Malcolm X* (New York: Grove Press, 1964).

5. Theodore H. White, *The Making of the President 1960* (New York: Atheneum, 1961), pp. 116–137.

6. See: Lupsha, "On Theories of Urban Violence."

7. Edward C. Banfield, "Rioting Mainly for Fun and Profit," in James Q. Wilson, ed., *The Metropolitan Enigma* (Garden City, N.Y.: Doubleday, Anchor 1970), pp. 312–341.

8. Thomas Hayden, *Rebellion in Newark* (New York: Vintage, 1967).

12. The Future of American Politics

INTRODUCTION

Given the complexities of the early 1970s, it is difficult to predict future developments and changes in American society. This chapter considers the factors influencing American society, types of possible change, indicators of future change, and individual obligation and responsibility in a changing society. Obvious fame and perhaps fortune await the individual who can "tell" the future, but how can society, specifically American society, "tell" its future?

Mankind has been fascinated with the study of the future during various historical periods; at the present time, interest in and concern about the future are again increasing.* Proponents of various population, social, and environmental causes warn of impending doom unless measures are taken to limit population, solve pressing issues, and/or conserve natural resources. Planners attempt to foresee the future; but the interesting and thought-provoking questions concern how the individual "tells" the future, and how he determines his role in it. Horoscopes, palm readings, and life signs supposedly aid the interested; two methods widely used by social scientists deserve consideration.

The first method will be labeled "futuristics" and involves the following. Assume an individual, group, or society decides it would like to change its present set of conditions (A) to another set of conditions (B). The result is a goal, a desired end state. Usually goals are thought of in concrete terms or definitions, such as income level, calories per person, or educational attainment levels; however, they can be as abstract as quality of life or improved morality. Using the futuristics approach, a number of distinct steps would be followed. As already mentioned, the first would be the establishment of a particular goal or set of goals. These can be broad or specific; in addition, time is a variable. Thus, goals can be differentiated into short- and long-run categories. The process of setting goals is not too difficult for an individual, since competing values and wants should be minimal, but a group or society may have a more difficult time setting goals as the number and diversity of participants increases. The group or society has to develop agreement and support for the goals it desires or sets. A group or society may have such diverse elements that it becomes impossible for it to set goals, but assuming goals are set, a number of specific steps usually follow. These are crucial if the goals are to be reached or if progress toward them is to be achieved.

Once goals have been established, it is necessary to assemble information on how far you are from a particular goal. This involves extensive information gathering and assessment. This second stage of futuristics emphasizes research and the interpretation of the research findings. What is studied and the interpretation of findings are both dependent on individual values and preferences. Any assessment of the present state of affairs must take these preferences into account if the resulting findings are to have significance. Another problem is that this second stage may be either too short to permit an accurate assessment of how things really are or conditions may be too involved to permit realistic changes to occur. One aspect of assessment is the discovery of trends; that is, are conditions such that they are moving the individual, group, or society, toward or away from the stated goal? In any case, upon completion of assessment, the third step follows.

Since one now has some idea of where he presently stands and has also set goals for the future, the third step involves the development of specific policies which are designed to increase the probability of reaching a stated goal. In other words, how one gets from A (present condition) to B (future goal) is considered. In developing policies, attention must be paid to the effects a policy in pursuit of one goal may have on other goals. For instance, if increased employment is a goal, but the policy to reach it involves environmental waste, consideration of policies other than those concerning employment are likely. Policies are not neutral; they involve the use of scarce resources and directly affect people. For these reasons, the development of specific policies, as earlier sections of this book have indicated, is likely to be a difficult and time-consuming process. Policies can vary; they may attempt to influence individual action, involve direct governmental action, or be a combination of both approaches. In addition, more than one policy may be utilized to reach a specific goal.

Once the specific policies have been set, the next aspect of futuristics involves two related steps. First, the policies must be implemented; that is, the policies are actually put into practice and attempted. Second, after a period of time which may vary from policy to policy or society to society, the effects of the implemented policies must be evaluated. Research is necessary to ascertain whether or not the policies have achieved the desired goal or are responsible for trends which make the realization of the goal possible. Based on this evaluation, policy makers may decide to discontinue policies which have had little impact or which appear to be establishing trends that make the attainment of the desired goal less likely. On the other hand, successful policies are also identified through evaluation; these can then be continued or supplemented with other similar policies to maximize the chances of reaching the goal.

After the previous four steps have been completed, societal evaluation and assessment would be undertaken. Decisions as to progress or the lack of it and other desired goals would be

Table 12-1
Futuristics: A Summary

STEP	DESCRIPTION OF ACTIVITY
1	Goal-setting
2	Assessment of present conditions and various trends
3	Policy development to reach goals based on assessment of conditions and trends
4	Implementation of specific policies and evaluation of the policies' effects in producing progress toward stated goals
5	Societal assessment and evaluation of specific policies, results, and ultimate goals; continuation of policies or the adoption of new goals

forthcoming. This final step provides for alternative resource allocations to reach other goals if new priorities or demands take precedence. Table 12-1 summarizes these steps.

While the theoretical aspects of futuristics are relatively straightforward, the practical application of the approach is more difficult. For instance, consider America's decision to place men on the moon or to pursue its Vietnam policy. These and other policies can be analyzed using the futuristics approach. Consider for a moment its use in developing future economic or social goals for the United States. One of the advantages of the futuristics method is that it permits analysis to be dynamic, to follow events and developments over periods of time. The futuristics approach is usually used to study a society or large collectivity; simulation, the second method for studying the future to be discussed, is useful in predicting organizational and smaller group behavior.

Simulation is an attempt to create "real-world" conditions in an experimental setting and to observe the results of the subsequent interaction and decision-making.* Organizations such as the United Nations and political units such as cities or metropolitan areas have had simulation exercises patterned after them. Individual roles are recreated, and an attempt is made to predict subsequent behavioral reactions to certain conditions and situations. Through the use of simulations, strategies and policies may be developed which prevent undesirable behavior. Consider the following example.

A city is chosen for a simulation exercise. Participants are assigned certain roles: one may be the mayor, another a councilman, another a private citizen. Situations are then created based on real-world facts and conditions. The participants, assuming the roles assigned them, react to the situation and make specific policy decisions as they are interacting with one another. One aim of simulation is to replicate accurately real-world conditions so that subsequent participant behavior will be either illustrative or predictive of real-world behavior. If you can simulate the real-world conditions, then you might be able to develop policies to change or influence the behavior of those in the real world, based on the behavior observed during the simulation.

While both futuristics and simulation have been widely discussed and often attempted, both have one major shortcoming. It is impossible to anticipate all future developments. For instance, would the United States have been different in the late 1960s if several prominent leaders, such as John and Robert Kennedy and Martin Luther King, had not been assassinated or if the late Lyndon Johnson had chosen to run again for president in 1968? Also, is it not possible that human society is so complicated, diverse, and unstable that any set of facts used to predict what may happen in the future may simply be so incomplete and inaccurate that projections or predictions based on it suffer the same fate? This is not meant to say that futuristics and simulation have no roles to play but that you should be cautious about accepting their predictive results without subjecting them to several important critical tests. Keeping in mind the nature and utility of both approaches, consider the present setting of American politics and the complexities it creates for anyone interested in either approach.

CURRENT SETTING

Chapter 11 considered the effects of environmental factors on systems analysis and pointed out the difficulties in fully understanding or measuring all of these factors. This chapter segment summarizes the various environmental forces which are influencing the American political system at this point in time. These environmental forces will be divided into internal and external categories for the sake of simplicity; however, the boundaries between the categories and the factors within each often merge with one another.

An internal factor which is important, but difficult to comprehend or isolate, is the "mood" of the country. Understanding the mood and its implications is essential if future events are to be anticipated with any reliability. Does the margin of Richard Nixon's electoral victory in November of 1972 or the Republican party's showing in House and Senate races in 1972 reflect the underlying national mood in American politics? If one accepts the Nixon margin as symbolic of the national mood, interpretations of the future are sure to be quite different from those that would be made if one accepts the second results as indicative of national mood. For if Nixon's margin represented basic national sentiment, then major changes in the country's outlook on racial and other important domestic and international issues might be forthcoming. If the margin reflects a general tendency toward conservatism, then one might expect governmental policy at various levels to reflect this change.

Perhaps an even more important aspect of the national mood is the underlying attitude American citizens have toward government and government action. Was President Nixon correct when he maintained:

> *Relying on bigger government is the wrong way to meet our nation's needs. Government has grown by leaps and bounds since the nineteen-thirties; but so have problems—problems like crime and blight and inflation and pollution. The bigger Government became, the more clumsy it became, until its attempt to help often proved a hindrance.*[1]

Has the American public decided that government, whether it be local, state, or national, is either ill-equiped to act or prevented from taking action in certain areas? If this is the case, not only is governmental action in new areas unlikely, but governmental programs in various areas are likely to be discontinued or permitted to lapse. If we assume (and, as it has been pointed out, this is a tentative assumption at best) that public officials are bound by constituent interests to some degree, it then becomes likely that this underlying disenchantment on the part of the American public will have an impact on subsequent policy formulation and implementation.

Another internal factor may also have profound effects. American attitudes toward the military involvement in Vietnam and the present completion of that involvement will have great impact. Will the American public be responsive to critics representing various positions regarding our policy, or will the public want to "forget" the war and America's role in it? If the critics can find a receptive audience, debate and accusations over the war may continue for an indefinite period of time. On the other hand, if the public is indifferent, it might be difficult to rally public support at times when the political leaders feel obligated to protect American national interests throughout the world. In either case, the Vietnam War will continue to have an impact on American politics and policies.

While the public's responsiveness and attitudes toward these issues are significant, various demographic and social trends within American society may have an equal or greater impact on the political system. For instance, population is becoming increasingly urbanized. The consequences for political representation and participation of this increased population density and the accompanying possible increase in societal tensions need to be fully considered. At some point, American society may be confronted with the need to institute managerial and other programs to control population growth and mobility. This possibility raises important questions for a society which emphasizes free choice and individual autonomy.

Accompanying the shift toward increased urbanization is the increased interdependency of American society. No longer can one sector of society take action or receive benefits without that action or benefits affecting other sectors. The United Auto Workers' decision to bargain for higher wages or improved working conditions affects not just the auto industry but most Americans. In similar fashion, the farmers' decisions on acreage plans and crop allocations directly affect most Americans. American society has become so complex and interrelated that individual and group autonomy in decisions is unlikely in most areas and on most issues.

Coupled with these internal conditions and attitudes, a variety of external environmental factors affect the United States. Foremost among these is the changing nature of the international arena and America's role in it. The continued development of the People's Republic of China as a major participant and power in world politics needs to be fully understood. At the minimum, the emergence of China has three important results. First, the United States and its representative democracy is being challenged as the model for political development. For many countries, the economic and political development exemplified in China's rise is attractive and perhaps better suited to their own position in the international setting than either the experiences of the Soviet Union or of the United States.

Second, China's emergence has affected the world's power relationships by changing the nature of international politics from a two-nation domination to a three-nation contest. Previously, international relations were split into the United States and its supporters versus the Soviet Union and its supporters. China and its supporters have become a potent force in the international arena and are to be reckoned with by both the Soviet Union and the United States. American leaders will be confronted with a series of difficult diplomatic and strategic choices in the next decade. American response to this changing international scene could well influence future world events.

Third, and finally, China presents a series of unique problems and particular opportunities to the world. Will its emergence as a major power be accomplished without the devastation of war? The Soviet Union and the United States evolved as world powers only after the turmoil and tragic events of the Second World War. The implications of future global military actions are so devastating that their contemplation results in despair. Despite this, the possibility of future military action among the three powers should not be dismissed lightly.

While China's emergence has had and will continue to have an impact on the United States, other factors in the international arena are also undergoing change. Our allies are in a state of flux, and the continued economic development of Germany and Japan poses important questions for the American system. American decisions and policies will have an impact on the world's economy and its nations, but that impact may be less significant in the future than it has been in the past. American response to the changing international environment will be a critical component of future political development in this country.

Technological and scientific developments will affect change in both the domestic and international environments as well as humanity in general. For instance, what are the ramifications if genetic engineering becomes possible and biologists are able to systematically breed in or out of human beings certain biological traits such as bravery, intelligence, violence, or responsibility? Even more imminent is the possibility of agricultural and industrial advances which could alter the amount of resources controlled by various people and result in increased conflict over the decisions in these areas. The possible impact of these changes on individual lifestyles and political systems is awesome. The next two chapter segments consider the changes likely to occur in American society by the year 2000 and the potential critical signs indicating such changes. Both sections rely heavily on the environmental factors just discussed.

INDICATORS OF CHANGE

Before the concluding discussion of participatory questions, consideration of indicators of change and possible future scenarios are in order. These will illustrate the range and variety of future possibilities. Each reader is encouraged to develop his own scenarios on the future of American politics. This particular segment describes several key areas which are likely to represent broad societal changes:

(1) Political parties in the United States have been meaningful indicators of general change. This has been true in two general areas: party leadership and the general structure of the political party. If American parties respond to their contemporary challenges by opening their leadership rather than continuing to be dominated by a few, American society itself will be affected. Events at both the 1968 and 1972 Democratic National Conventions signaled

major unrest in parts of that party. In similar fashion, although more muted, the 1972 Republican National Convention considered liberalizing the party's guidelines for representation to the convention; if this had been adopted, the party would have been truly reformed. The outcomes of these and other challenges to both parties are significant. In the case of the Republican party, the defeat of this particular measure may mean more conservative factions within the party will be assured of control in the 1976 convention, which could mean control over who gets nominated. In the case of the Democrats, the ensuing in-fighting and bitterness prompted by the reforms at the 1972 convention may have disrupted various alliances beyond repair. The nature of internal party leadership and each party's responses to demands for reform have implications not only for that particular party but for the American party structure as well.

Traditionally, change in the American party structure has meant that third parties develop in an attempt to influence the other parties or to offer viable candidates of their own. The George Wallace phenomenon is an excellent example of this. It is doubtful, given the underlying institutional and behavioral predispositions toward the two-party system as discussed earlier, that third parties will have any major impact over a prolonged period of time. They may be successful in influencing certain elections or policy decisions but it is unlikely that they will replace either of the two major parties or become a long tenured competitor to the two major parties. Despite this, the American party structure may still undergo major change.

If increasing numbers of citizens were to become alienated and/or apathetic toward both political parties, then the party structure might be affected. Most Americans, for a variety of personal and social reasons, have very little interest in politics.[2] Evidence of this is the general lack of information most citizens have toward politics and the relatively low percentage of voting turnout in the United States. Imagine the impact on the party structure if the apathetic public suddenly became either concerned with politics or actively antipolitical. In the latter case, they would oppose politics because of what it meant, or the methods used, or the results obtained. If increased apathy were to occur, then the party professionals, a relatively small number in each party, could dominate the party's decisions. In either case, the party structure would be profoundly affected, as would the rest of society.

(2) The second area indicative of broader social change would be majority-minority relationships; this category would include not only racial relationships but also economic majority-minority relationships.

Most Americans would agree that the United States has a serious problem involving white-nonwhite relationships. In the nonwhite group are Negroes, American Indians, Chicanos, Puerto Ricans, and Orientals. Unless American society, and especially the white majority of society, reaches some rapprochement with these various groups, hostility and conflict may result in the disintegration of societal institutions and in general societal failure in dealing with complex problems. One indicator of the status of majority-minority racial relationships is the extent of racial integration within American society and the extent of conflict generated by attempts at racial integration. Consider for a moment the explosive issue of school bussing and the magnitude of the problem becomes clear. In addition, keep in mind that the racial groups involved are not in agreement as to the end state they desire. For instance, do nonwhite groups desire integration within the white society, or do they want to be able to control the neighborhoods and communities in which they are a majority?

A related aspect of the majority-minority question is the extent to which it applies to economic concerns. What would happen if the economically dispossessed exercised their potential political power to do away with the advantages presently given the large economic interests in American society? Even more important, what if the lower and middle income groups were to unite politically in order to gain various economic benefits at the expense of the upper economic groups? Would violence and strife dominate, or would the institutions of American society be able to accommodate the tremendous change involved? For instance, imagine the societal implications if the upper and lower income groups combined political forces to restrict or reduce the economic and political gains of the middle income groups. Other possible pairings can be envisioned. As America passes into the 21st century, majority-minority relationships, both economic and racial, will become increasingly complicated and important.

(3) The nature of political leadership is the third general area which will be indicative of broader societal change. A variety of forces and conditions will be important in the future. Whether or not political leaders are capable of developing and utilizing technological expertise is crucial. Since technical expertise involves both ability and training, this is not an insignificant point. As our society becomes more technically oriented, leaders must be capable of considering these technical factors if rational and proper decisions are to be reached.

A second aspect of leadership trends is whether leaders are open to citizen input, and, even more important, what leaders have done to encourage or discourage it. It is not necessary that leaders respond to every citizen input, but it is necessary, if the political system is to have any degree of openness, that they be aware of citizen interests and needs. In a complex and dynamic society, it may become increasingly difficult for the political leader to be both open and responsive unless he consciously accepts the practice of frequent citizen access.

Finally, the quality of leadership will depend on the political leader's perception of the responsibility of his leadership. Is he responsive to narrow interests which bring specific power to bear when necessary, or does he consider the general "public interest" whenever it conflicts with the desires of a private sector? In short, who are leaders going to respond to? Future answers to this question and the first two will illustrate the quality of leadership found in American society.

(4) Future patterns of violence, often overlooked and ignored, will serve as general indicators of change in American society. In this case, future violence may fall into one of two categories. The first and most commonly accepted pattern is violence against the system. This is reflected in general crime rates, but more importantly in the specific acts against political leaders or institutions of the country. If violent acts, including political assassinations, were to increase drastically, America's stability might be endangered, and one would be justified in inquiring about the political responsiveness of a system which has such a great number of violent acts committed against its leaders. The analysis would then have to center on why this is the case.

A second, and often overlooked, type of political violence is system-perpetuated violence. This can be of two types. The first would be harsh and/or repressive measures used to deal with dissident groups seen to be posing a threat in power. Acts of violence designed to punish participants in dissident groups or to discourage others from participating in their activities would be common. The second type of violence is the overuse of counterforce when authorities are confronted with potentially violent or actually violent situations. For instance, the countermeasures used by Southern law enforcement agencies during the civil rights struggle and by the Chicago police during the 1968 Democratic National Convention were seen by many as being overreactions to the actual threats the various demonstrations posed. In both cases, the contention was that the overreaction was prompted because of the symbolic nature of the protest.

(5) Finally, the role of individual responsibility will indicate

Figure 12-2
A Continuum of Individual Responsibility

A	B	C
SOCIAL CONSCIOUSNESS	MIXED	INDIVIDUALISM

the nature of future American society. Figure 12-2 depicts a responsibility continuum.

Points A, B, and C represent various dominant attitudes on a responsibility continuum. If one finds most individuals at Point A rather than B or C, then that society will be marked by vastly different social relationships than if most individuals were found to be at points B or C. One can argue that American society and the American people have historically been closer to Point C than Point A but that various historical periods have seen movement towards Point B. Future developments regarding individual responsibility will have profound effects on the society and deserve careful consideration.

THREE POSSIBLE FUTURE SCENARIOS

Table 12-3 summarizes the preceding discussion and offers insights into the three scenarios to be discussed in this chapter segment.

Using Table 12-3 as a reference point, one can foresee a variety of possible future scenarios. The five variables taken together provide the minimum theoretical possibility of 120 future scenarios. For our purposes, three will be considered.

The first scenario is most likely to be described as a utopia: problems within the political system and society in general are

Table 12-3
Possible Future Scenarios

VARIABLE	SCENARIO 1	SCENARIO 2	SCENARIO 3
Party leadership and party structures	Open	Closed and rigid	Varies with issues
Majority-minority relationships	Fluid; resolved	Hierarchical; unresolved	Bargaining; withdrawn
Political leadership	Public-interest oriented	Special-interest oriented	Flexible; firm
Violence	Minimal	Frequent and self-generating	Sporadic but intense
Individual responsibility	Social-consciousness oriented	Self-interest stressed	Occasional social consciousness

minimal, and the system is responsive to public demands and interests. In this scenario, political parties are open to new leadership; that is, as an issue succeeds in gaining broadly based support, the party that fails to be responsive on that issue is open enough to let those who organize for it carry the issue within the party. Hierarchical relationships in the parties are minimized; emphasis is on the party structure being responsive to public-interest demands. In addition, relationships between majority-minority groups are marked by compromise and mutually acceptable agreements. The result is an increase in public-interest orientation of political leaders; no longer do they feel compelled to respond to narrow, special interests. Instead, the emphasis is on public desires and wants. Problems with broad societal appeal are resolved, and the emphasis is on reaching solutions which benefit the majority of citizens. Political leaders are able to respond to citizen desires and are also free from the need of utilizing the resources large private interests are capable of mustering. In essence, political leadership becomes independent of large vested interests.

The result of this increased fluidity and openness within the system is a decline in both acts of violence against the system and acts of violence perpetuated by the system. Since the citizenry perceives the system as responsive, it feels less need to organize and actively test the system. This trust and acceptance of the system's legitimacy eliminates the conditions in which violence toward the system encourages excessive violence by authorities within the system. Finally, under these circumstances, the individual is able to be socially conscious instead of concerned only with problems which directly affect him. His concern for others and for societal needs helps to provide the system with a dynamic force which stresses common good over individual needs or wants. The citizenry provides the dynamic aspect for the system described in the scenario; the prevailing social consciousness permits the system to find outlets for its collective energy.

The scenario just outlined is readily contrasted with a second scenario that might also be extrapolated from Table 12-3. In the latter, party leadership and party structure are closed to public demands and are unwilling to be reflective of underlying public sentiment. The party structure is characterized by the iron law of oligarchy; that is, party leadership has as its main goal the perpetuation of itself in positions of dominance and power. Any attempt to organize a faction in the hope of influencing party policy is seen as a definitive threat, and the party leadership takes whatever steps it feels necessary to prevent that faction or organization from being effective. The party structure remains closed, and those interested in expressing a position through the party system are ignored and overlooked.

In scenario 2, majority-minority relationships are hierarchical, mutual respect is absent, and the groups involved view each other with extreme mistrust and are unlikely to modify a given position. Thus, compromise and negotiation become rarities; instead, deadlock and refusal to modify positions dominate the relationship. The end result is a heightening of tensions throughout the political system, because each group is concerned with its own vested interests.

Political leadership in this scenario fails to respond to public-interest questions unless they also correspond to the private interests it seeks to serve. Political leaders stress that they must "deliver" for those who helped place them in office; societal consequences of this position are obvious. With political leaders responding to vested interests, who is left to protect or champion issues affecting the general public? The result is that these issues are largely ignored. Thus, the public becomes even more fractured, with groups forming to support leaders who cater to their special needs and interests. Elections become bitter contests characterized by tension and by strategies designed to win at any cost.

These three aspects contribute to increased and self-generating violence in the system. Dissident groups are frustrated whenever they attempt to influence decisions or reform political structures. Those in power are fearful that the dissidents may succeed and are therefore likely to take countermeasures which often provoke greater violence. Violence begets violent reaction, and the result is that both challengers to the system and system authorities use violence against one another either to gain an objective or to prevent others from gaining theirs. The end result is a society torn by internal strife and much violence.

Under these circumstances, it is natural for the individual citizen to be concerned only with his own self-interest. He quickly realizes that it is up to him to protect his own interests and that any policy or program which helps others without affecting him is undesirable, since it takes potential resources away from him. As a result, individuals stress the negative aspects of any program which does not directly benefit them. In sum, scenario 2 stresses constant friction and tension, with special emphasis on individual self-interest and realization of one's own goals at the expense of all others. Its contrast to scenario 1 is apparent.

Scenario 3 provides an interesting contrast to both 1 and 2. As extracted from Table 12-3, this scenario is characterized by party leadership and structure which varies in openness, depending upon the issue under consideration. If party leadership feels the issue can be resolved without threatening its dominant position in the party, then resolution is sought. This strategy permits party leadership to appear flexible on questions it feels are unimportant or to take a firm position on questions it feels are decisive. The party structure is similar: it is capable of permitting short-run deviations, such as third-party candidates and insurgent parties, only as long as they do not seriously alter the existing structure.

Majority-minority relationships are characterized by intense bargaining among the various groups. Each attempts to gain concessions from the other, without giving up anything in return. In addition, the various majority and minority groups become withdrawn; little attempt is made to interact with one another, and individual suspicion becomes dominant. The result is increased tension and periodic breakdown in attempts to reach bargaining agreement on specific changes.

Political leadership responds to the forces at work in this system by maintaining a flexible air on the surface; that is, emphasis is on the public interest, and issues with broad appeal are actively supported when these issues coincide with the leadership's self-interest. At the same time, any issue which the political leadership feels would be detrimental to the special interests supporting it is opposed. In many cases, the opposition is intense and dogmatic.

Violence is sporadic, but intense when it occurs. It results from increased tensions, due to a breakdown in the bargaining process and growth in mistrust between supporters and opponents of the system. Extensive casualties and property damage are common. In addition, violence does little to alter things in the society. For all practical purposes, violence is a safety valve; as pressure increases, frustrations, desires, and needs are vented in forms of violence rather than in effective, permanent change within the society.

In response to societal conditions, the individual citizen would take a rational position on most issues. If he felt a particular issue would benefit him directly or indirectly, he would be supportive. In other cases, he would do all that was possible to defeat an issue. Thus, public interest would have to be sold to him on the basis of his own self-interest; if this could not be shown, he would not be supportive, but he might also not be antipathetic.

All three scenarios and many others are possible, given the dynamic nature of American politics and the system's propensity to change over time. Given your knowledge of the system, which scenario is most likely to occur? Your response should be carefully studied; it will foreshadow your future participation and role in political society.

INDIVIDUAL FUTURE PARTICIPATION

Obviously, if the individual citizen feels his participation in any of the preceding scenarios or other possible scenarios will have little, if any, impact, he will be unlikely to participate. If he feels his participation may make a significant difference, then the probability of his participation will increase. In both instances, traditional definitions of participation are assumed; that is, voting, organizing, and other legal acts are expected. Future participation may involve other "nontraditional" acts. Both categories require explanation.

Under traditional political behavior would come such oft-expected and practiced techniques as voting, petitioning leaders for action, contributing to campaigns, and the like. As pointed out earlier, it seems reasonable to expect participatory rates to be related to the perceived importance of issues being discussed and the perceived chances of affecting a decision. If both are low, then participation is unlikely; if both are high, then participation is probably assured. This will vary if a mixed situation develops according to the outlook and values of the individual citizen. In any case, traditional participation signifies several additional points. Most important of these is that the individual participant has at least some faith that participation will have a chance of making some difference; that is, his participation *may* result in the end he desires. Thus, if participatory rates were to increase, one would be justified in assuming there still was belief in the general system of government and belief that efforts should be concentrated on trying to influence that system.

Such is not the case with nontraditional methods of participation. If one decides the system is hopelessly closed or incapable of responding to individual needs or public desires, he may take other means of action. One form of action might be passive; that is, the individual simply withdraws from political decision-making or any attempt to influence it. He may become apathetic or apolitical, simply ignoring political events about him. Another type of non-traditional behavior would be active; that is, one might adopt measures and tactics which are designed to change the nature of government completely. Thus, one might develop various strategies, in most cases involving various degrees of violence, which would abolish existing forms of government and replace them with others.

In concluding this volume, two additional points need to be pointed out. First, one can take different positions according to the level of government at which one wishes to influence change. Thus, one might advocate violence as the only means to change the local level of government while accepting traditional forms of behavior and participation at other levels. In similar fashion, the reverse could be true for national versus local governmental institutions. Second, these choices are largely individual. The type, extent, and energy each individual devotes to his participation in the political process will be determined by his assessment both of the present situation and of his role in future developments.

SUGGESTED READINGS

Future Orientation: See the following for a discussion of possible, probable, and desirable future states: Bertrand de Jouvenal, *The Art of Conjecture* (New York: Basic Books, 1967); Harold D. Lasswell, *The Future of Political Science* (New York: Atherton Press, 1964); Harold D. Lasswell, "Technique of Decision Seminars," *Midwest Journal of Political Science* 4, no. 3 (August 1960): 213–236; and Theodore Roszak, *The Making of a Counter Culture* (Garden City, N.Y.: Doubleday, 1969).

Simulation: For a discussion of the uses of simulation and modeling, see: Albert Ando, Franklin M. Fisher, and Herbert Simon, *Essays on the Structure of Social Science Models* (Cambridge: Massachusetts Institute of Technology Press, 1963); Garry D. Brewer and Owen P. Hall,

Jr., *Policy Analysis by Computer Simulation: The Need for Appraisal* (Santa Monica: Rand Corporation, August 1972); Harold Guetzkow, ed., *Simulation in Social Science* (Englewood Cliffs, N.J.: Prentice-Hall, 1963); and G. Arthur Mirham, *Simulation: Statistical Foundation and Methodology* (New York: Academic Press, 1972). For specific examples of simulation and modeling applied to actual social conditions, see: John P. Crecine, *Governmental Problem Solving* (Chicago: Rand-McNally, 1969); Jay W. Forrester, *Urban Dynamics* (Cambridge: Massachusetts Institute of Technology Press, 1969); and I. Pool and Robert Abelson, "The Simulmantics Project," *Public Opinion Quarterly* 25 (1961): 167–183.

NOTES

1. Richard Nixon's "Budget Message," January 29, 1973.
2. Lester Milbrath has divided political participation by the American public into four types: apathy, spectator, transitional, and gladiatorial. Less than ten percent of the public was classified as being in the gladiatorial (most active) group. See: Lester Milbrath, *Political Participation* (Skokie, Ill.: Rand-McNally, 1965), pp. 16–22.

APPENDIX

The Constitution of the United States

WE, THE PEOPLE OF THE UNITED STATES, in Order to form a more perfect Union, establish Justice, Insure domestic Tranquility, provide for the common defense, promote the general Welfare, and secure the Blessings of Liberty to ourselves and our Posterity, do ordain and establish this Constitution for, the United States of America.

ARTICLE 1

Section 1

All legislative Powers herein granted shall be vested in a Congress of the United States, which shall consist of a Senate and a House of Representatives.

Section 2

The House of Representatives shall be composed of Members chosen every second Year by the People of the several States, and the electors in each State shall have (the) Qualifications requisite for Electors of the most numerous Branch of the State Legislature.

No Person shall be a Representative who shall not have attained to the Age of twenty five Years and been seven Years a Citizen of the United States, and who shall not when elected, be an inhabitant of that State in which he shall be chosen.

Representatives and direct Taxes shall be apportioned among the several States which may be included within this Union, according to their respective Numbers, which shall be determined by adding to the whole Number of free Persons, including those bound to Service for a Term of Years and excluding Indians not taxed, three fifths of all other Persons. The actual Enumeration shall be made within three Years after the First Meeting of the Congress of the United States, and within every subsequent Term of ten Years, in such Manner as they shall by Law direct. The Number of Representatives shall not exceed one for every thirty Thousand, but each State shall have at Least one Representative; and until such enumeration shall be made, the state of New Hampshire shall be entitled to chuse three, Massachusetts eight, Rhode Island and Providence Plantations one, Connecticut five, New York six, New Jersey four, Pennsylvania eight, Delaware one, Maryland six, Virginia ten, North Carolina five, South Carolina five, and Georgia three.

When vacancies happen in the Representation from any State, the Executive Authority thereof shall issue Writs of Election to fill such Vacancies.

The House of Representatives shall chuse their Speaker and other Officers; and shall have the sole Power of impeachment.

Section 3

The Senate of the United States shall be composed of Two Senators from each State, chosen by the Legislature thereof, for six Years; and each Senator shall have one Vote.

Immediately after they shall be assembled in Consequence of the first Election, they shall be divided as equally as may be into three Classes. The Seats of the Senators of the first Class shall be vacated at the Expiration of the second Year, of the second Class at the Expiration of the fourth Year, and of the third Class at the Expiration of the sixth Year, so that one third may be chosen every second Year and if Vacancies happen by Resignation, or otherwise, during the Recess of the Legislature of any State, the Executive thereof may make temporary Appointments until the next Meeting of the Legislature, which shall then fill such Vacancies.

No person shall be a Senator who shall not have attained to the Age of thirty Years, and been nine Years a Citizen of the United States, and who shall not, when elected, be an inhabitant of that State for which he shall be chosen.

The Vice-President of the United States shall be President of the Senate, but shall have no Vote, unless they be equally divided.

The Senate shall chuse their other Officers, and also a President pro tempore, in the Absence of the Vice-President, or when he shall exercise the Office of President of the United States.

The Senate shall have the sole power to try all impeachments. When sitting for that Purpose, they shall be on Oath or Affirmation. When the President of the United States (is tried) the Chief Justice shall preside. And no Person shall be convicted without the Concurrence of two thirds of the Members present.

Judgment in Cases of Impeachment shall not extend further than to removal from Office, and disqualification to hold and enjoy any Office of honor, Trust or Profit under the United States; but the Party convicted shall nevertheless be liable and subject to indictment, Trial, Judgment and Punishment according to Law.

Section 4

The Times, Places, and Manner of holding Elections for Senators and Representatives shall be prescribed in each State by the Legislature thereof, but the Congress may at any time by Law make or alter such Regulations, except as to the Places of chusing Senators.

The Congress shall assemble at least once in every Year, and such Meeting shall be on the first Monday in December, unless they shall by Law appoint a different Day.

Section 5

Each House shall be the Judge of the Elections, Returns and Qualifications of its own Members, and a Majority of each shall constitute a Quorum to do Business; but a smaller Number may adjourn from day to day, and may be authorized to compel the Attendance of absent Members, in such Manner, and under such penalties as each House may provide.

Each House may determine the Rules of its Proceedings, punish its Members for disorderly Behaviour, and, with the Concurrence of two thirds, expel a Member.

Each House shall keep a Journal of its Proceedings, and from time to time publish the same, excepting such Parts as may in their Judgment require Secrecy; and the Yeas and Nays of the Members of either House on any question shall, at the Desire of one fifth of those Present, be entered on the Journal.

Neither House, during the Session of Congress, shall, without the Consent of the other, adjourn for more than three days, nor to any other Place than that in which the two Houses shall be sitting.

Section 6

The Senators and Representatives shall receive a Compensation for their Services, to be ascertained by Law, and paid out of the Treasury of the United States. They shall in all Cases, except Treason, Felony and Breach of the Peace, be privileged from Arrest during their Attendance at the Session of their respective Houses, and in going to and returning from the same; and for any Speech or Debate in either House, they shall not be questioned in any other Place.

No Senator or Representative shall, during the Time for which he was elected, be appointed to any civil Office under the Authority of the United States, which shall have been created, or the Emoluments where of shall have been encreased during such time; and no Person holding any Office under the United States, shall be a Member of either House during his Continuance in Office.

Section 7

All Bills for raising Revenue shall originate in the House of Representatives; but the Senate may propose or concur with Amendments as on other Bills.

Every Bill which shall have passed the House of Representatives and the Senate, shall, before it becomes a Law, be presented to the President of the United States; if he approve he shall sign it, but if not he shall return it, with his Objections to that House in which it shall have originated, who shall enter the Objections at large on their Journal, and proceed to reconsider it. If after such Reconsideration two thirds of that House shall agree to pass the Bill, it shall be sent, together with the Objections, to the other House, by which it shall likewise be reconsidered, and if approved by two thirds of that House, it shall become a Law. But in all such Cases the Voted of both Houses shall be determined by yeas and Nays, and the Names of the Persons voting for an against the Bill shall be entered on the Journal of each House respectively. If any Bill shall not be returned by the President within ten Days (Sundays excepted) after it shall have been presented to him the Same shall be a Law, in like Manner as if he had signed it, unless the Congress by their Adjournment prevent its Return, in which Case it shall not be a Law.

Every Order, Resolution, or Vote to which the Concurrence of the Senate and House of Representatives may be necessary (except on a question of Adjournment) shall be presented to the President of the United States, and before the Same shall take Effect, shall be approved by him, or being disapproved by him, shall be repassed by two thirds of the Senate and House of Representatives according to the Rules and Limitations prescribed in the Case of a Bill.

Section 8

The Congress shall have the Power To lay and collect Taxes, Duties, Imposts and Excises, to pay the Debts and provide for the common Defence and general Welfare of the United States; but all Duties, Imposts and Excises shall be uniform throughout the United States.

To borrow Money on the credit of the United States;

To regulate Commerce with foreign Nations and among the several States, and with the Indian Tribes;

To establish an uniform Rule of Naturalization, and uniform Laws on the subject of Bankruptices throughout the United States;

To Coin Money, regulate the Value thereof, and of foreign Coin, and fix the Standard of Weights and Measures;

To provide for the Punishment of counterfeiting the Securities and current Coin of the United States;

To establish Post Offices and post Roads;

To promote the Progress of Science and useful Arts, by securing for limited Times to Authors and inventors the exclusive Right to their respective Writings and Discoveries;

To constitute Tribunals inferior to the supreme Court;

To define and punish Piracies and Felonies committed on the High Seas and Offences against the Law of Nations;

To declare War, grant Letters of Marque and Reprisal and make Rules concerning Captures on Land and Water;

To raise and support Armies, but no Appropriation of Money to that Use shall be for a longer Term than two Years;

To provide and maintain a Navy;

To make Rules for Government and Regulation of the land and naval Forces;

To provide for calling forth the Militia to execute the Laws of the Union, suppress insurrections and repel Invasions;

To provide for organizing, arming, and disciplining the Militia, and for governing such Part of them as may be employed in the Service of the United States, reserving to the States respectively the Appointment of the Officers, and the Authority of training the Militia according to the discipline prescribed by Congress.

To exercise exclusive Legislation in all Cases whatsoever, over such District (not exceeding ten Miles square) as may, by Cession of particular States, and the Acceptance of Congress, become the Seat of the Government of the United States, and to exercise like Authority over all Places purchased by the Consent of the Legislature of the State in which the Same shall be, for the Erection of Forts, Magazines, Arsenals, dock-Yards, and other needful Buildings; —And

To make all Laws which shall be necessary and proper for carrying into Execution the foregoing Powers, and all other Powers vested by this Constitution in the Government of the United States, or in any Department or Officer thereof.

Section 9

The Migration or Importation of such Persons as any of the States now existing shall think proper to admit, shall not be prohibited by the Congress prior to the Year one thousand eight hundred and eight, but a Tax or duty may be imposed on such Importation, not exceeding ten dollars for each Person.

The Privilege of the Writ of Habeas Corpus shall not be suspended, unless when in Cases of Rebellion or Invasion the public Safety may require it.

No Bill of Attainder or ex post facto Law shall be passed.

No Capitation, or other direct, Tax shall be laid, unless in Proportion to the Census or Enumeration herein before directed to be taken.

No tax or Duty shall be laid on Articles exported from any State.

No Preference shall be given by any Regulation of Commerce or Revenue to the Ports of State over those of another, nor shall vessels bound to, or from, one State be obliged to enter, clear, or pay Duties in another.

No Money shall be drawn from the Treasury, but in Consequence of Appropriations made by Law, and a regular Statement and Account of the Receipts and Expenditures of all public Money shall be published from time to time.

No title of Nobility shall be granted by the United States. And no Person holding any Office of Profit or Trust under them, shall, without the Consent of the Congress, accept of any present, Emolument, Office, or Title, of any kind whatever, from any King, Prince, or foreign State.

Section 10

No State shall enter into any Treaty, Alliance, or Confederation; grant Letters of Marque and Reprisal; coin Money; emit Bills of Credit; make any Thing but gold and silver Coin a Tender in Payment of Debts; pass any Bill of Attainder, ex post facto Law, or Law impairing the Obligation of Contracts, or grant any Title of Nobility.

No State shall, without the Consent of the Congress, lay any imposts or Duties on Imports or Exports, except what may be absolutely necessary for executing its inspection Laws and the net Produce of all Duties and Imposts, laid by any State on Imports or Exports, shall be for the use of the Treasury of the United States, and all such Laws shall be subject to the Revision and Controul of (the) Congress.

No State shall, without the Consent of Congress, lay any Duty of Tonnage, keep Troops, or Ships of War in time of Peace, enter into any Agreement or Compact with another State, or with a foreign Power, or engage in War, unless actually invaded, or in such imminent Danger as will not admit of delay.

ARTICLE 2

Section 1

The executive Power shall be vested in a President of the United States of America. He shall hold his office during the Term of four Years, and together with the Vice-President, chosen for the same Term, be elected as follows.

Each State shall appoint, in such Manner as the Legislature thereof may direct, a Number of Electors, equal to the whole Number of Senators and Representatives to which the State may be entitled in the Congress; but no Senator or Representative, or Person holding an Office of Trust or Profit under the United States, shall be appointed an Elector.

The Electors shall meet in their respective States, and vote by Ballot for two Persons of whom one at least shall not be an inhabitant of the same State with themselves. And they shall make a List of all the Persons voted for, and of the Number of Votes for each; which List they shall sign and certify, and transmit sealed to the Seat of the Government of the United States, directed to the President of the Senate. The President of the Senate shall, in the Presence of the Senate and House of Representatives, open all the Certificates, and the Votes shall then be counted. The Person having the greatest Number of Votes shall be the President, if such Number be a Majority of the whole Number of Electors appointed; and if there be more than one who have such Majority, and have an equal Number of Votes, then the House of Representatives shall immediately chuse by Ballot one of them for President, and if no Person have a Majority, then from the five highest in the List the said House shall in like Manner chuse the President. But in chusing the President, the Votes shall be taken by States, the Representation from each State having one Vote. A quorum for this purpose shall consist of a Member or Members from two thirds of the States, and a Majority of all the States shall be necessary to a Choice in every Case, after the choice of the President, the Person having the greatest Numbet of Votes of the Electors shall be the Vice-President. But if there should remain two or more who have equal Votes, the Senate shall chuse from them by Ballot the Vice President.

The Congress may determine the Time of chusing the Electors, and the Day on which they shall give their votes; which Day shall be the same throughout the United States.

No person except a natural born Citizen, or a Citizen of the United States, at the time of the Adoption of this Constitution, shall be eligible to the Office of President; neither shall any Person be eligible to that Office who shall not have attained to the Age of thirty five Years, and been fourteen Years a Resident within the United States.

In Case of the Removal of the President from Office, or of his Death, Resignation, or inability to discharge the Powers and Duties of the said Office, the Same shall devolve on the Vice-President and the Congress may by Law provide for the Case of Removal, Death, Resignation or inability, both of the President and Vice-President, declaring what Officer shall then act as President, and such Officer shall act accordingly, until the Disability be removed, or a President shall be elected.

The President shall, at stated Times, receive for his Services, a Compensation, which shall neither be encreased not diminished during the Period for which he shall have been elected, and he shall not receive within that Period any other Emolument from the United States, or any of them.

Before he entered on the Execution of his Office, he shall take the following Oath or Affirmation—"I do solemnly swear (or affirm) that I will faithfully execute the Office of the President of the United States, and will to the best of my Ability, preserve, protect and defend the Constitution of the United States."

Section 2

The President shall be Commander in Chief of the Army and Navy of the United States and the Militia of the several States, when called into the actual Service of the United States, he may require the Opinion, in writing, of the principal Officer in each of the executive Departments, upon any subject relating to the Duties of their respective Offices and he shall have Power to grant Reprieves and Pardons for Offences against the United States, except in Cases of Impeachment.

He shall have Power, by and with the Advice and Consent of the Senate, to make Treaties, provided two thirds of the Senators present concur; and he shall nominate, and by and with the Advice and Consent of the Senate, shall appoint Ambassadors, other public Ministers and Consuls, Judges of the supreme Court, and all other Officers of the United States, whose Appointments are not herein otherwise provided for and which shall be established by Law, but the Congress may by Law vest the Appointment of such inferior Officers, as they think proper in the President alone, in the Courts of Law, or in the Heads of Departments.

The President shall have Power to fill up all Vacancies that may happen during the Recess of the Senate, by granting Commissions which shall expire at the End of their next Session.

Section 3

He shall from time to time give to the Congress information of the State of the Union, and recommend to their Consideration such Measures as he shall judge necessary and expedient; he may, on extraordinary Occassions, convene both Houses, or either of them, and in Case of Disagreement between them, with Respect to the Time of Adjournment, he may adjourn them to such Time as he shall think proper; he shall receive Ambassadors and other public Ministers; he shall take care that the Laws be faithfully executed, and shall commission all the Officers of the United States.

Section 4

The President, Vice-President, and all civil Officers of the United States, shall be removed from Office on Impeachment for, and Conviction of, Treason, Bribery, or other high Crimes and Misdemeanors.

ARTICLE 3

Section 1

The judicial Power of the United States, shall be vested in one supreme Court, and in such inferior Courts as the Congress may from time to time ordain and establish. The judges, both of the supreme and inferior Courts, shall hold their Offices during good Behavior, and shall, at stated Times, receive for their Services, a Compensation, which shall not be diminished during their Continuance in Office.

Section 2

The judicial Power shall extend to all Cases, in Law and Equity, arising under this Constitution, the Laws of the United States, and Treaties made, or which shall be made, under their Authority;—to all Cases affecting Ambassadors, other public Ministers and Consuls;—to all Cases of admiralty and maritime Jurisdiction—to Controversies to which the United States shall be a Party—to Controversies between two or more States;—between a State and Citizens of another State;—between Citizens of different States;—between Citizens of the same State claiming Lands under Grants of different States, and between a State, or the Citizens thereof, and foreign States, Citizens or Subjects.

In all Cases affecting Ambassadors, other public Ministers and Consuls, and those to which a State shall be Party, the supreme Court shall have original Jurisdiction. In all the other Cases before mentioned, the supreme Court shall have appellate Jurisdiction, both as to Law and Fact, with such Exceptions, and under such Regulations as the Congress shall make.

The trial of all Crimes, except in Cases of impeachment shall be by Jury; and such Trial shall be held in the State where the said Crimes shall have been committed; but when not committed within any State, the Trial shall be at such Place or Places as the Congress may by Law have directed.

Section 3

Treason against the United States, shall consist only in levying War against them, or in adhering to their Enemies, giving them Aid and Comfort. No Person shall be convicted of Treason unless on the Testimony of two Witnesses to the same overt Act, or on Confession in open Court.

The Congress shall have Power to declare the Punishment of Treason, but no Attainder of Treason shall work Corruption of Blood, or Forfeiture except during the Life of the Person attainted.

ARTICLE 4

Section 1

Full Faith and Credit shall be given in each State to the public Acts, Records, and judicial Proceedings of every other State. And the Congress may by general Laws prescribe the Manner in which such Acts, Records and Proceedings shall be proved, and the Effect thereof.

Section 2

The citizens of each State shall be entitled to all Privileges and Immunities of Citizens in the several States.

A Person charged in any State with Treason, Felony, or other Crime, who shall flee from Justice, and be found in another State, shall on Demand of the executive Authority of the State from which he fled, be delivered up, to be removed to the State having Jurisdiction of the Crime.

No Person held to Service or Labour in one State, under the laws thereof, escaping into another, shall, in Consequence of any Law or Regulation therein, be discharged from such Service or Labour, but shall be delivered upon Claim of the Party to whom such Serivce or Labour may be due.

Section 3

New States may be admitted by the Congress into this Union, but no new State shall be formed or erected within the Jurisdiction of any other State, nor any State be formed by the Junction of two or more States, or Parts of States, without the Consent of the Legislature of the States concerned as well as of the Congress.

The Congress shall have Power to dispose of and make all needful Rules and Regulations respecting the Territory or other Property belonging to the United States, and nothing in this Constitution shall be so construed as to Prejudice any Claims of the United States, or of any particular State.

Section 4

The United States shall guarantee to every State in this Union a Republican Form of Government, and shall protect each of them against Invasion; and on Application of the Legislature, or of the Executive (when the Legislature cannot be convened) against domestic Violence.

ARTICLE 5

The Congress, whenever two thirds of both Houses shall deem it necessary, shall propose Amendments to this Constitution, or, on the Application of the Legislatures of two thirds of the several States, shall call a Convention for proposing Amendments which, in either case, shall be valid to all Intents and Purposes, as Part of this Constitution, when ratified by the Legislatures of three fourths of the several States, or by Conventions in three fourths thereof, as the one or the other Mode of Ratification may be proposed by the Congress. Provided that no Amendment which may be made prior to the Year One thousand eight hundred and eight shall in any Manner affect the first and fourth Clauses in the Ninth Section of the first Article, and that no State, without its Consent, shall be deprived of its equal Suffrage in the Senate.

ARTICLE 6

All Debts contracted and Engagements entered into, before the Adoption of this Constitution, shall be as valid against the United States under this Constitution, as under the Confederation.

This Constitution, and the Laws of the United States which shall be made in Pursuance thereof, and all Treaties made, or which shall be made, under the Authority of the United States, shall be the supreme Law of the Land, and the Judges in every State be bound thereby, any Thing in the Constitution or Laws of any State to the Contrary notwithstanding.

The Senators and Representatives before mentioned, and the Members of the several State Legislatures, and all executive and judicial Officers, both of the United States and of the several States, shall be bound by Oath or Affirmation to support this Constitution; but no religious Test shall ever be required as a Qualification to any Office or public Trust under the United States.

ARTICLE 7

The Ratification of the Conventions of nine States, shall be sufficient for the Establishment of this Constitution between the States so ratifying the Same.

done in Convention by the Unanimous Consent of the States present the Seventeenth Day of September in the Year of our Lord one thousand seven hundred and Eighty Seven and of the Independence of the United States of America the Twelfth in witness whereof We have hereunto subscribed our Names.

GO. WASHINGTON
Presidt and deputy from Virginia

New Hampshire: *John Langdon, Nicholas Gilman*
Massachusetts: *Nathaniel Gorham, Rufus King*
Connecticut: *Wm. Saml. Johnson, Roger Sherman*
New York: *Alexander Hamilton*
New Jersey: *Wil. Livingston, David Brearley, Wm. Paterson, Jona. Dayton*
Pennsylvania: *B. Franklin, Thomas Mifflin, Robt. Morris, Geo. Clymer, Thos. FitzSimons, Jared Ingersoll, James Wilson, Gouv. Morris*
Delaware: *Geo. Read, Gunning Bedford jun, John Dickinson, Richard Bassett, Jaco. Broom*
Maryland: *James McHenry, Dan of St. Thos. Jenifer, Danl. Carroll*
Virginia: *John Blair, James Madison, Jr.*
North Carolina: *Wm. Blount, Richd. Dobbs Spaight, Hu Williamson*
South Carolina: *J. Rutledge, Charles Cotesworth Pinckney, Charles Pinckney, Pierce Butler*
Georgia: *Silliam Few, Abr. Baldwin*

AMENDMENTS TO THE CONSTITUTION

(The first ten amendments were proposed by Congress on September 25, 1789; ratified and adoption certified on December 15, 1791.)

AMENDMENT I

(Freedom of Religion, of Speech, of the Press, and Right of Petition)

Congress shall make no law respecting an establishment of religion, or prohibiting the free exercise thereof, or abridging the freedom of speech, or of the press, or the right of the people peaceably to assemble, and to petition the Government for a redress of grievances.

AMENDMENT II

(Right to Keep and Bear Arms)
A well regulated Militia being necessary to the security of a Free State, the right of the people to keep and bear Arms, shall not be infringed.

AMENDMENT III

(Quartering of Soldiers)
No Soldier shall, in time of peace be quartered in any house, without the consent of the Owner, nor in time of war, but in a manner to be prescribed by law.

AMENDMENT IV

(Security from Unwarrantable Search and Seizure)
The right of the people to be secure in their persons, houses, papers, and effects, against unreasonable searches and seizures, shall not be violated, and no Warrants shall issue, but upon probable cause, supported by Oath or Affirmation, and particularly describing the place to be searched, and the persons or things to be seized.

AMENDMENT V

(Rights of Accused in Criminal Proceedings)
No person shall be held to answer for a capital, or otherwise infamous crime, unless on a presentment or indictment of a Grand

Jury, except in cases arising in the land or naval forces, or in the Militia, when in actual service in time of War or public danger; nor shall any person be subjected for the same offense to be twice put in jeopardy of life or limb; nor shall be compelled in any criminal case to be a witness against himself, nor be deprived of life, liberty, or property, without due process of law; nor shall private property be taken for public use, without just compensation.

AMENDMENT VI

(Right to Speedy Trial, Witnesses, etc.)

In all criminal prosecutions, the accused shall enjoy the right to a speedy and public trial, by an impartial jury of the State and district wherein the crime shall have been committed, which district shall have been previously ascertained by law, and to be informed of the nature and cause of the accusation; to be confronted with the witnesses against him; to have compulsory process for obtaining witnesses in his favor, and to have the Assistance of Counsel for his defence.

AMENDMENT VII

(Trial by Jury in Civil Cases)

In Suits at common law, where the value in controversy shall exceed twenty dollars, the right of trial by jury shall be preserved, and no fact tried by a jury, shall be otherwise reexamined in any Court of the United States, then according to the rules of the common law.

AMENDMENT VIII

(Bails, Fines, Punishments)

Excessive bail shall not be required, nor excessive fines imposed, nor cruel and unusual punishments inflicted.

AMENDMENT IX

(Reservation of Rights of the People)
The enumeration in the Constitution, of certain rights, shall not be construed to deny or disparage others retained by the people.

AMENDMENT X

(Powers Reserved to States or People)
The powers not delegated to the United States by the Constitution, nor prohibited by it to the States, are reserved to the States respectively, or to the people.

AMENDMENT XI

(Proposed by Congress on March 4, 1794; declared ratified on January 8, 1798.)

(Restriction of Judicial Power)
The Judicial power of the United States shall not be construed to extend to any suit in law or equity, commenced or prosecuted against one of the United States by Citizens of another State, or by Citizens or Subjects of any Foreign State.

AMENDMENT XIII

(Proposed by Congress on December 9, 1803; declared ratified on September 25, 1804.)

(Election of President and Vice-President)
The Electors shall meet in their respective states, and vote by

ballot for President and Vice-President, one of whom, at least, shall not be an inhabitant of the same state with themselves; they shall name in their ballots the person voted for as President, and in distinct ballots the person voted for as Vice-President and they shall make distinct lists of all persons voted for as President, and of all persons voted for as Vice-President, and of the number of votes for each, which lists they shall sign and certify, and transmit sealed to the seat of the government of the United States, directed to the President of the Senate;—The President of the Senate shall, in the presence of the Senate and House of Representatives, open all the certificates and the votes shall then be counted;—The person having the greatest number of votes for President, shall be the President, if such number be a majority of the whole number of Electors appointed; and if no person have such majority, then from the persons having the highest numbers not exceeding three on the list of those voted for as President, the House of Representatives shall choose immediately, by ballot, the President. But in choosing the President, the votes shall be taken by states, the representation from each state having one vote; a quorum for this purpose shall consist of a member or members from two-thirds of the states, and a majority of all the states shall be necessary to a choice. And if the House of Representatives shall not choose a President whenever the right of choice shall devolve upon them, before the fourth day of March next following, then the Vice-President shall act as President, as in the case of the death or other constitutional disability of the President—The person having the greatest number of votes as Vice-President, shall be the Vice-President, if such number be a majority of the whole number of Electors appointed, and if no person have a majority, then from the two highest numbers on the list, the Senate shall choose the Vice-President; a quorum for the purpose shall consist of two-thirds of the whole number of Senators, and a majority of the whole number shall be necessary to a choice. But no person constitutionally ineligible to the office of President shall be eligible to that of Vice-President of the United States.

AMENDMENT XIII

(Proposed by Congress on January 31, 1865, declared ratified on December 18, 1865.)

Section 1

(Abolition of Slavery)

Neither slavery nor involuntary servitude, except as a punishment for a crime whereof the party shall have been duly convicted, shall exist within the United States, or any place subject to their jurisdiction.

Section 2

(Power to Enforce This Article)

Congress shall have power to enforce this article by appropriate legislation.

AMENDMENT XIV

(Proposed by Congress on June 16, 1866; declared ratified on July 28, 1868.)

Section 1

(Citizenship Rights Not to Be abridged by States)

All persons born or naturalized in the United States, and subject to the jurisdiction thereof are citizens of the United States and of the State wherein they reside. No State shall make or enforce any law which shall abridge the privileges or immunities of citizens of the United States; nor shall any State deprive any person of life, liberty, or property, without due process of law; nor deny to any person within its jurisdiction the equal protection of the laws.

Section 2

(Appointment of Representatives in Congress)

Representatives shall be apportioned among the several States according to their respective numbers, counting the whole number of persons in each state, excluding Indians not taxed. But when the right to vote at any election for the choice of electors for President and Vice-President of the United States, Representatives in Congress the Executive and Judicial officers of a state, or the members of the Legislature thereof, is denied to any of the male inhabitants of such State being twenty-one years of age and citizens of the United States, or in any way abridged, except for participation in rebellion, or other crime, the basis of representation therein shall be reduced in the proportion which the number of such male citizens shall bear to the whole number of male citizens twenty-one years of age in such State.

Section 3

(Persons Disqualified from Holding Office)

No person shall be a Senator or Representative in Congress, or elector of President and Vice-President, or hold any office, civil or military, under the United States, or under any State, who, having previously taken an oath, as a member of Congress, or as an officer of the United States, or as a member of any State legislature, or as an executive or judicial officer of any State to support the Constitution of the United States, shall have engaged in insurrection or rebellion against the same or given aid or comfort to the enemies thereof. But Congress may by a vote of two-thirds of each House remove such disability.

Section 4

(What Public Debts are Valid)

The validity of the public debt of the United States, authorized by law, including debts incurred for payment of pensions and bounties for services in suppressing insurrection or rebellion, shall not be questioned. But neither the United States nor any State shall assume or pay any debt or obligation incurred in aid of insurrection or rebellion against the United States, or any claim for the loss or emancipation of any slave, but all such debts, obligations and claims shall be held illegal and void.

Section 5

(Power to Enforce This Article)
The Congress shall have power to enforce, by appropriate legislation, the provisions of this article.

AMENDMENT XV

(Proposed by Congress on February 26, 1869; declared ratified on March 30, 1870.)

Section 1

(Negro Suffrage)
The right of citizens of the United States to vote shall not be denied or abridged by the United States or by any State on account of race, color, or previous condition of servitude.

Section 2

(Power to Enforce This Article)
The Congress shall have power to enforce this article by appropriate legislation.

AMENDMENT XVI
(Proposed by Congress on July 12, 1909; declared ratified on February 25, 1913.)

(Authorizing Income Taxes)
The Congress shall have power to lay and collect taxes on incomes, from whatever source derived, without apportionment among the several States, and without regard to any census or enumeration.

AMENDMENT XVII
(Proposed by Congress on May 13, 1912; declared ratified on May 31, 1913.)

(Popular Election of Senators)
The Senate of the United States shall be composed of two Senators from each State, elected by the people thereof, for six years; and each Senator shall have one vote. The electors in each State shall have the qualifications requisite for electors of the most numerous branch of the State legislatures.

When vacancies happen in the representation of any State in the Senate, the executive authority of such State shall issue writs of election to fill such vacancies; Provided, That the legislature of any State may empower the executive thereof to make temporary appointments until the people fill the vacancies by election as the legislature may direct.

This amendment shall not be so construed as to affect the election or term of any Senator chosen before it becomes valid as part of the Constitution.

AMENDMENT XVIII
(Proposed by Congress on December 18, 1917; declared ratified on January 16, 1919.)

Section 1

(National Liquor Prohibition)

After one year from the ratification of this article the manufacture, sale, or transportation of intoxicating liquors within, the importation thereof into or the exportation thereof from the United States and all territory subject to the jurisdiction thereof for beverage purposes is hereby prohibited.

Section 2

(Power to Enforce This Article)

The Congress and the several States shall have concurrent power to enforce this article by appropriate legislation.

Section 3

(Ratification Within Seven Years)

This article shall be inoperative unless it shall have been ratified as an amendment to the Constitution by the legislatures of the several States, as provided in the Constitution, within seven years from the date of the submission hereof to the States by the Congress.

AMENDMENT XIX

(Proposed by Congress on June 4, 1919; declared ratified on August 26, 1920.)

(Woman Suffrage)

The right of citizens of the United States to vote shall not be denied or abridged by the United States or by any State on account of sex.

Congress shall have power to enforce this article by appropriate legislation.

AMENDMENT XX

(Proposed by Congress on March 2, 1932; declared ratified on February 6, 1933.)

Section 1

(Terms of Office)

The terms of the President and Vice-President shall end at noon on the 20th day of January and the terms of Senators and Representatives at noon on the 3rd day of January, of the years in which such terms would have ended if this article had not been ratified; and the terms of their successors shall then begin.

Section 2

(Time of Convening Congress)

The Congress shall assemble at least once in every year, and such meeting shall begin at noon on the 3rd day of January, unless they shall by law appoint a different day.

Section 3

(Death of President Elect)

If, at the time fixed for the beginning of the term of the President, the President elect shall have died, the Vice-President elect shall become President. If a President shall not have been chosen before the time fixed for the beginning of his term, or if the President elect shall have failed to qualify, then the Vice-President elect shall act as President until a President shall have qualified; and the Congress may by law provide for the case wherein neither a President elect nor a Vice-President elect shall have qualified, declaring who shall then act as President, or the manner in which one is to act shall be selected, and such person shall act accordingly until a President or Vice-President shall have qualified.

Section 4

(Election of President)
The Congress may by law provide for the case of the death of any of the persons from whom the House of Representatives may choose a President whenever the right of choice shall have devolved upon them, and for the case of the death of any of the persons from whom the Senate may choose a Vice-President whenever the right of choice shall have devolved upon them.

Section 5

Section 1 and 2 shall take effect on the 15th day of October following the ratification of this article.

Section 6

This article shall be inoperative unless it shall have been ratified as an amendment to the Constitution by the legislatures of three-fourths of the several States within seven years from the date of its submission.

AMENDMENT XXI
(Proposed by Congress on February 20, 1933; declared ratified on December 5, 1933.)

Section 1

(National Liquor Prohibition Repealed)
The eighteenth article of amendment to the Constitution of the United States is hereby repealed.

Section 2

(Transportation of Liquor into "Dry" States)

The transportation or importation into any States, Territory, or possession of the United States for delivery or use therein of intoxicating liquors, in violation of the laws thereof, is hereby prohibited.

Section 3

This article shall be inoperative unless it shall have been ratified as an amendment to the Constitution by conventions in the several States, as provided in the Constitution, within seven years from the date of the submission hereof to the States by the Congress.

AMENDMENT XXII
(Proposed by Congress on March 21, 1947; declared ratified on February 26, 1951.)

Section 1

(Tenure of President Limited)

No person shall be elected to the office of the President more than twice, and no person who has held the office of President, or acted as President, for more than two years of a term to which some other person was elected President shall be elected to the office of the President more than once. But this Article shall not apply to any person holding the office of President when this Article was proposed by the Congress, and shall not prevent any person who may be holding the office of President, or acting as President, during the term which this Article becomes operative from holding the office of President, for acting as President during the remainder of such term.

Section 2

This article shall be inoperative unless it shall have been ratified as an amendment to the Constitution by the legislatures of three-fourths of the several States within seven years from the date of its submission to the States by the Congress.

AMENDMENT XXIII
(Proposed by Congress on June 17, 1960; declared ratified on May 29, 1961.)

Section 1

(District of Columbia Suffrage in Presidential Elections)

The District constituting the seat of Government of the United States shall appoint in such manner as the Congress may direct:

A number of electors of President and Vice-President equal to the whole number of Senators and Representatives in Congress to which the District would be entitled if it were a State, but in no event more than the least populous State; they shall be in addition to those appointed by the States, but they shall be considered, for the purposes of the election of President and Vice-President, to be electors appointed by a State; and they shall meet in the District and perform such duties as provided by the twelfth article of amendment.

Section 2

The Congress shall have power to enforce this article by appropriate legislation.

AMENDMENT XXIV
(Proposed by Congress on August 27, 1962; declared ratified on January 23, 1964.)

Section 1

(Bars Poll Tax in Federal Elections)
The right of citizens of the United States to vote in any primary or other election for President or Vice-President, for electors for President or Vice-President, or for Senator or Representative in Congress, shall not be denied or abridged by the United States or any State by reason of failure to pay any poll tax or other tax.

Section 2

The Congress shall have power to enforce this article by appropriate legislation.

AMENDMENT XXV
(Proposed by Congress on July 6, 1965; declared ratified on February 10, 1967.)

Section 1

(Succession of Vice-President to Presidency)
In case of the removal of the President from office or of his death or resignation, the Vice-President shall become President.

Section 2

(Vacancy in Office of Vice-President)
Whenever there is a vacancy in the office of the Vice-President the President shall nominate a Vice-President who shall take office upon confirmation by a majority vote of both Houses of Congress.

Section 3

(Vice-President as Acting President)

Whenever the President transmits to the President pro tempore of the Senate and the Speaker of the House of Representatives his written declaration that he is unable to discharge the powers and duties of his office, and until he transmits to them a written declaration to the contrary, such powers and duties shall be discharged by the Vice-President as Acting President.

Section 4

(Vice-President as Acting President)

Whenever the Vice-President and a majority of either the principal officers of the executive departments or of such other body as Congress may by law provide transmit to the President pro tempore of the Senate and the Speaker of the House of Representatives their written declaration that the President is unable to discharge the powers and duties of his office, the Vice-President shall immediately assume the powers and duties of the office as Acting President.

Thereafter, when the President transmits to the President pro tempore of the Senate and the Speaker of the House of Representatives his written declaration that no inability exists, he shall resume the powers and duties of his office unless the Vice-President and a majority of either the principal officers of the executive department or of such other body as Congress may by law provide, transmit within four days to the President pro tempore of the Senate and the Speaker of the House of Representatives their written declaration that the President is unable to discharge the powers and duties of his office. Thereupon Congress shall decide the issue, assembling within forty-eight hours for that purpose if not in session. If the Congress, within twenty-one days after receipt of the latter written declaration, or, if Congress is not in session, within twenty-one days after Congress is required to assemble, determines by two-thirds vote of both Houses that the

President is unable to discharge the powers and duties of his office, the Vice-President shall continue to discharge the same as Acting President; otherwise, the President shall resume the powers and duties of his office.

AMENDMENT XXVI
(Adopted June 30, 1971)

Section 1

The right of citizens of the United States, who are 18 years of age or older, to vote shall not be denied or abridged by the United States or by any State on account of age.

Section 2

The Congress shall have power to enforce this article by appropriate legislation.

Index

NAMES

Agnew, S., 193, 197
Ashbrook, J., 189

Bremmer, A., 191

Carswell, G. H., 50, 75
Chisholm, S., 190
Clemens, S., 36
Colt, S., 36
Connolly, J. W., 196

Dahl, R., 177
Daley, R. J., 127, 174, 194
Dirkson, E., 112

Eagleton, T., 195–196
Elizabeth, Q., 88

Flood, C., 73–74
Fortas, A., 75
Fraser, D., 188
Fulbright, J. W., 97

Garfield, J., 36, 107
Garvey, M., 28

Hayden, T., 216
Haynesworth, C. F., Jr., 50, 75

Humphrey, H. H., 182, 190–191, 194
Hunter, F., 175–176

Jackson, H., 190, 193–194
Johnson, L. B., 75, 85, 98, 157, 189, 221, 237

Kennedy, J. F., 36, 85, 97, 112, 214, 237
Kennedy, R., 237
Kennedy, T., 193
King, M. L., 212, 214, 237
Kissinger, H., 112

Lincoln, A., 36

Malcolm X, 214
McCarthy, E., 189, 221
McCloskey, R., 189
McGovern, G., 88–89, 188, 190–191, 193–197
McKinley, J., 36
Mills, C. W., 178
Morse, S., 36
Muskie, E., 190–191, 194–195

Neustadt, R., 93

Nixon, R. M., 31, 50, 64, 85, 87–88, 94–95, 112, 134–137, 152, 182, 188–190, 193, 196–197, 199, 222, 238–239

Reuss, H., 134–135
Ribicoff, A., 195
Roosevelt, F. D., 70, 86

Scott, D., 151
Shriver, S., 195

Truman, H. S, 28
Turner, F. J., 35

Wallace, G. W., 182, 188, 191, 194, 243
Washington, G., 181
Whitney, J., 36
Wilson, W., 87

Yorty, S., 190, 193

SUBJECTS

affirmative action, 29
Alaska, 25
allies, U.S. relations with, 241
aggression, American, 222
America, American (See, United States)
American Independent Party, 182
Andromeda Strain, 36
Anti-Federalist Party, 182
aristocracy, absence of in U.S., 173
arms limitation talks (1972), 87
assassination:
    attempt on George Wallace, 191
    presidential, 36
Atlanta, 175–176

baseball, organized, 74
bicameral legislature, 49
big business, 21, 60
big labor, 60

Bill of Rights, 71, 274–277
    (See also, Constitution, U.S.)
black nationalism, 28
black urban populations, 29
Boston Tea Party, 21
Brave New World, 36
Brown decision, 152
bugging, 32, 196
bureaucracy:
    and the civil service, 107
    extent of, 105
    federal, 41
    historical perspective of, 106
    policy making vs. administration by, 110
    red tape in, 106
    size and scope of federal, 109
    spoils system in, 107
bussing, 28–29, 152, 183

California, 25, 197

California—*continued*
  and 1972 Democratic delegates fight, 194
  role in 1972 primaries, 193
campaigns, 1972:
  presidential, 152
  strategies, 195–197
change:
  incremental, 12
  indicators of, 242–247
  in politics, 33–34
  major, 12
  revolutionary, 12
  types of, 10–13
Chicago, 127, 188
China, 112, 189, 220
  implications for U.S., 240–241
citizen responsibility, 16
city council and party politics, 184
civil disturbances:
  causes in the 1960s, 214–215
  major conclusions, 212–213
  precipitating/spark event, 211–212
  (See also, Violence)
civil rights, 26, 29
  acts, 28
  amendments, 27
civil service:
  benefits, 108
  insulation of, 108–109
Civil War, 27, 34, 36
  and state politics, 151
community action programs (CAPS), 157
community power, 175–178
competition, executive vs. Congress, 113

Congress, 12, 27, 46, 61, 110, 152, 184
  and change, 67
  and compromise, 63
  and fiscal problems, 63
  and foreign affairs, 46
  and presidential involvement in foreign policy, 113
  and revenue sharing, 14–15
  and social security legislation, 64
  and state legislatures, 67
  and war powers, 45
  appropriation and authorization bills, 62
  committee chairmen, 53–57
  criticisms of, 60
  legislative process, 49
  national vs. personal interests in, 65
  Ninety-third, 58
  partisan organization of, 53
  relationship between houses of, 64–65
  selection process, 67
  seniority system, 53, 58
  standing committees, 50–52
congressional districts, Indiana, 66
Connecticut, 44
Constitution, United States, 21–22, 43, 105, 122–123, 259–290
  amendments to, 43
  and congressional selection, 67
  and federal courts, 78
  "checks and balances" concept, 45
Constitutional Convention, 23, 25, 70, 119

conventions, presidential, 193–195
cost of living, 94–95
courts:
  federal circuit, 78–89
  federal district, 69
  of appeal, 69, 79
  specialized, 69
  state, 69, 78
  trial, 69
crime, organized, 32

decentralization and the 1972 elections, 199
Declaration of Independence, 16
demands, political, 206–207, 209
democracy, 9
Democratic National Committee, 195
Democratic National Conventions:
  1968: 188, 242, 246
  1972: 194, 242
Democratic Party, 163, 183, 243
  advantages over Republican Party, 187
  1972 reforms, 188–189
  presidential primaries of, 191
Democrats for Nixon, 196
Detroit, 211
disenchantment, impact on policy, 239
domino theory, 218
Dred Scott decision, 151
drugs, illegal possession of, 32

"ebb and flow" theory, 199
economics:
  and nonwhite gains, 169
  and resources, 171–173
  as indicator of change, 244–245
education, legislation for higher, 61
elections (1972):
  and the future, 238–239
  coattails, 196
  decentralization, 199
  (See also, Presidential Election 1972)
electoral college, 89, 182
electronic eavesdropping and crime, 32, 196
elitism, 9–10
Environmental Protection Act (1970), 109
environmental quality, 121, 156–157
equal rights amendment, 43–44
Escobedo decision, 33
ethnic:
  consciousness, 168
  integration, consequences of, 169
  jokes, 165
executive vs. congressional competition, 113

federalism, 119, 156
  and bloc grants, 134
  and constitutional powers, 121
  and coordination of policy problems, 125
  and courts, 122
  and fiscal distribution of resources, 130–131
  and intergovernmental relations, 123

federalism—*continued*
  and metropolitan decision-making, 158
  and national legislative powers, 120
  and participation, 159
  and pollution, 122
  and revenue sharing, 134
  and size of governmental unit, 130
  and state responsiveness, 129
  and urban centers, 123
  defined, 119
  dynamic aspects of, 137
  in the U.S., 119
  layer cake theory of, 119
  marble cake theory of, 122
  national powers under, 124
  problems of integration, 124
  reserve clause, 121
  responsiveness of, 127
  two contrasting views of American, 120
  two-tier nature, 123
Federalist Party, 182
Fifteenth Amendment, 22, 281
  (See also, Constitution, U.S.)
First Amendment, 111, 274–275
  (See also, Constitution, U.S.)
floods, 207, 210
Florida, 193
focal points, 4–17
foreign policy, Congress vs. president, 113
Founding Fathers, 22–23, 26, 45, 78
Fourth Amendment, 32, 275
  (See also, Constitution, U.S.)

frontier theory, 35
future scenarios, 247–252
  illustrated, 248
Future Shock, 36
futuristics, 233–236
  limitations of, 237–238
  men on the moon, 236
  practical applications of, 236–238

Germany, 88, 241
Gideon decision, 32
goal-setting, 233–234
government, ideal types of, 8
government, United States:
  attitudes toward action of, 239
  nature of, 7
  political interaction among units of, 111
  units of, 144
  (See also, Federalism)
Great Depression, 187
groups, formal and informal, 163

Harlem, 211
Hatch Acts, 107
House of Representatives, 25, 41, 43, 69, 238
  and Senate rules, 62
  interaction with president, 50
  membership, 49
  (See also, Congress and Constitution, U.S.)

Illinois, 197
immigration:
  and assimilation, 168

immigration—*continued*
  and political integration, 126
  and social unrest, 167
  by groups, 165–166
  reasons for and consequences of in U.S., 165, 167
Indiana, 66, 154
individual:
  participation, 253–254
  power, 170
  rationality, 252
  responsibility, 246–247
  rights, 4
  self-interest, 251
institutions, American:
  and political problems, 114
  comparative information on, 42
  future of, 114–115
  role of violence in, 115
  types of change in, 114–115
integration, 29, 152
  political, 124–126
intensity of feelings, 117
interaction among branches of government, 111
interdependency in American society, 240
interest articulation, 183

Japan, 241
judicial process:
  avenues of litigation, 80
  delays, 74, 81
  fairness to participants, 81
judicial system, 69
  judge selection, 80

labor, organized, 61

layer cake theory, 119
  (See also, Federalism)
layers of government, 14
  defined, 13–14
leadership, political:
  flexibility, 252
  nature and quality of, 245–246
  responsibility, types of, 15–16
legislative process:
  and "have-nots," 60
  and organized labor, 61
  bill into law, 58
  cloture, 62–63
  lobbying, 61
  pigeonholing, 59
  time involved, 60
legislature, bicameral, 49
legitimacy, 5, 7
lynching, 27

machines, political, 127–129
majority-minority relationships:
  defined, 244–245
  hierarchical nature of, 250
  intense bargaining between, 246–249
marble cake theory, 119
  (See also, Federalism)
Marion County, Indiana, 67
McGovern–Fraser Commission, 188, 194
melting pot, 168
Memphis, 212
metropolitan America, 145–150
  and race, 158–159
  problems of decision-making in, 157–159
Mexican-Americans, 169

military power, United States, 45
minority rights:
   and Congress, 63
   defined, 26
Miranda decision, 33

National Association for the Advancement of Colored People (NAACP), 28
Nebraska, 44
Newark, 211–212, 216
New Hampshire primaries, 189–190
New Haven, 177
New York, 197
   Board of Regents' prayer, 111
Nineteenth Amendment, 22, 283
   (See also, Constitution, U.S.)
nonwhites:
   and affirmative action in employment, 29
   and economic gains, 169–170
   and whites, relations between, 149–159, 214, 244

Ohio, 197
one man–one vote, 67, 154
"open" society, 174

parliamentary selection of chief executives, 88
participation, 23, 159
   individual, 253–254
   rates, 253
parties, political (See, Political Parties)
partisan organizations, role of, 53

Plessy vs. *Ferguson*, 152
pluralism, 9–10
policy:
   evaluation, 235–236
   impact of disenchantment on future, 239
   implementation, 235
   prediction of, 208
   public, 205–229
political parties, 178
   affiliation with, 184
   and conflict resolution, 184
   and congressional organization, 53
   and electoral law, 182
   and ideology, 183
   and 1972 elections, 181–199
   as indicators of change, 242–243
   as interest articulators, 183
   closed and rigid structure of, 248, 250–251
   George Washington's attitudes toward, 181
   leadership issue, variations in, 251
   organization, 183
   participation, 185
   preferences, 186
   socialization, 185
   third parties in future, 243
   turnout, 186
   two-party system, 183, 185
   Wallace movement in, 243
political party identification, 183–184
   and the 1972 elections, 196
   how established, 187–188

political party identification—
continued
  partisan decisions, 184
  stability, 187
political system:
  closed and rigid structure of, 248, 250–251
  openness of, 149, 178
politics, United States
  alienation to, 243–244
  and domestic environmental factors, 238–240
  and external environmental factors, 240–242
  apathy to, 243–244
  change in, 33–34
  demands in, 206–207, 209
  demographic trends affecting, 240
  expediency in, 64
  future of, 233
  leadership in, 245–246, 252
  loyalty in 206–207, 209
  needs in, 206
  resources in, 174
  role of partisan, 53
  scenarios of future, 229
  (See also, Presidential Politics)
population:
  metropolitan growth in U.S., 148
  rural to urban movement, 145
  state, proportions in metropolitan counties, 147
poverty program, 157
power:
  and corporate assets, 171–173
  and resources, 171
  and social resources, 173
  community, 175–178
  defined, 5–7
  elite, 178
  (See also, Presidential Power)
presidency:
  and electoral college, 88
  and electoral college and popular votes, 90–92
  and selection process, 88
  as head of state, 85
  assassinations in, 36
  contemporary, 100
  political nature of, 86
  problems of, 99–100
  role of chief executive, 86
  (See also, Presidential Politics and Presidential Power)
presidential election (1972), 75
  campaign, 152
  compared with others, 197–198
  conventions before, 193–195
  explanations of, 198–199
  outcome, 197–199
  primaries before, 190–193
presidential politics:
  and the 1972 race, 189–197
  impact on other offices, 197–198
presidential power, 93
  discipline, punishment, inducements, 101
  in foreign affairs, 46, 97, 112
  limitations on, 96
  over public opinion, 99
  persuasion vs. force, 93
public opinion, 96, 99
Puerto Ricans, 169

race (See, Nonwhites)

radio in 1972 campaign, 197
reapportionment, 25–26
Republican National Convention (1972), 194, 243
Republican Party, 163, 183, 243
   as dominant party, 199
   disadvantages in elections, 187
reserve clause:
   constitutional, 121
   in organized baseball, 73
resources:
   political, 174
   social, 173
responsibility:
   citizen, 16
   individual, 246–247
revenue sharing, 134–137
rights:
   civil, 29
   individual, 4
   minority, 26
   to counsel, 32–33

scientific developments and the future, 242
search and seizure, 31–32
segregation:
   de jure, 152
   in the armed forces, 28
Selective Service, 13, 45
Senate, 41, 43, 69, 238
   Foreign Relations Committee, 97
   membership, 49
   selection of members, 23
   (See also, Congress and Constitution, U.S.)

"separate but equal" doctrine, 152
separation of powers, 45, 111
   (See also, Government, U.S.)
Seventeenth Amendment, 23, 43, 282
   (See also, Constitution, U.S.)
simulation, 236–238
slavery, 26–27, 151
social security:
   administration, 107
   benefits, 12
society:
   interdependency in American, 240
   openness of, 174–175
   resources in, 173
   trends of, affecting U.S. politics, 240
South Dakota, 210
Southeast Asia, 86, 217, 220
   and domestic demonstrations, 220
   and domestic destruction, 223–225
   and domestic polarization, 221–222
   and national security, 218–220
   and 1972 campaign, 217, 223
   and presidential power, 97
   and Richard M. Nixon, 222
   Gulf of Tonkin resolution, 98
   Saigon government, 98
   systems approach to, 224
   Vietcong, 98
   war casualties, 222–223
   (See also, Vietnam)
Soviet Union, 87, 112, 189, 241

spark events and urban violence, 211–212
special courts, 79
speech, freedom of, 31
spoils system and Andrew Jackson, 107
Standard Metropolitan Statistical Area (SMSA), 146
state:
- constitutional authority, 151
- courts, 79–80
- government, 153–154
- governmental expenditures by function, 153
- historical roles of, 151
- legislatures, 43–44, 67, 154
- politics, 150–154
- (See also, Constitution, U.S. and Federalism)

St. Louis Cardinals, 73
suffragettes, 22
Supreme Court, 27, 45–56, 69, 151
- alternative justice selection process, 77
- and bussing, 75
- and changing position, 71
- and Congress, 77
- caseload, 69
- constitutional authority, 70
- corporate decisions, 71
- criminal cases, 72
- criminal rights, 75
- Eighth Amendment, 71
- external pressures, 73
- Fifth Amendment, 71
- Fourteenth Amendment, 71–72
- Fourth Amendment, 71
- freedom of speech, 31
- industrial development, 71
- justices' characteristics, 76–77
- judicial process, 74
- New Deal impact, 70
- number of justices, 70
- "one man–one vote" concept, 67
- original jurisdiction, 78
- partisan politics, 75–77
- political aspects, 75
- position changes over time, 72
- presidential appointment to, 75–76
- procedural cases, 73
- reapportionment, 154
- religious freedoms, 111
- role of precedent, 70
- Sixth Amendment, 71
- substantive cases, 73
- (See also, Constitution, U.S.; Federalism; and cases under their legal names)

systems analysis, 205–207
- and civil disturbances, 210–217
- and decision-making, 206, 208
- and dynamism, 209
- and environment, 209–210, 214
- and feedback, 206, 209
- and policy impact, 206, 209, 215
- and Southeast Asia, 217–224
- illustrated, 206
- predictability of, 207
- statistical tools, 205

systems model:
- and change analysis, 228–229
- and complexity, 225

systems model—*continued*
  and data, 225
  and evaluation, 226–227
  and limitations, 225
  and linkages, 225–226
  and the 1976 presidential election, 228
  implications, 224–229
  practical applications of, 226–227

technological developments:
  and change, 35–36
  and the future, 242
television and the 1972 presidential campaign, 197
Tenth Amendment, 120, 277
  (See also, Constitution, U.S.)
Tet offensive, 221–222
  (See also, Southeast Asia and Vietnam)
Third World nations, 35
ticket balancing, 168
tokenism, 215
Treaty of Versailles, 87
Twenty-sixth Amendment, 22, 290
  (See also, Constitution, U.S.)

unit rule and the 1972 Democratic National Convention, 194
United Auto Workers, 240
United States:
  changing relations with allies, 241
  Constitution (See, Constitution, U.S.)
  government, nature of, 7
  (See also, Government, U.S.)

urban:
  needs, 214
  unrest in 1960s, 36, 211–212
  violence, 14
  violence and race, 211
urbanization of American society, 240
utopia, 247–249

Vietcong, 221
  (See also, Southeast Asia and Vietnam)
Vietnam, 190, 194, 196, 220–221
  and 1972 presidential campaign, 189
  and presidential power, 97
  and systems analysis, 208
  and the Nixon administration, 31
  U.S. military commitment to, 218–219
  (See also, Southeast Asia)
violence, 152, 245, 251–252
  against the system, 246
  and change, 17
  and U.S. politics, 136–137
  future patterns, of, 246
  spark event of, 211–212
  system-perpetuated, 246
  urban-centered, 207, 211–212
  various defenses against, 254
voting, 253
  and representation, 22
  18-to-20 year olds, 141–143
  residency requirements, 23
  rights, 21–22
  turnout in 1972, 199
  turnout rates, 23–24

voting—*continued*
  working class, 196–197
  youth, role in 1972 elections, 197

Wage and Price Commission, 95–96

wage-price freeze, 94
War on Poverty, 215
Washington, D.C., 211–212
Watts, 211–212, 216
West Virginia, 214
Who Governs?, 177
Wisconsin, 193, 197